Encounters with God

THE FRANK S. AND ELIZABETH D. BREWER PRIZE ESSAY OF
THE AMERICAN SOCIETY OF CHURCH HISTORY

Encounters with God

*An Approach to the Theology of
Jonathan Edwards*

Michael J. McClymond

New York   Oxford
OXFORD UNIVERSITY PRESS
1998

Oxford University Press

Oxford   New York

Athens   Auckland   Bangkok   Bogota   Bombay   Buenos Aires
Calcutta   Cape Town   Dar es Salaam   Delhi   Florence   Hong Kong
Istanbul   Karachi   Kuala Lumpur   Madras   Madrid   Melbourne
Mexico City   Nairobi   Paris   Singapore
Taipei   Tokyo   Toronto   Warsaw

and associated companies in
Berlin   Ibadan

Copyright © 1998 by Michael J. McClymond

Published by Oxford University Press, Inc.
198 Madison Avenue, New York, New York 10016

Oxford is a registered trademark of Oxford University Press

Library of Congress Cataloging-in-Publication Data
McClymond, Michael James, 1958–
Encounters with God : an approach to the theology of Jonathan
Edwards / Michael J. McClymond.
p.   cm.—(Religion in America series)
Includes bibliographical references and index.
ISBN 0-19-511822-7
1. Edwards, Jonathan, 1703–1758.   I. Title.   II. Series: Religion
in America series (Oxford University Press)
BX7260.E3M33   1998
230'.58'092—dc21   97-9358

1 3 5 7 9 8 6 4 2

Printed in the United States of America
on acid-free paper

Preface

In one of his memorable analogies, Jonathan Edwards compared the course of history to a "large and long river, having innumerable branches" that follow "diverse and contrary courses" yet finally "unite at last and all come to the same issue."[1] The same image might be applied to this book. Though its chapters originated at different times and in relative independence from one another, they come together to form a new picture of Edwards as a religious thinker. My aim in this book has been to delineate a new paradigm for understanding Edwards's theology. Doctoral research introduced me to the imposing body of Edwards's writings and the equally imposing body of secondary studies—some *three thousand* books, articles, and stray references, as tabulated in the two-volume bibliography by M. X. Lesser.[2] Yet my early studies of Edwards's *The Mind* and *End of Creation* (summarized in chapters 2 and 4) seemed a bare torso and left me unsatisfied. I wanted to develop a picture of Edwards based on a wider scrutiny of the texts.

During the last decade, Yale University Press has accelerated its output in the series *The Works of Jonathan Edwards*, and now an extensive and rapidly growing set of texts exists in a splendid, critical edition. Yet relatively little has been done recently to provide a broader and better portrait of Edwards as a religious thinker. Few scholars have attempted to make connections across Edwards's corpus, and some of those who made the attempt have done so by reading into Edwards ideas derived from contemporary thinkers. Generally speaking, the best recent research is highly focused and rarely inquires into the connections between Edwards the historian, the philosopher, the ethicist, the typologist, the preacher, and so on. By contrast I have sought to uncover these connections, while attempting to be scrupulously faithful to Edwards's texts in their specific literary and historical contexts.

As I studied Edwards's writings I found my interpretations clustering around two themes—spiritual perception and apologetics—and found that these two could not really be discussed in isolation from one another. Edwards's conception of religious experience as a form of perception was, in effect, an apology for the Christian faith and a response to the Enlightenment's challenge to see with one's own eyes and not rely on external authority. Conversely his apology for the Christian faith—more often implicit than explicit—amounted to a new way of seeing, an effort to rethink intellectual traditions so that the reality and activity of God could become visible in them and through them. To adapt and extend the river analogy, one might say that spiritual perception is the Blue Nile and apologetics the White Nile of Edwards's thought, two major tributaries of one river.

Perhaps this study can serve as an impetus toward rethinking the basic contours of eighteenth- and nineteenth-century Christian thought. Beginning with the European Enlightenment, or more specifically the deist controversy in England, theologians of varying shades were increasingly concerned to demonstrate the credibility of Christianity vis-à-vis the claims of reason. Christian thinkers during the period from 1700 to 1900 might be located at either the top or the bottom of the following diagram:

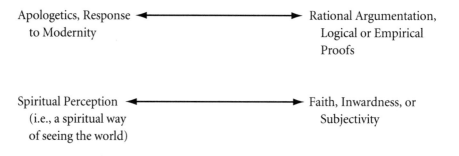

Apologetics, Response ⟵————————⟶ Rational Argumentation,
  to Modernity   Logical or Empirical
                                       Proofs

Spiritual Perception ⟵————————⟶ Faith, Inwardness, or
  (i.e., a spiritual way   Subjectivity
  of seeing the world)

Theological conservatives responded to the Enlightenment with logical and empirical arguments on behalf of faith. They are represented in the top half of the diagram. Theological romantics, represented in the bottom half, repudiated the whole enterprise of proving Chrisitianity. A sea change occurred in the early part of the nineteenth century, as the latter group rejected objective and rational argumentation as a basis for defending the faith in the post-Enlightenment context. Coleridge declared himself weary of the very phrase "evidences of Christianity," and insisted that people needed to "look into their own souls" and not look without for proof of God's reality (see chapter 6). Schleiermacher in Germany, much like Coleridge in the English-speaking world, did much to promote the notion that religion consists in a unique spiritual perception of the world that has little to do with empirical evidences, historical conjectures, or rational arguments. On the other side of the divide, William Paley and other theological conservatives continued the tradition of rational apologetics through the nineteenth and early twentieth centuries.

One of the most interesting things about Edwards is how he breaks the pattern. The diagram must be redrawn to describe him:

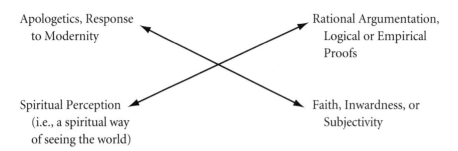

Apologetics, Response to Modernity → Rational Argumentation, Logical or Empirical Proofs

Spiritual Perception (i.e., a spiritual way of seeing the world) → Faith, Inwardness, or Subjectivity

As the subsequent chapters show, Edwards formulated his notion of spiritual perception not in distinction from rational argumentation but rather as a direct response to the Enlightenment's challenge to provide proofs for God that were not based on biblical texts, church traditions, or papal pronouncements. Thus spiritual perception and rational argumentation are connected with a double-pointed arrow. At the same time, Edwards developed an apology for Christianity that reinterpreted metaphysics, ethics, history, and so forth, so that God's reality became apparent in and through each of these disciplines. Even when engaged in the most esoteric and abstract reasoning, he did not lose touch with the issue of religious sensibility. Apologetics, in other words, was never a pen-and-paper proof but rather an encounter with God. Thus apologetics is linked with faith or inwardness in the diagram, and Edwards's distinctive theology emerges as a criss-crossing of customary categories.

Acknowledgments are due to a number of individuals who were early influences and mentors. Sarah Maza set a high standard of excellence in her course on modern European intellectual history at Northwestern University. Three others deserve mention, representing the fields of classics, biblical studies, and philosophy: Stuart Small of Northwestern University, D. A. Carson of Trinity Evangelical Divinity School, and William Lane Craig of Talbot School of Theology. I got started with Edwards in a seminar taught by David Kelsey of Yale Divinity School. My first in-depth research took place in a reading course with W. Clark Gilpin, now Dean of the University of Chicago Divinity School. For all-around excellence in teaching the history of Christian thought, I should mention several professors at Yale University—Rowan Greer, George Lindbeck, Paul Holmer, and the late Hans Frei—and several others at the University of Chicago—Langdon Gilkey, David Tracy, Susan Schreiner, Brian Gerrish, and Bernard McGinn. Special thanks are due to my dissertation committee members: W. Clark Gilpin, Jerald Brauer, and Langdon Gilkey. I would particularly like to thank Clark Gilpin for encouraging me to persist in efforts toward suitable academic employment and a completed book manuscript.

Along with other workers in the vineyard, I owe an enormous debt to Thomas Schafer, the dean of Edwards studies and a most helpful, accessible, and gracious man. I thank him for sharing his knowledge with me so freely, and for allowing me to examine his transcriptions of Edwards's *Miscellanies* at his house on the north side of Chicago. It was an unlikely spot for such meetings, but whenever I visited I was welcomed, schmoozed, fêted, and further initiated into the mysteries of Edwardseana. To the students who enrolled in my seminar on Edwards at Wheaton College, I send my thanks and add this wish: May they chance upon this volume somewhere and find it an improvement on the lectures. I thank my dear friend Charles Sikorovsky for reading the manuscript through at an early stage, and for his many thought-provoking comments on it.

Numerous colleagues and friends at Westmont College, both inside and outside the Religious Studies Department, deserve to be mentioned here, especially Bob and Lois Gundry, Jonathan Wilson, Bill Nelson, Ron Tappy (now of Pittsburgh Theological Seminary), Joseph Huffman (now of Messiah College), Jim Taylor, and Warren Rogers. Westmont College granted me a summer stipend that financed a trip to New Haven in 1991 to examine the Edwards manuscripts. Ned Divilbiss processed an inordinate number of interlibrary loan requests over the years, and showed as much interest and enthusiasm in my research as any of my colleagues. I thank Stephen Crocco of Princeton Theological Seminary for several helpful conversations, Wilson Kimnach of the University of Bridgeport for encouragement and counsel in seeking a publisher, and Stephen Stein of Indiana University for giving me the opportunity to present a paper at the 1994 conference in Bloomington. Harry Stout of Yale University, along with Ken Minkema and Doug Sweeney, deserve thanks for hosting me in New Haven in 1996 and for enlightening me regarding *The Works of Jonathan Edwards.*

Acknowledgments are due to Scottish Academic Press, Walter de Gruyter, and the University of Chicago Press for granting permission to reprint articles that appeared in the periodicals *Scottish Journal of Theology, Zeitschrift für neuere Theologiegeschichte / Journal for the History of Modern Theology,* and *The Journal of Religion.* I especially thank Dick Crouter of Carleton College, editor of *ZNThG/ JHMT,* for publishing my essay on Edwards's *End of Creation.* Appreciation goes to Barbara Holdrege of the University of California, Santa Barbara, for her collegiality and encouragement. Special thanks are due to Vicki Sullivan in Florida, or wherever she is, for taking Sarah to the beach or park almost daily in the summer of 1995, while I was transfixed at my word processor. I wish to acknowledge and thank Kathryn for her friendship and support during our years together and especially during my doctoral study.

Encounters With God is affectionately dedicated to my parents, James and Janet McClymond, and to my daughter, Sarah.

San Diego, California   M. J. M.
January 1998

Contents

Abbreviations for Primary Texts

Works 1   *Freedom of the Will.* Vol. 1 of *The Works of Jonathan Edwards.* Edited by Paul Ramsey. New Haven: Yale University Press, 1957.

Works 2   *Religious Affections.* Vol. 2 of *The Works of Jonathan Edwards.* Edited by John E. Smith. New Haven: Yale University Press, 1959.

Works 3   *Original Sin.* Vol. 3 of *The Works of Jonathan Edwards.* Edited by Clyde A. Holbrook. New Haven: Yale University Press, 1970.

Works 4   *The Great Awakening.* Vol. 4 of *The Works of Jonathan Edwards.* Edited by C. C. Goen. New Haven: Yale University Press, 1972.

Works 5   *Apocalyptic Writings.* Vol. 5 of *The Works of Jonathan Edwards.* Edited by Stephen J. Stein. New Haven: Yale University Press, 1977.

Works 6   *Scientific and Philosophical Writings.* Vol. 6 of *The Works of Jonathan Edwards.* Edited by Wallace E. Anderson. New Haven: Yale University Press, 1980.

Works 7   *The Life of David Brainerd.* Vol. 7 of *The Works of Jonathan Edwards.* Edited by Norman Pettit. New Haven: Yale University Press, 1985.

Works 8   *Ethical Writings.* Vol. 8 of *The Works of Jonathan Edwards.* Edited by Paul Ramsey. New Haven: Yale University Press, 1989.

Works 9   *A History of the Work of Redemption.* Vol. 9 of *The Works of Jonathan Edwards.* Edited by John F. Wilson. New Haven: Yale University Press, 1989.

Works 10   *Sermons and Discourses, 1720–1723.* Vol. 10 of *The Works of Jonathan Edwards.* Edited by Wilson H. Kimnach. New Haven: Yale University Press, 1992.

Works 11   *Typological Writings.* Vol. 11 of *The Works of Jonathan Edwards.* Edited by Wallace E. Anderson, Mason I. Lowance, and David H. Watters. New Haven: Yale University Press, 1993.

Works 12   *Ecclesiastical Writings. Vol. 12 of The Works of Jonathan Edwards.* Edited by David D. Hall. New Haven: Yale University Press, 1994.

Works 13   *The "Miscellanies" (Entry Nos. a–z, aa–zz, 1–500). Vol. 13 of The Works of Jonathan Edwards.* Edited by Thomas A. Schafer. New Haven: Yale University Press, 1994.

Works 14   *Sermons and Discourses, 1723–1729. Vol. 14 of the Works of Jonathan Edwards.* Edited by Kenneth P. Minkema. New Haven: Yale University Press, 1997.

Works 15   *Notes on Scripture. Vol. 15 of The Works of Jonathan Edwards.* Edited by Stephen J. Stein. New Haven: Yale University Press, 1998.

Works 16   *Letters and Personal Writings. Vol. 16 of The Works of Jonathan Edwards.* Edited by George S. Claghorn. New Haven: Yale University Press, 1998.

Works (Hickman)   *The Works of Jonathan Edwards.* With a Memoir by Sereno E. Dwight. Revised by Edward Hickman. 2 vols. Edinburgh: Banner of Truth Trust, 1984 reprint [1834].

PJE   *The Philosophy of Jonathan Edwards from His Private Notebooks.* Edited by Harvey G. Townsend. Eugene: University of Oregon Press, 1955.

Divine Light   "A Divine and Supernatural Light." In *Selected Writings of Jonathan Edwards.* Edited by Harold P. Simonson. New York: Frederick Ungar, 1970.

Personal Narrative   "Personal Narrative." In *Selected Writings of Jonathan Edwards.* Edited by Harold P. Simonson. New York: Frederick Ungar, 1970.

Yale MSS.   Typed transcripts of the "Miscellanies" collection, Beinecke Rare Book and Manuscripts Library, Yale University.

Encounters with God

Introduction

Edwards as an "Artful Theologian"

SINCE PERRY MILLER'S biography of Jonathan Edwards began a new cycle of study almost fifty years ago, research into Edwards's life and thought has advanced considerably.[1] No longer is the intellectual giant of colonial America surrounded by the obscurity to which early generations had consigned him. Yale University Press is steadily producing a definitive and critical edition of his works, with sixteen sizeable volumes to date.[2] New secondary studies on Edwards appear regularly. Academics from a range of disciplines—history, American studies, theology, philosophy, and literary criticism—have given Edwards serious scholarly attention. As an index to the quickening tempo of research, the total number of dissertations on Edwards increased in geometrical proportion during much of the last half century, *doubling* during each successive decade from 1940 to 1980.[3]

Perry Miller set the tone for the renaissance in Edwards studies with his claim that the Northampton sage was "infinitely more than a theologian" and "one of America's major . . . artists."[4] In Miller's brilliant reinterpretation, Edwards's mind shaped theological doctrines into beautiful forms much as a sculptor molds clay. It just so happened that the medium of his artwork was concepts, rather than verse, paint, or musical notes. Hence an appreciation of Edwards no longer hinged upon one's response to, or measure of agreement with, his doctrinal Calvinism. Most of the literature on Edwards until the early twentieth century was devoted to testing the truth of his teachings, not to appraising the beauty of his "artistry."[5] If Edwards was praised—as he was by nineteenth-century conservatives at Princeton and Andover seminaries—he was praised for his resolute orthodoxy and unstinting Calvinism.[6] If Edwards was condemned—as he was by Boston liberals such as Oliver Wendell Holmes—he was condemned for negating human values, for asserting God at the expense of humanity.[7] Perry Miller changed the rules of the game. One could learn from Edwards without adhering to his creed.

Despite its obvious attractiveness for university academics interested in Edwards, Miller's style of scholarship brought a disadvantage, since it separated

3

Edwards the "theologian" from Edwards the "artist." The new research paradigm could not bring to light the way in which Edwards's theology was in effect a form of artistry, and conversely, his artistry was a form of theology. What Miller put asunder, I seek here to join together: Edwards was an "artful theologian." It is better to say artful theologian than theological artist, since, as I attempt to show throughout this book, Edwards's artistry was ever at the service of his theology, rather than vice versa.

Following Miller's lead, much of the recent scholarship on Edwards tends toward a secularizing and naturalizing interpretation of his ideas. Thus Edwards's Christian sermonizing becomes rhetorical theory, while his reflections on the beauty of God translate into general aesthetics, and his typological worldview becomes semiotics. To some extent it is perfectly acceptable to interpret Edwards in terms of the currently regnant academic disciplines, with political scientists, historians, philosophers, literary critics, and other specialists all viewing his writings through different lenses. Decontextualizing and detheologizing Edwards's ideas may be a help in understanding the individual segments of the corpus. Yet such a procedure fails conspicuously to yield a sense of the whole. The recent, cutting-edge research tends to be highly specialized, with the result that Edwards the theologian remains separate from Edwards the historian, the typologist, the spiritual seeker, the preacher, the pastor, the revivalist, and the metaphysician. In this book, I assess a large portion of the corpus, building on an excellent, existing body of scholarship yet going beyond it to show how the various texts within Edwards's oeuvre reflect his underlying theological purposes.

While Conrad Cherry's classic work *The Theology of Jonathan Edwards: A Reappraisal*[8] interpreted Edwards largely in relation to his Puritan and Calvinist forebears, this study examines him in relation to the eighteenth-century intellectual context. Each of the six chapters contextualizes and interprets some text or issue in Edwards within the emergent post-Lockean, post-Newtonian culture of the English-speaking world of the early 1700s. The first chapter opens with an analysis of spiritual perception in Edwards and seeks to move beyond the impasse between naturalistic and supernaturalistic interpretations. I show that the simplistic contrast between Puritanism and the Enlightenment does not apply, and that Edwards's position is a complex synthesis of the two. Once Edwards is seen as an apologist, attempting to bridge the hiatus between distinctively Christian claims and the broader culture of his day, it becomes clear why his notion of spiritual perception shows both continuities and discontinuities with natural human experience. Chapters 2 through 5 build on this first chapter, with an examination of metaphysics in *The Mind*, spirituality in the *Personal Narrative* and *Diary*, ethics in the *Two Dissertations*, and history in *History of Redemption*. The final chapter, on the Christian apology of the *Miscellanies*, summarizes and interprets the results of the preceding chapters. A brief conclusion to the book treats Edwards's general religious outlook. The gist of the argument is contained in the final section of the first chapter, the last two sections of the sixth chapter, and the general conclusion to the book.

A word of explanation is needed about the themes of spiritual perception and apologetics and the choice of texts for discussion in the book. One of the distinctive features of Edwards's thought was its careful attunement to both the subjective and objective aspects of religion. In contrast to much of modern religious thought, his theology shows no tug-of-war between the subjective and the objective. As the first chapter on spiritual perception should make clear, he was concerned not merely with the rational validity of the Christian faith, but also with religious sensibility and an awareness of God's overwhelming holiness and beauty. This concern set him apart from the more prosaic and stereotypical eighteenth-century Christian apologist. However, as chapter 6, on Edwards as apologist, should make equally clear, he never abandoned the task of rational argument for Christianity. This attribute set him apart from later theological Romantics in general, and Friedrich Schleiermacher in particular.

The first and sixth chapters thus frame the book, and are interrelated. One finds in Edwards an apologetically oriented notion of spiritual perception, and a perceptually oriented notion of Christian apologetics. The spiritual sense is itself an evidence for the reality and character of God; therefore, Edwards's teaching on spiritual perception is to some extent coopted by his apologetic enterprise. The saints' "new sense" of God's "excellency" is itself a proof for God. Conversely, the arguments and evidence provided by apologetics serve as a means not only of attaining rational assurance of God's existence but also of *seeing* the world in its profound unity with God. Daniel Shea speaks of Edwards's "pious passion for unity" and adds: "It is appropriate to consider Edwards's thought, not as a system, but as the expression of a profound experience of the interrelatedness of things."[9] The unity of the world is a unity in relation to God. Throughout his writings, Edwards is unfailingly theocentric. As the subsequent chapters demonstrate, Edwards's religious thought constantly shuttles back and forth between a preoccupation with the *experiential manifestation* of God and an impulse toward *cosmic integration* centered on the idea of God. The manifestation of God is the basic thrust of his teaching on spiritual perception, and the integration of the world is the thrust of his apologetics. Yet these two formal aspects of his religious thought modify and condition one another.

The particular texts selected for analysis are those that to my mind best exemplify the two themes of spiritual perception and apologetics, or experiential manifestation and cosmic integration. These include *Religious Affections, Divine Light, The Mind, Personal Narrative, Diary, Two Dissertations, History of Redemption,* and the *Miscellanies.* Neither Edwards's sermons nor his revival writings and ecclesiastical treatises are treated here. While the writing of sermons—Edwards's "sermon mill," as Wilson Kimnach calls it—was in many ways his central literary activity,[10] the individual sermon did not generally give sufficient scope for Edwards to develop his distinctive themes of spiritual perception and apologetics. The sermon *Divine Light* is an exception to this principle, and so is *History of Redemption*, a sermon series revised into a full-length book. The revival writings and ecclesiastical texts, such as *Thoughts on the Revival, Humble Attempt*, and *Humble Inquiry*, are occasional pieces that embody Edwards's response to particular historical circumstances and shed little light on his larger intellectual ambitions. The typological writings, though not discussed here, could perhaps be included within the interpretive framework set out in this book.

Readers may be surprised by the virtual absence of *Freedom of the Will* from my discussion. In studying the corpus, I have become convinced that this work, for all its dialectical virtuosity, is not nearly as central to Edwards's lifelong intellectual concerns as is commonly thought.[11] The same holds true for *Original Sin*. Much like the revival and ecclesiastical treatises, these were occasional writings, even though grandly conceived and executed, as one would expect from Edwards. "Arminianism" compelled him to write. Yet even if I am wrong in this judgment, it is clear that neither *Freedom of the Will* nor *Original Sin* had much relation to the vast magnum opus that Edwards planned to write but died without commencing. It was to be entitled *A History of the Work of Redemption*, and Edwards's 1758 letter to trustees at the College of New Jersey (later Princeton University) shows his excitement at the prospect of producing this work and his reluctance at taking on administrative responsibilities that might hinder him from completing it. Scholars differ as to just what was to be included within the magnum opus, yet from the intriguing intimations within Edwards's letter it is reasonable to assume that it would have been a massive synthesis of his preceding work, "thrown into the form of a history."[12]

One major conclusion coming out of this study is that Edwards was modern, yet with a twist. He was deeply engaged with characteristically eighteenth-century intellectual issues—for example, empiricism, British moral philosophy, and the deistic controversy. While the German philosopher Johann Gottlieb Fichte once referred to him ruefully as "this lonely North American thinker,"[13] the recent scholarship on Edwards indicates how deeply enmeshed he was in the European high culture of his day. As James Hoopes observes, "Edwards was not intellectually isolated in the colonial hinterland but wrote in response to numerous British and continental thinkers—not only Locke but also René Descartes, John Norris, Samuel Clarke, Antoine Arnauld, Henry More, Nicholas Malebranche, and others."[14] Among the others whose writings Edwards knew were Thomas Hobbes, Lord Shaftesbury, Francis Hutcheson, William Wollaston, Isaac Newton, Ralph Cudworth, Hugo Grotius, Joseph Addison, Richard Steele, Lord Kames, John Tillotson, Joseph Butler, Matthew Tindal, John Toland, Thomas Chubb, David Hume, and Lord Bolingbroke.[15] In responding apologetically to early modernity, Edwards was necessarily drawn into its circle of ideas. It takes a modern to debate a modern. The impact of modernity on Edwards is especially clear in chapter 4, where I show how he used the British moral philosophy of Hutcheson and Shaftesbury to anthropomorphize and ethicize God, without however eliminating the Calvinist elements from his conception of God.

Just as important as Edwards's modernity, however, is the unique way in which he engaged the intellectual traditions of the eighteenth century. He was not a passive recipient of the new ideas but responded with a novel strategy of appropriating and modifying entire intellectual traditions, reinterpreting them so as to make them subservient to his theological purposes. In a brief but tantalizing note left behind at his death, entitled *A Rational Account of the Main Doctrines of the Christian Religion Attempted*, Edwards said he intended "to shew how all arts and sciences, the more they are perfected, the more they issue in divinity, and coincide with it, and appear to be as parts of it."[16] Though Edwards did not live to write the *Rational Account*, his published works and unpublished notebooks reflect his desire to turn the best thought of his day to the advantage of God. Such disciplines as metaphysics, moral philosophy, and autobiography were all pressed into the service of religion.

This strategy, which I call Edwards's "implicit apology" for Christianity, has gone unnoticed in previous literature. Scholars have emphasized the presence of particular modern conceptions in Edwards's texts but have often failed to note the specific use to which Edwards marshalled these conceptions.[17] Some decades ago, there was a minor academic skirmish between those who interpreted Edwards as a "medieval" and those who read him as a "modern."[18] According to my analysis, neither viewpoint is quite accurate (though, if pressed, I would favor the latter), because neither does justice to the root-and-branch transformation of modern conceptions in Edwards's thinking. For many religious thinkers of the last two centuries, and especially the self-styled liberals, Christian theology took the form of a mediation between tradition and modernity in which compromise was reached by the mutual modification of both. Edwards developed a different and quite audacious form of mediation. Rather than starting from the accepted *results* of the various intellectual disciplines of his day, he delved back to their fundamental *principles* and sought to reconstruct the very disciplines themselves so as to make them congruent with Christian truth as he understood it. Hence Edwards was modern, though with a twist.

A second major insight of this book, expounded in the general conclusion, is that Edwards mediates between two different understandings of God's presence and activity in the world—the dichotomous supernaturalism represented by William Paley, and the religious naturalism exhibited in the younger Schleiermacher. Although both Paley and Schleiermacher flourished and wrote *subsequent* to Edwards, a comparison of their thought with that of Edwards serves in this book as a heuristic device for understanding Edwards's Christian apology. Paley's *A View of the Evidences of Christianity* (1794) relied on discrete, supernatural acts of God. It ran the risk of limiting God's presence and activity in the world to a special class of miraculous events. Schleiermacher's *Speeches* (1799) reinterpreted the miraculous as a mode of apprehension, so that all events were miracles if seen from a religious perspective. His viewpoint veered dangerously close to secularity, since a God who does everything is functionally indistinguishable from a God who does nothing. Edwards's religious thought, by contrast, includes both senses of the miraculous. Consequently, Edwards sits at the juncture between conservative and liberalizing tendencies in modern religious thought, as I argue in the book's conclusion.

Interpreted in its historical and cultural context, Edwards's religious thought was a brilliant exercise in "artful theology," and its artistry was shown most tellingly in his prodigious attempt to alter, reinterpret, and "baptize" the intellectual traditions of the eighteenth century, to make them serve the Christian message as he understood it.

1

Apprehension

Spiritual Perception in Jonathan Edwards

O NE OF THE most contentious issues in the interpretation of Jonathan Edwards has been the nature and significance of his teaching on the "new sense," "spiritual sense," or "sense of the heart." Nearly half a century ago, Perry Miller published his groundbreaking article "Jonathan Edwards on the Sense of the Heart,"[1] and since that time virtually all writers have agreed on the centrality of the spiritual sense to Edwards's thought. References to it crop up throughout the primary texts, including the *Personal Narrative, Religious Affections, Miscellanies,* the various revival writings, and the sermon *A Divine and Supernatural Light.* In part because of the pivotal status of the spiritual sense in Edwards's thought, a sizeable number of authors have written on it recently.[2] At the heart of the debate lies a disagreement over whether the spiritual sense should be seen as basically continuous with, and integral to, the sphere of everyday sense experience, or as discontinuous with ordinary perception, and thus distinct and separate from it.[3]

Those who argue for discontinuity describe Edwards's spiritual sense as the apprehension of a mental content that is entirely different from the content of ordinary consciousness. Because Edwards in one notable passage in *Religious Affections* connects the spiritual sense with the Lockean notion of a "new simple idea,"[4] they hold that Edwards's position implies the existence of a sixth sense distinct from the usual mental faculties or channels of sense experience. Thus the spiritual sense has no direct link with the five faculties of seeing, hearing, tasting, touching, and smelling. It is not in any sense a modification or extension of everyday experience. Consequently, the presence or absence of the spiritual sense creates an epistemological cleavage between the regenerate and the unregenerate, who live in two altogether different worlds. Viewed in historical context, the spiritual sense is Edwards's restatement, in the language of eighteenth-century philosophy, of the Puritan conviction that the unregenerate are spiritually blind and that conversion is the opening of one's eyes to God. Paul Helm and David Lyttle, among others, support this discontinuous interpretation of the spiritual sense.

Those who make a case for the continuity of Edwards's spiritual sense with everyday experience describe it as the apprehension of a content that is already accessible and known through everyday experience. The new sense may be a *deeper* vision of the world, but it is not the vision of a different world or of a different object in the world. These scholars interpret Edwards's reference to the "new simple idea" in *Religious Affections* in a quite different fashion, as implying that grace is an "idea" that becomes accessible to the individual through the usual channels of sense experience. Grace is sensible, not supersensible. Moreover, the mental content of the spiritual sense—the greatness and goodness of God—is already known in everyday experience, though perhaps less clearly and distinctly. There is no sixth sense. The spiritual sense is interwoven throughout mundane experience and is integrally related to ethics, aesthetics, and ordinary perception. The spiritual sense is not a way of looking at certain things, but rather a certain way of looking at everything. The unregenerate and the regenerate live in the very same world, though only the latter properly perceive its spiritual depth and breadth. Edwards's spiritual sense, according to their argument, connects him not with the Puritans, but with the Romantics, who like him sought a deeper insight into reality.[5] Perry Miller originated this continuous interpretation of the spiritual sense, and he has been followed by such later writers as Edward Davidson.

Previous interpretations of Edwards's spiritual sense have tended toward one-sidedness, in one of the two indicated directions. Yet if one understands Edwards's Puritan convictions, his post-Lockean intellectual context, and his specifically apologetic motivations in writing, then it becomes clear why his teaching on the spiritual sense has a double-sided, Janus-faced appearance. As a good apologete, bridging distinctively Christian convictions and wider human experience, Edwards sought duality without duplicity, and it is not surprising that his later readers have tended to lay hold of one or the other side of his formulations. In what he wrote on the spiritual sense, there is a tacit tug-of-war between the distinctiveness and uniqueness of Christian experience as he conceived it, and the Enlightenment's appeal to general human experience as the basis for all legitimate claims to knowledge. The varied motives at work in Edwards's teaching on the spiritual sense help to explain the complexity of his position. He insisted on God's immediate presence to each believer, and on the indispensability of divine grace. Yet simultaneously he asserted that the spiritual sense was a kind of evidence for God's reality, and that the perception of God's beauty and truth enabled the human mind to perceive truth and beauty wherever it appears.

In what follows, I will first summarize the discussion of Edwards's spiritual sense in Perry Miller and a number of later writers. We may now be able to go beyond Miller, but we cannot—at least in Edwards studies—go around him. Following that, a brief look at the post-Lockean intellectual situation will provide a backdrop for an examination of the primary texts. A comparison of Edwards and Schleiermacher will be drawn out, with a view to clarifying Edwards's position. I will conclude with some reflections on Edwards's use of perception as a model for religion, and the broader implications of spiritual perception for Edwards as a religious thinker.

Perry Miller and His Critics

Perry Miller insisted that Edwards was inspired by Locke in the most important and most distinctive aspects of his thought. Edwards's reading of Locke's *Essay Concerning Human Understanding,* according to Miller, was "the central and decisive event of his intellectual life." Moreover, "the simplest, and most precise, definition of Edwards's thought is that it was Puritanism recast in the idiom of empirical psychology."[6] Miller interpreted Edwards's metaphysics, rhetoric, and teaching on spiritual experience in reference to Lockean empiricism. He held that Edwards both continued the tradition of Lockean empiricism and also significantly modified it. Because Locke's "way of ideas" traced the origins of all our mental conceptions back to their roots in sense experience, Edwards sought to interpret the experience of divine grace as itself a kind of sensation. "Conversion is a perception," wrote Miller, "a form of apprehension, derived exactly as Locke said mankind gets all simple ideas, out of sensory experience."[7]

Locke's basic insight on language, according to Miller, was that words are *separable* from things themselves, and thus it was quite possible for verbal discussion to occur without anyone knowing what they were talking about.[8] The "simple idea" is the basic building block of experience in Locke's philosophy, and no words can convey to a person a "simple idea" he or she does not already possess. Although a name is normally affixed to an idea that is itself derived from experience, the process can also operate in the reverse order, so that the name excites an idea even before the object corresponding to the word has ever been encountered. This reversal, according to Miller, engendered the profound religious problem of Edwards's day: the words used to speak of God and spiritual things had become divorced from the ideas and affections to which they referred.[9] Much of the church's talk was just empty verbiage. Edwards's use of vivid and concrete imagery in his preaching—what Miller calls "the rhetoric of sensation"—was an ambitious attempt to overcome the separation of word from idea and word from affection, so that religious language might evoke the appropriate experiential response among Edwards's hearers. One might say that religious language itself had to be regenerated before Edwards's parishioners could be.

Miller asserts that Edwards, in developing his "rhetoric of sensation," achieved a "dramatic refashioning" of Lockean empiricism by insisting that "an idea in the mind is not only a form of perception but is also a determination of love and hate." Thus apprehension occurs "not only intellectually but passionately." Locke, by restricting the validity of words to their matching ideas, intended to prevent words from ever becoming the goads of passion, and he self-consciously downplayed the emotive and affective dimension of language. Edwards, in contrast, in elaborating his "sense of the heart," explicitly invoked the volition and the affections and thus established the inseparability of idea from emotion. He denied that an appeal to the emotions must always be made at the detriment of the idea, for "an idea is a unit of experience, and experience is as much love and dread as it is logic."[10]

Miller interpreted Edwards's teaching on spiritual perception in terms of natural, sense experience: "In Edwards' 'sense of the heart' there is nothing transcendental; it is rather a sensuous apprehension of the total situation." Edwards's fundamental insight, according to Miller, was that the "sense of the heart" is a "second stage" that "depends on and presumes the first." That is, the "saving conviction" arises out of the ideas derived from sense experience, and "the supernatural effect thus becomes, in Edwards' vision of the cosmos, integrated 'naturally and immediately' in nature."[11] There was little, if anything, in Miller's interpretation that suggested that either the content or the mode of spiritual perception in Edwards was markedly different from that of everyday experience.[12]

Reactions to Perry Miller during the last generation have mingled praise for his eloquence and imagination with serious reservations about his scholarly accuracy, his insistence on Locke's dominant influence on Edwards, and his tendency toward an anachronistic reading of the past in light of more recent developments.[13] Some have charged that Miller "naturalized" Edwards by minimizing the role of God and supernatural grace in Edwards's theology in general and in his notion of the spiritual sense in particular. James Hoopes—among the most trenchant critics—speaks of "Miller's persistent attempts to make Edwards not only 'modern' but also a materialist like Miller himself."[14] A decisive departure from Miller's teaching on the spiritual sense first came in Conrad Cherry's 1966 book, *The Theology of Jonathan Edwards: A Reappraisal*. Cherry highlighted many aspects of Edwards that Miller had glossed over, such as Edwards's adherence to doctrinal Calvinism, his unitary model of the self, and his teaching on divine illumination.[15]

Cherry demonstrated that Edwards's entire interpretation of the human self was designed to break down the customary dichotomy of cognition and affection, of head and heart. Edwards retained a twofold distinction in the powers of the self (i.e., understanding and will) yet subordinated it to a more basic unity and integrity of the self.[16] The upshot of Cherry's analysis was that any interpretation of Edwards that set mind and emotion against one another was fundamentally flawed. Ola Winslow got it completely wrong when she wrote: "The 'sense of God' is an emotional, not an intellectual experience." Perry Miller was almost as mistaken in claiming that "Edwards fully intended to subordinate understanding to feeling."[17]

Cherry focussed attention on Edwards's doctrine of divine illumination and his teaching that the spiritual sense only becomes possible through the inner enablement of the Holy Spirit. Devoting an entire chapter to the Holy Spirit as "the internal possibility of the act" of faith, Cherry showed in effect, that Edwards's notion of spiritual perception is not dyadic but triadic.[18] That is, this form of perception is unique in involving not only a perceiving subject and a perceived object, but also a "divine light" or "communication of the Spirit." A special enablement or empowerment, conferred through the agency of the Holy Spirit, is an indispensable requirement for any human perception of God and spiritual things.

The most difficult issue of all, as Cherry acknowledged, was "the rather thorny problem . . . of how the *Divine* Light is related to the *human* seeing."[19] Edwards repeatedly states that the divine light does not merely shine upon the minds of the elect but is communicated to them, and enters into them, in such a way that it becomes an "indwelling principle" that enables their natural faculties to operate in a new and unprecedented fashion. The Spirit pervades the saint's mind. Yet Edwards does not wish to portray the connection of the divine light and the human vision as so intimate that the light is mystically absorbed into human nature, or the human nature into the divine light. As Edwards says, the human being is not "Godded with God" or "Christed with Christ."[20] A distinction between God and humanity remains at all times, even though the Spirit and the natural human faculties operate conjointly and coordinately in the process of spiritual perception. The Spirit is "immediately" from God, and therefore the divine light is always a gift of grace and never a simple human power or prerogative. Perhaps the Neoplatonic notion of participation is the best way of grasping this relationship of the regenerate human and the divine.[21] In any case, the relation between the divine and human agencies in salvation is a characteristic dilemma for the Augustinian-Calvinist tradition, and so for Edwards as well.

A number of recent authors have dissented from Perry Miller's interpretation of the spiritual sense even more sharply than Cherry did. Despite his emphasis on divine illumination, Cherry never contested Miller's claim that Edwards's supernatural light operates in and through the natural faculties, for, as Cherry writes, "New faculties are not given in illumination, but a new basis is given to the mind from which the natural faculties operate in a new way."[22] In contrast to Miller and Cherry, Paul Helm wrote that Edwards's spiritual sense is "God-given," it is "qualitatively different from the other five," and "its subject matter is strictly non-empirical." It is a "sixth sense." Lockean empiricism was thus not a *theory* of religious experience for Edwards but merely a *model* of religious experience. Edwards used Locke's terminology to highlight the peculiar character of religious experience, not to reduce it to the level of sense experience.[23] For Helm, Edwards's epistemology is that of a late-blooming Puritan rather than an incipient modernist.

James Hoopes essentially concurred with Helm, against Perry Miller, that for Edwards "religious knowledge is entirely new knowledge," and that his teaching on the spiritual sense is fundamentally indebted to Puritanism. Yet "Edwards differed from those earlier theologians in the rigor of his insistence that utterly new knowledge requires a new sense."[24] Edwards, for Hoopes, was more Puritanical than the Puritans themselves in safeguarding the uniqueness of the saint's knowledge of God. Hoopes argues that "redemption is not a matter merely of achieving ideal apprehension generally but rather of achieving it with respect to a single new idea—holiness—resulting from a divine influx."[25] Other writers support the position of Helm and Hoopes. Terence Erdt finds the background to Edwards's spiritual sense in John Calvin's *sensus suavitas*, and David Lyttle judges that the "supernatural light" was radically different from ordinary sense experience. Steven R. Yarbrough and John C. Adams summarize this viewpoint: "Saints did not simply disagree with sinners: they *saw* differently, they *felt* differently, they *thought* differently. In short, they lived in a different world altogether."[26]

Epistemology and Religion after Locke

An understanding of Edwards's spiritual sense requires that we see it in relation to Locke's philosophy, which dominated the Anglo-American intellectual scene in Edwards's day. "Men of the eighteenth century," wrote Perry Miller, "were not so much the beneficiaries of Locke as they were his prisoners." Voltaire dubbed Locke "the Hercules of metaphysics."[27] Yet in the flush of enthusiasm over Locke's new "way of ideas," not many perceived the subtlety of the challenge it posed to orthodox Christianity. Because for Locke all ideas derived ultimately from sensation or reflection, there could be no direct knowledge of any spiritual or material "substance." Thus Locke's philosophy created a conundrum vis-à-vis *divine* "substance." The consequence of Locke's epistemology seemed to be that that no idea could ever be perceived as directly coming from God. Moreover, since the Bible does not speak of any new organs of sensation given in conversion, it would seem that all people have the very same resources for acquiring ideas, and that regenerate persons have no special knowledge of God.[28] It was fitting therefore that Locke viewed revelation as simply an "enlarged" version of "natural reason."[29]

Locke's more radical disciples grasped the full implication of their master's teaching sooner than others. Deists and rationalists, such as Matthew Tindal and Samuel Clarke, used Lockean empiricism to deny that there could be any distinctive religious experience reserved for saints alone. Since all thought originated in sensation, divine revelation could only reinforce and reiterate principles already known and recognized through ordinary sense experience. Thus the freethinker John Toland wrote that "God should lose his End in speaking to them, if what he said did not agree with their common notions."[30]

Unlike some of the later deists, Locke left room in his thinking for a work of divine "inspiration" that communicates new knowledge to the mind of an inspired individual or prophet. This phenomenon he referred to as "original revelation," to distinguish it from the body of truths passed along by the inspired person to others, in oral or written form, which he called "traditional revelation."[31] Yet for Locke it was only the "original revelation," as it existed in the mind of the prophet, that constituted knowledge in the full sense of the term. As he wrote:

> For whatsoever truth we come to the clear discovery of, from the knowledge and contemplation of our own ideas, will always be certainer to us than those which are conveyed to us by *traditional revelation*. For the knowledge we have that this revelation came at first from God can never be so sure as the knowledge we have from the clear and distinct perception of the agreement or disagreement of our own ideas.[32]

Locke's position, as David Laurence explains, created a chasm between the inspired prophet and the rest of humanity: "Inspiration was knowledge to him who experienced it; but to anyone else it was but the diffracted analogies of the report of it. . . . Original revelations were experiences; yet they were not properly human experiences because they could not be shared."[33] Any alleged knowledge of God through revelation had to be based either on "original revelation" or "traditional revelation." Yet to claim "original revelation" was to leave oneself open to the charge of "enthusiasm," while "traditional revelation," as I have shown, was not knowledge in the full sense.[34]

A final aspect of Locke's philosophy to which Edwards responded was the disparagement of emotions or affections in the sphere of religion. The chapter "Enthusiasm" in the *Essay* set the tone for Locke's entire treatment of religion and for many readers' treatment of it as well. He was acutely suspicious of religious responses that were not carefully controlled by cool and dispassionate reason. An idea, for Locke, was an object of mental contemplation, not of emotional engagement. By defining "revelation" as an "enlarged" version of "natural reason" (rather than "natural emotion"), Locke privileged the intellect and invalidated the affections. Some decades later, opponents of the Great Awakening in New England concurred with Locke that reasonable religion had to be dispassionate. "One of the most *essential* Things," wrote Charles Chauncy, "is the Reduction of their *Passions* to a proper Regimen. . . . *Reasonable* Beings are not to be guided by *Passion* or *Affection*, though the Object of it should be God, and the Things of another World."[35]

For an orthodox Protestant such as Edwards, Locke's philosophy was thick with unacceptable implications. For Edwards, the soul in conversion comes into immediate contact with God and gains a new knowledge that it could never have attained previously.[36] As Edwards was fond of pointing out, the Bible describes conversion as the opening of the eyes of the blind, the unstopping of the ears of the deaf, and even the raising of the dead back to life.[37] God "illumines" the mind of the saint, "infuses" his grace, and even "indwells" the body of the believer by his Holy Spirit. Revelation does not merely "enlarge" natural reason but transcends it, conferring that which the human mind could never attain by its own resources. Edwards sought to vindicate a genuine religious knowledge— knowledge in the full sense—based on a direct encounter with God, which was yet not an instance of "inspiration" or "enthusiasm."[38] One reason that Edwards took such pains in formulating his position on spiritual perception is that the logic of Locke's position tended to collapse it into "enthusiasm."[39] In his complex response to Locke, Edwards provided, in Hoopes's words, "the eighteenth century's most thorough and philosophical defense of traditional religion against these impious implications."[40]

Edwards's Spiritual Sense: An Exposition

I turn now to the primary texts in which Edwards discusses spiritual perception.[41] An appropriate starting point for analysis is the divine object of experience. Despite his pervasive interest in the human affections, in spiritual "delight" and "sweetness," in the vigorous engagement or "consent" of the will, in the human response to divine beauty, and in the inward feel of religious experience, Edwards nonetheless insisted that the spiritual sense is a human response to God as God is in Godself.[42] He writes in *Religious Affections*: "The first objective ground of gracious affections, is the transcendently excellent and amiable nature of divine things, as they are in themselves."[43] Some writers have even gone so far as to label Edwards as an objectivist, more interested in the divine object of religious experience than in its subjective feel.[44] Though this description is an exaggeration, there is no question that Edwards links his carefully crafted theory of human religious sensibility with an equally nuanced theory of divine objectivity. The subjective and objective aspects of religious experience come together in the notion of spiritual perception.

One of Edwards's early reflections, Miscellany aa, shows the apologetic context and apologetic motivation of his teaching on spiritual perception. He argues that the perception of God in faith is itself a "testimony" to God's reality and character:

There may undoubtedly be such a thing as is called the testimony of faith, and a sort of certainty of faith that is different from reason, that is, is different from discourse by a chain of arguments, a certainty that is given by the Holy Spirit; and yet such a belief may be altogether agreeable to reason, agreeable to the exactest rules of philosophy. Such ideas of religion

may be in the mind, as a man may feel divinity in them, and so may
know they are from God, know that religion is of divine original. . . . he
is certain that what he sees and feels, he sees and feels; and he knows that
what he then sees and feels is the same thing he used to call God. . . . Now
no man can deny but that such an idea of religion may possibly be
wrought by the Holy Spirit. 'Tis not unphilosophical to think so.[45]

This brief entry in the early notebooks captures the basic insight that Edwards
later developed in *A Divine and Supernatural Light, Religious Affections,* and elsewhere in his writings.[46] In the passage quoted and in these other texts, one is
struck by the frequent occurrence of the words "testimony" and "evidence," by
the contrast between the remote conclusions achieved by "a chain of arguments"
(or "ratiocination") and the immediate certainty conferred in spiritual perception, and by Edwards's repeated assertions that spiritual perception is "rational,"
is "not unphilosophical," and cannot be ruled out by "the exactest rules of philosophy." As the truism goes, seeing is believing, and there is no use arguing
against someone who is a firsthand witness: "When persons see a thing with their
own eyes, it gives them the greatest certainty they can have of it, greater than
they can have by any information of others."[47]

Divine Light shows the same apologetic thrust as "Miscellany aa," attempting
to prove that the doctrine of illumination is not only scriptural but rational as
well: "The evidence that is this way obtained, is vastly better and more satisfying,
than all that can be obtained by the arguings of those that are most learned."[48]
Here Edwards stands Locke on his head, for he uses Locke's empiricist principle—that everyone must see with his own eyes—to establish, against Locke, that
the intellectual certitude of the believer's spiritual perception is *greater* than the
certitude gained by mere human reasoning about God. As Edwards writes: "The
gospel of the blessed God don't go abroad a begging for its evidence, so much
as some think; it has its highest and most proper evidence in itself."[49] The upshot
is that Edwards's doctrine of spiritual perception is misunderstood if interpreted
merely as a description of religious experience—by the believers, of the believers,
and for the believers. It was also directed to the unbelievers, as a self-conscious
response to the Enlightenment challenge of providing a rationally justified evidence of God.

To understand accurately Edwards's notion of spiritual perception, some important distinctions must be drawn. In one of his defining statements, Edwards
writes: "This spiritual and divine light is . . . a true sense of the divine excellency
of the things revealed in the word of God, and a conviction of the truth and
reality of them thence arising."[50] Several of Edwards's key terms are encapsulated
in this brief statement: "spiritual and divine light," "true sense," and "divine
excellency." Edwards's notion of spiritual perception involves three discrete
though related aspects: content, mode, and sensibility. The *content* of perception

is divine or spiritual "excellency" (also called "holiness," "beauty," or "amiability") The *mode* of perception is the "divine light," operating in and alongside the natural human faculties. The *sensibility* of perception is the "spiritual sense" or "new sense," whose essence is "delight" in God. In part because these discrete aspects of Edwards's teaching have not generally been distinguished from one another, previous discussions of the spiritual sense have ended up, as I have already shown, in an unresolved contest between the continuous interpretation of Miller and the discontinuous interpretation of Helm and Hoopes.

A first crucial point regarding spiritual perception is that it has definite intellectual *content*. Not only are the affections moved, but the mind or reason is active. For Edwards writes, "The heart cannot be set upon an object of which there is no idea in the understanding."[51] Miller was correct therefore in claiming that the spiritual sense is based on the rational understanding. There can be no spiritual sense apart from the exercise of the "notional" or "speculative understanding."[52] At the same time, the content of spiritual perception differs from the content of ordinary sense perception. "The spiritual and divine light," says Edwards, "does not consist in any impression made upon the imagination. It is no impression upon the mind, as though one saw any thing with bodily eyes."[53] The question therefore arises: What then is "seen" by the saint, if it is not a physical object that strikes the eye? To this Edwards provided a consistent answer: the saint sees the "excellency," "holiness," "glory," "amiability," or "beauty" of God and divine things. "To see God," he writes, "is to have an immediate, sensible, and certain understanding of God's glorious excellency and love."[54] As Edwards says in the *Miscellanies*, "For it is not only the mere presence of ideas in the mind, but it is the mind's sense of their excellency."[55]

In speaking of the "excellency" of God we are not dealing with an entity in the physical universe, and therefore it becomes difficult to say whether the saints see a new *object* that the reprobate do not and cannot see or whether they see a new *quality* of an object that both they and the reprobate can see. It all depends on whether one hypostatizes excellency, considers it a thing-in-itself, or rather treats it as accessory to other things. Much of the debate on Edwards's spiritual sense has hinged on this essentially semantic quibble, with Paul Helm and James Hoopes inclining to view excellency as a new object of experience, and Perry Miller tending to think of it as a new quality of already familiar objects. Yet the idealist premises of Edwards's thought rule out any dichotomy between external things, on the one hand, and perceived qualities or mental ideas, on the other. What matters for Edwards is that the excellency of God *appears* in the mind of the saint and not in the mind of the reprobate. Interpreting excellency as quality rather than object, though, agrees better with Edwards's clear statements in *Divine Light* that believer and unbeliever share alike in a "notional" or "speculative understanding" of God and spiritual things. The Word of God provides "notions" of God and spiritual things to all who read or hear it with rational understanding.[56] The unbeliever has a notion of God but lacks a perception of God's excellency.[57] Hence one could say that the saint and the reprobate live in the same universe and have access to the same speculative understanding of God, but only the saints perceive God's quality of excellency. Satan and the demons, according to Edwards, have speculative knowledge of God's truth, but they have no sense whatsoever of God's holiness.[58]

While the content of spiritual perception in Edwards is excellency or holiness, the mode of spiritual perception in Edwards is "the divine and supernatural light." In God's light we see light, as Augustine also taught.[59] Yet the modus operandi of spiritual perception is twofold, since Edwards specifically states that the natural human faculties operate along with the divine light.

> It is not intended that the natural faculties are not made use of in it. The natural faculties are the subject of this light: and they are the subject in such a manner, that they are not merely passive, but active in it; the acts and exercises of man's understanding are concerned and made use of in it. God, in letting in this light into the soul, deals with man according to his nature, or as a rational creature; and makes use of his human faculties. But yet this light is not the less immediately from God for that; though the faculties are made use of, it is as the subject and not as the cause. . . . As the use that we make of our eyes in beholding various objects, when the sun arises, is not the cause of the light that discovers those objects to us.[60]

The "human faculty" in question here is the "understanding" that belongs to "man . . . as a rational creature." The final sentence regarding "the use . . . of our eyes" is merely a helpful illustration for the divine light, for already in *Divine Light* Edwards ruled out any involvement of the bodily eyes in the process of spiritual perception. Thus the overall picture of perception is triadic, since it involves a human perceiver, a perceived spiritual object (God or spiritual things), and the presence of divine illumination in the perceiver's mind.

Edwards's statements on the divine light contain an obscurity: The light clearly comes from God, but what does it *shine on*? At various points it appears that that light shines on the human mind itself, while on other occasions (as in the passage just quoted) the light shines on the perceived objects, and at still other times it seems that the light becomes one with the mind that perceives. The texts provide no clear-cut answer. If there is a mystical dimension to Edwards's teaching on illumination, it lies in his insistence that the divine light not only gives knowledge but also becomes one with the knower and transforms him or her. Edwards concludes *Divine Light* by saying, "This light . . . assimilates the nature to the divine nature, and changes the soul into an image of the same glory that is beheld."[61] Like is known by like; only a spiritual mind can understand spiritual things. It may be impossible to specify just where human reason ceases and spiritual illumination commences, for the effect of the divine light is precisely to unify the human mind with the mind of God. In some measure, the human being is lifted up to see as God sees. As noted earlier, Edwards appeals to the notion of participation: like a diamond sparkling in the sunlight, so the human mind is illumined as it shares in God's own light.[62]

Edwards constantly associates the divine light with the presence of the Holy Spirit, who is manifest to the mind of the regenerate in a unique fashion. "The Holy Ghost influences the godly as dwelling in them as a vital principle, or as a new supernatural principle," while "in unregenerate men, he operates only by assisting natural principles to do the same work which they do of themselves, to a greater degree." For "the Spirit of God may operate upon a mind and produce effects in it, and yet not communicate itself in its nature in the soul." After conversion, however, "the Spirit of God . . . dwells in the soul and becomes there a principle of life and action."[63] Ultimately, the work of the Holy Spirit is inscrutable, because the giving or withholding of divine illumination from human minds depends on nothing other than the will of God. There is no human explanation as to why God illumines one mind and not another, and so the teaching on the divine light leads one back to Edwards's Calvinistic belief in election.

The Spirit's action in illumination is "arbitrary"—something of a technical term for Edwards, which he uses not with its contemporary connotation of "capricious," but in its Latin etymological meaning of "a matter of the [arbiter's] will." Edwards writes: " 'Tis the glory of God that He is an arbitrary being . . . [and] acts as being limited and directed in nothing but His own wisdom."[64] He argues in numerous passages that the "arbitrary" conferral of illumination is a suitable expression of the preciousness of grace. If God had tied grace to some kind of mechanical process, grace would have been diminished. Because it comes immediately from God, the divine light has superlative value.[65]

The final aspect of spiritual perception is sensibility, that is, the affective human response to God. The stress on sensibility reflects Edwards's preoccupation with the *impact* of spiritual things on the mind, for, in terms of philosophical idealism, God is only as real to humans as God appears to be. For Edwards, the defining issue in spiritual sensibility is enjoyment. The objective notion of "excellency" corresponds to the subjective experience of "delight."[66] So intrinsic to spiritual perception is this "delight" or "sweetness," that one can say unequivocally that where there is no "delight" at all, there is no genuine perception of God or spiritual things. Whenever someone has a true spiritual sense, "the heart is sensible of pleasure or delight in the presence of the idea." Thus the saint "does not merely rationally believe that God is glorious, but he has a sense of the gloriousness of God in his heart."[67] Edwards speaks autobiographically in his *Personal Narrative* of how he gradually passed from grudging acquiescence in the doctrine of divine election to a rational belief, and then finally to a "delightful conviction."[68] Only this last stage involved a "sense of the heart" and an affective engagement of his mind. Throughout his writings, Edwards never deviated from his insistence that the "delightful sense" of God belongs to the regenerate alone, never to the unregenerate.[69]

Edwards's most celebrated and most quoted statement on spiritual sensibility may well be his comment in *Divine Light* on the taste of honey: "There is a difference between having a rational judgment that honey is sweet, and having a sense of its sweetness. A man may have the former, that knows not how honey tastes; but a man cannot have the latter unless he has an idea of the taste of honey in his mind."[70] Here Edwards breaks away from his usual reliance on the metaphor of seeing God and spiritual things, and instead adopts—following certain Puritan precedents—the analogy of tasting.[71] What makes the honey passage in *Divine Light* so memorable and so effective is that it appeals to perhaps the most intimate of the five senses. The visible object remains at a distance; the tasted substance touches our very tongue. We commonly touch with our fingers, and sniff with our noses, things that we would never dream of putting into our mouths! What better way to emphasize that spiritual perception is the knowledge of a participant, and not that of a spectator, than to describe it as a kind of "tasting"? Later in his sermon Edwards refers to honey once again, and his intent is to distinguish the spectator from the participant: "Reason . . . may determine that honey is sweet to others; but it will never give me a perception of its sweetness."[72] If it is hard to imagine how another person could do my seeing for me, it is is even less conceivable that somebody else should do my tasting. There is no sweetness at second hand.

Each of the three aspects of spiritual perception just examined—content, mode, and sensibility—shows the existence of both continuity and discontinuity between believers and unbelievers. The regenerate and the unregenerate alike have mental notions or ideas of God, conveyed to them through the Word of God or by other means. Yet only the regenerate perceive the divine excellency, and the unregenerate remain wholly insensible to it. The regenerate and the unregenerate alike possess the natural faculty of reason, and both employ their reason with respect to spiritual things. Yet only the regenerate receive that divine and supernatural light that enables their natural reason to see God as God truly is. The regenerate and the unregenerate alike receive the influences of the Holy Spirit, for the Spirit does not act only on the elect. Yet only the regenerate have the Spirit communicated in such a way that the Spirit becomes united with them and acts in and through them as a "new vital principle." The regenerate and the unregenerate alike have affective sensibility, and both experience the "sense of the heart" with respect to those objects that engage them. Yet only the regenerate have that "spiritual sense" or "new sense" that consists in "delight" and in a "sweet sense" of God and spiritual things. This subtle interplay of continuity and discontinuity is essential for Edwards to achieve his theological and apologetic purposes. On the one hand, he vindicates the epistemological distinctiveness of the religious, or rather Christian, experience of God and the necessity of divine grace as a prerequisite to this experience. On the other hand, he attempts to show that religious experience is not the nullification of ordinary sense experience but rather its fulfillment. For Edwards, grace does not destroy nature but perfects it.

Edwards and Schleiermacher: A Comparison

Jonathan Edwards and Friedrich Schleiermacher invite comparison with one another, since both were early modern theologians who developed highly nuanced theories of religious sensibility and both were apologetically motivated in doing so.[73] Edwards's 1734 sermon *Divine Light* and Schleiermacher's 1799 treatise *On Religion: Speeches to Its Cultured Despisers* were both written against a backdrop of Enlightenment rationalism and broke beyond the narrowness of the existing interpretations of religion as an intellectual assent to doctrinal propositions. Both men highlighted the element of immediacy in religious experience; insisted that religion contained something not reducible to ordinary sense experience; and showed an awareness of the unity of the world in God and a receptivity to God or the transcendent in nature. For all these reasons Edwards's "spiritual sense" has something in common with Schleiermacher's "intuition" (*Anschauung*) or "feeling" (*Gefühl*) of the Infinite.

However, the resemblances between the two thinkers recede on closer examination. Schleiermacher's basic strategy for vindicating religion was to declare its independence from the spheres of knowledge, metaphysics, and morality. One might even say with Wayne Proudfoot that Schleiermacher invented religion, if by that term one refers to an autonomous dimension or aspect of human life that cannot be captured by beliefs, social practices, or institutions.[74] One implication of Schleiermacher's position was that religion could not be identified with knowledge in the usual sense. He writes in his *Speeches*: "Religion is not knowledge and science, either of the world or of God. . . . In itself it is an affection, a revelation of the Infinite in the finite, God being seen in it and it in God." In another passage he adds: "I cannot hold religion the highest knowledge, or indeed knowledge at all."[75] Some writers have described his position as noncognitivist, since it seems to posit the existence of a distinct religious faculty in human nature that is separate from reason or intellect.[76]

Confronted with the blistering assault on traditional theology by Spinoza, Kant, and the Neologists of the German *Auflklärung*, the young Schleiermacher preserved a place for religion, but only by defining and isolating the religious sensibility in such a way that it had little connection with rationality and knowledge. Ultimately, religious experience for Schleiermacher did not tell us anything about the world per se but only about our mode of intuiting the world: "What we feel and are conscious of in religious emotions is not the nature of things, but their operation upon us. What you may know or believe about the nature of things is far beneath the sphere of religion."[77] In his *Speeches*, especially in the outspoken and controversial first edition of the work, Schleiermacher broadmindedly suggested that the religious feeling or intuition could be interpreted doctrinally in various ways—in reference to a personal God, an impersonal deity, or even no God at all.[78]

A further distinctive of religion for Schleiermacher was its universality. Religion, as an orientation toward God or the Infinite, was an invariant feature of human existence. Sometimes the consciousness of God was explicit, and sometimes implicit, yet it existed in some fashion among all persons and within all cultures. Yet because some persons may never be aware of God at all, and perhaps no persons are conscious of God at all times, Schleiermacher in *The Christian Faith* hypothesized that all persons have a "sense of absolute dependence" that points back to God as the ultimate causally conditioning factor in every human experience. God is the "Whence" of this experience of "absolute dependence," even when God is not overtly recognized as such.[79] For Schleiermacher, there were differing levels of human consciousness, and so it was conceivable that one might be experientially in relation to God without being fully aware of this fact.

Schleiermacher exhibits one of the most important strategies in modern Western religious thought, namely, the effort to preserve a place for religion in the context of a highly critical post-Enlightenment culture by either severing or weakening the link between faith (or religion) and knowledge. In varying ways, a wide variety of modern thinkers adopted this approach. Immanuel Kant, in the preface to his *Critique of Pure Reason*, commented: "I have therefore found it necessary to deny *knowledge*, in order to make room for *faith*."[80] By consigning God to the realm of the supersensible, Kant effectively placed the deity beyond the sphere of direct human knowing. Though the dichotomy of faith and knowledge was somewhat less acute among English-language thinkers than among the post-Kantians in Germany, Locke too, as we have seen, did not think that faith provided knowledge in the full sense of the term. "For our simple ideas, then, which are the foundation, and sole matter of all our notions and knowledge," wrote Locke, "we must depend wholly on our reason; I mean, our natural faculties."[81] Faith for Locke was believing what another told you, while reason meant seeing something for yourself.[82]

Edwards, in contrast to Locke, thought of faith as a way of seeing for oneself.[83] Among the major religious thinkers of the eighteenth and nineteenth centuries, Edwards held to the minority view that faith is itself a form of knowledge and that it implies a direct and cognitive relationship to God. "Excellency" was an objective property of God, and therefore spiritual perception gives a glimpse of God as God truly is.[84] Moreover, Edwards clearly would not have accepted Schleiermacher's notion of an implicit awareness of God, that is, a state in which the subject does not recognize God as the object of his or her experience. The mark of genuine spiritual perception is seeing the very "divinity" of God.[85] What also decisively separated Edwards from Schleiermacher, and the Romantics generally, was his sharp distinction between the mentality of the regenerate and that of the unregenerate. For Schleiermacher, the capacity for religious feeling was an intrinsic aspect of human nature per se, and not a special gift that God confers on selected individuals.

Edwards's position was conservative, since the equation of faith with knowledge was a theological tenet extending back through the Puritans and orthodox Protestants to the Reformers, the medieval scholastics, and early Christian writers. Yet, despite its conservative intent, Edwards's theory of spiritual perception was novel both in its form and in much of its substance. There were wide ramifications, to be explored hereafter, in Edwards's interpretation of the Christian religion as consisting in a new form of perception.

Reflections on Religion and Perception

By way of summary, let me distinguish the key elements in Edwards's teaching on spiritual perception. Three points pertain primarily to his Christian convictions, and three to his engagement with Enlightenment thought. First, Edwards stressed the immediacy of the religious life. God not only spoke and acted in distant times and places but ineffably and unmistakably touches each believer here and now through the Holy Spirit. There is no place for secondhand religion. Second, Edwards underscored the uniqueness and indispensability of grace. The divine light of grace enables a person to see what he or she could not otherwise see. Just as Edwards in *Freedom of the Will* and elsewhere insisted that the unregenerate person cannot *obey* God apart from grace, so in his teaching on the divine light he insisted that the unregenerate cannot *know* God apart from grace. Conrad Cherry comments: "Edwards is irredeemably 'supernaturalist,' if we take this now hackneyed and ambiguous term to mean that whatever human nature is and does from itself is qualitatively different from what it is and does from beyond itself or from the Spirit of God."[86] Third, Edwards constantly stressed the affective and volitional aspect of the spiritual sense, so that true religion was more than cognitive assent to doctrinal propositions.

Fourth, in the face of counterclaims by Enlightenment thinkers, Edwards wished to establish that the believer's awareness of God is an evidence for God's reality and is in fact the firmest and least vulnerable kind of evidence. Fifth, he sought to formulate a conception of religious sensibility that was not subjectivistic. His theology was, in Wilson Kimnach's apt phrasing, a "pursuit of reality," and for Edwards this meant above all the *divine* reality.[87] At this point he differed markedly from Schleiermacher, who held a subjectively oriented theory of religious sensibility. Edwards's notion of spiritual perception served as a safeguard against subjectivism, since the very notion of perception requires a perceived object as well as a perceiving subject. The model of religion as perception enabled Edwards to uphold his assertion that faith involves a genuine knowledge of a distinct object, namely, God. Sixth, and finally, Edwards was insistent that the spiritual sense is not an epistemological quirk, disconnected from the rest of human experience. The Spirit of God activates and quickens the natural human faculties and in no way circumvents or negates them.

This brings us to a final interpretive question: What happens when the Christian religion is conceived as *a new form of perception*? Edwards's concern for spiritual perception gave a meditative atmosphere to his life, religion, and thought. Benjamin Franklin's *Autobiography* exhibits a familiar image of the American as someone concerned with working, doing, earning, and generally getting ahead. Yet Edwards was preoccupied with seeing God.[88] Despite the mundaneness of his perception of God—that is, seeing God in and not apart from the world—his visionary aspirations pulled him steadily toward stillness and receptivity. One has to stop in order to look. Not surprisingly, the vision of God is a Christian theme traditionally associated with mystical experience and with heaven. Seeing God is what occurs beyond this world, in an experiential realm that transcends normal awareness or else in an eschatological realm that transcends human history.[89] Chapter 3 will examine Edwards's contemplative aspect; yet it is already implied in his core notion of spiritual perception.

Edwards's writings contain oblique indications that the perception of God's supreme excellency opens the human mind to perceive excellency in its lesser, creaturely manifestations. In his *Personal Narrative*, he describes his first experience of the "sense of the glory of the Divine Being; a new sense, quite different from any thing I ever experienced before." Yet very quickly after describing this moment of experience, he moves on to speak of a change in his entire perspective on the world:

> The appearance of every thing was altered; there seemed to be, as it were, a calm, sweet cast, or appearance of divine glory, in almost every thing. God's excellency, his wisdom, his purity and love, seemed to appear in every thing; in the sun, and moon, and stars; in the clouds and blue sky; in the grass, flowers, trees; in the water, and all nature; which used greatly to fix my mind. I often used to sit and view the moon for continuance; and in the day spent much time in viewing the clouds and sky, to behold the sweet glory of God in these things; in the mean time, singing forth, with a low voice, my contemplations of the Creator and Redeemer.[90]

Outside of the lovely lyricism of the passage, one is struck by Edwards's mundane mysticism, his capacity for seeing God in and through the world of nature. This could be explained with reference to the Neoplatonic notion of participation. Because the creaturely ectype or copy of excellency shares in the nature of the divine archetype, an acquaintaince with the archetype is all that one needs to discern excellency in any of its manifestations. Thus the spiritual sense of the elect is directly linked with the natural human experience of the true, the good, and the beautiful. It is crucial to note, however, that in the *Personal Narrative* the new sense of God *precedes* the transformed and renewed perspective on nature.[91] In experiential terms, Edwards does not ascend from the "secondary beauty" of creatures to the "primary beauty" of God, but rather travels in the opposite direction. In this way, he establishes the priority of regenerate experience while also connecting it with the natural human experience of the beautiful.[92]

Spiritual perception is one of Edwards's most encompassing themes. It links idea and emotion, the cognitive and the affective. It meshes experiential manifestation with philosophical reflection. It brings together God and nature. It joins the beautiful to the divine. It connects theology with spirituality. As Robert Jenson aptly commented, "Edwards' free metaphysical speculation is precisely his way of 'viewing' God's beauty."[93] There is no dichotomy in Edwards between the spiritual sense of divine things and the philosophical, theological, and historical reflection that may be engendered by it. The succeeding chapters will examine the varied ways in which Edwards's entire body of thought may be interpreted as a reflection on, or expression of, the processes of spiritual perception.

2

Speculation

The Theocentric Metaphysics of *The Mind*

Wᴵᴛʜ ᴛʜᴇ ᴘᴜʙʟɪᴄᴀᴛɪᴏɴ of *Freedom of the Will* in 1754, Edwards gained a reputation for metaphysical genius. Writing in the early 1800s, Dugald Stewart referred to Edwards as the "*one* metaphysician of whom America has to boast, who, in logical acuteness and subtility, does not yield to any disputant bred in the universities of Europe."[1] *The Mind*, published in Sereno Dwight's *Life of President Edwards* (1829),[2] provoked many nineteenth- and twentieth-century scholars to amazement at Edwards's precocity and to puzzlement over the sources of his idealism or immaterialism. Though *The Mind* was not written quite as early in Edwards's life as Dwight presumed, it still ranks as a major philosophical accomplishment and attests to Edwards's force and independence of mind.[3] Perry Miller deemphasized Edwards's idealism and focussed instead on his indebtedness to Locke yet was no less laudatory than earlier writers on the subject of Edwards's metaphysical brilliance. In launching the republication of Edwards's works in the 1950s, Miller called Edwards "the greatest philosopher-theologian yet to grace the American scene."[4]

Despite the consensus regarding Edwards's metaphysical genius, some scholars question whether his writings contain any proper philosophy at all and, if so, whether it bears any relation to the rest of his thought. Stephen Daniel correctly notes that Edwards's philosophical agenda differed markedly from that of modern philosophy in general. He seems to have been engaged in an altogether different intellectual project than that of Descartes, Locke, Berkeley, and Hume.[5] Frederick J. E. Woodbridge depicted Edwards as a philosopher manqué, whose religious experience was intellectually "disrupting" and whose promising metaphysical mind was sadly "arrested by emotional experiences for which Edwards himself could not account." Woodridge concluded: "It is futile to try to understand Edwards's Calvinism from his philosophy or his philosophy from his Calvinism. In him they are juxtaposed, not united."[6] In a similar vein, James Carse saw Edwards's metaphysical speculations as disconnected from the rest of his life and thought and as limited largely to such juvenilia as *The Mind*.[7] These authors intimate the ironic conclusion that Edwards was a philosophical genius but not a philosopher.

An imposing difficulty in interpreting Edwards as a philosopher is the mind-numbing complexity and variety in his metaphysical reflections. One is led to ask: Is the diversity of these writings a mere heterogeneity, or is there some underlying principle of coherence that binds them together? Where is the Ariadne's thread through the labyrinth of Edwards's metaphysics? Commonly the question has been posed in terms of a search for a "fundamental motif": Is there any single concept that could serve as a point of reference for the whole of Edwards's philosophy?[8]

A scrutiny of the secondary literature should induce skepticism with regard to isolating and identifying such a fundamental motif or its equivalent. Past claims to having discovered one have not been accepted and assimilated into the ongoing scholarship on Edwards. Instead each new researcher has gone on with his or her own focus while neglecting the others. Thus Douglas Elwood stresses "immediacy," Roland Delattre accents "beauty and sensibility," Norman Fiering emphasizes "moral philosophy," Sang Lee examines "dispositional ontology," and Stephen Daniel speaks in terms of "semiotics."[9] All these authors have produced substantial studies that enrich our general understanding of Edwards. Since a diversity of approaches has proved fruitful in studying Edwards's philosophy, it is unlikely that any one approach can claim ultimate priority over all others. Conrad Cherry comments: "In a theologian of Edwards' stature there are a number of fundamental and distinctive motifs operative, and his outlook cannot be reduced to any one of them. Nevertheless, any one of a number of motifs may serve as a window through which we may observe other aspects of his thought."[10]

The Theocentric Motif

Bearing in mind my own caveats regarding the search for a fundamental motif, I suggest that a hitherto neglected aspect of Edwards has special relevance for the interpretation of his metaphysical writings: the often noted but rarely explained phenomenon of Edwards's "theocentrism."[11] The existing studies of Edwards's metaphysics, as extensive and insightful as some of them are,[12] fail to show the intimate connection between his metaphysical and his theological interests, or what Robert Jenson has aptly termed "the native unity of speculation and adoration in his life."[13] The principle of theocentrism is important in showing how Edwards's metaphysics derives from essentially theological impulses and how the early philosophical texts such as *The Mind* are of a piece with the later works.[14] Theocentrism is also important in enabling us to see that Edwards's convoluted and often confusing strands of metaphysical speculation cohere with one another as parts of a recognizable pattern. What might otherwise seem a copious but chaotic profusion of ideas appears as an intelligible whole when interpreted in light of theocentrism. After elaborating briefly on the principle of theocentrism, I will apply it to the interpretation of Edwards's metaphysics, specifically his ontology, idealism, aesthetics, and causality, and then draw out some conclusions.

The term "theocentrism" expresses a point commonly agreed on: Edwards's strong and even overweening preoccupation with deity. Elwood claims that "he was a man of one idea, and that one idea was God."[15] The unsympathetic interpreter V. L. Parrington commented: "To one cardinal principle Edwards was faithful—the conception of the majesty and sufficiency of God; and this polar idea provides the clue to both his philosophical and theological systems."[16] Another scholar says that "Edwards never lost this vivid sense of God, His Reality, His Immediacy. It is the first, the fundamental thing to be taken into account in an understanding of his theology."[17] Thomas Schafer finds his theology to converge on "the acceptance and affirmation of God as he is."[18] Edwards's whole corpus of writings attests to his theocentrism. His first publication, the sermon "God Glorified in Man's Dependence," explores and explains the "absolute and universal dependence of the redeemed on him [God]."[19] One of his last works, *End of Creation*, is chiefly devoted to showing that the world exists for the glory of God.[20] Edwards, in short, was God-intoxicated.

Theocentrism means that God for Edwards is the measure of all things. God is not merely one instance of being, truth, beauty, or goodness, nor even the supreme exemplification of these categories. Instead God defines what is meant with such words. God's own self is the yardstick of measurement. As Edwards says: "Now God is the prime and original being, the first and last, and the pattern of all, and has the sum of all perfection."[21] Reiterating a biblical phrase but assigning it full ontological import, Edwards avers: "God is, and there is none else."[22] And as God's existence is the only fully realized existence, all else seems shadowy in comparison with God. Thus Edwards does not begin his thinking near at hand, with the reality of the creature. On the contrary he regards God's reality as *axiomatic* and that of the creature as *problematic*, as something in need of explanation.[23] The fact that God is the canonical instance of being and truth and goodness and beauty carries the epistemological implication that all reality must be interpreted in light of the divine reality. Nothing in the world can be comprehended unless it has been related back to God. Edwards's theologizing is a many-sided effort to bring all reality into explicit relation to God as the measure of all things.

Edwards's theocentrism represents a turning of the tables on Enlightenment anthropocentrism and has therefore a polemical aspect. "Theocentrism," as H. Richard Niebuhr comments, "no more begins by asking what is God good for than humanistic and vitalistic ethics begins with the inquiry what man or life is good for." As Paul Ramsey adds, it "asks rather what man is good for, what is the good for man and what are his responsibilities in the light of his being in relation to God."[24] Yet Edwards's theocentrism has constructive as well as critical intent. As the center and measure of reality, God stands in a positive and affirmative relation with all creatures, which live from God and to God, and exist under an ultimate divine "yes" and permission to be what they are. His is a world-affirming philosophy, which never lapses into dour otherworldliness or gnostic transcendentalism. The Creator does not disparage or depotentiate the creature, but on the contrary provides the only secure grounding for the creature's reality.[25]

Edwards's theocentrism suggests an inclusive rather than exclusive posture of God vis-à-vis the world. God is not only the measure but the source from which created reality continually derives its existence. Wherever one finds truth, goodness, or beauty, God is present.[26] Standing in the classical tradition of Christian Platonism, Edwards uses the notion of participation to explain how all truth, beauty, and goodness are related back to God. The creature's knowledge of God, he writes in *End of Creation*, is "most properly a communication of God's infinite knowledge," "a conformity to God," "the image of God's knowledge of himself," "a participation of the same . . . as beams of the sun communicated, are the light and glory of the sun in part."[27] With reference to the divine beauty, he comments: "All the beauty to be found throughout the whole creation, is but the reflection of the diffused beams of that Being who hath an infinite fullness of brightness and glory."[28] Edwards consistently strives to exalt God but not to distance God from the world.

In the next section, I will trace Edwards's theocentrism through the various aspects of his metaphysics and show that theocentrism is a hidden agenda in the speculations of *The Mind*.[29]

God and Being

God as being, as the great "I AM," is the foundation of Edwards's metaphysics and an appropriate starting point for its explication.[30] In developing his ontology Edwards showed independence from the Puritan tradition, which gave the nod to God as being but did not assign this notion any constitutive theological importance. He also departed from the main line of early modern English philosophy, which maintained a certain reserve regarding the meaningfulness and utility of such highly generalized conceptions as being. Thus Locke held it vain to "let loose our thoughts into the vast Ocean of *Being*"—just the thing that Edwards set out to do in *The Mind*.[31] In terms of his ontology (though not his empiricism), the philosophical flavor of Edwards's metaphysics is decidedly Continental rather than English.[32]

The most striking thing in Edwards's ontology is the way that his various lines of reasoning all converge on God. He shows almost no interest in explicating the ontological distinctions between creatures but concerns himself with the distinction between God and creatures. God's distinctiveness for Edwards is captured in his key identification of God as "Being in general." He speaks also of God as *ens entium* ("the Being of beings") and declares that "God is the sum of all being and there is no being without his being."[33] Sayings like this have led some to characterize Edwards as a pantheist.[34] Yet a careful readings of the texts in context leads to a different conclusion, as correctly stated by George Rupp: "Edwards' contention that God is coextensive with all reality implies the corollary that whatever ontological status finite individuals may have is derivative from that divine reality."[35] Similarly Miklos Vetö speaks of Edwards's "profound religious intuition of the essential deficiency of the creature" and comments: "The nonbeing of the creature is not the absence of all reality but rather the precarious, fluctuating, and unstable condition that does not deserve to be designated with the great name of 'being.' "[36]

The whole intent of Edwards's ontology is not to minimize or obliterate the distinction between God and the world in pantheistic fashion, but rather to enforce and accentuate this distinction. Surprising as it seems today, given the repudiation of metaphysics by many twentieth-century theologians, Edwards's identification of God as "Being in general" is designed chiefly to highlight the utter uniqueness and incommensurability of God. Precisely because of God's own infinite Being, God transcends creatures that exist only in partial and particular ways. Ontology is a safeguard for divine transcendence and most certainly not a means of reducing God to creaturely dimensions, of knocking God down to our size. The theocentric tendency of Edwards's ontology is perhaps most tellingly conveyed in a passage in *End of Creation*, where he suggests the thought experiment of weighing God and the world in opposite pans of a vast balance. The conclusion, as one might expect, is that "as the Creator is infinite, and has all possible existence, perfection and excellence, so he must have all possible regard."[37] Ontology serves doxology. The analogy of the balance illustrates graphically the process that is constantly occuring in Edwards's writings: the weighing of God's being and reality over against that of the world.

Occasionally Edwards invokes the idea of a "chain of being."[38] "An *Archangel*," he tells us, "must be supposed to have more existence . . . than a *worm* or a *flea*."[39] Yet his specific application of the chain of being shows once again that his chief concern is to highlight the ontological supremacy of God. He has in fact precious little to say regarding comparisons among creatures. He proposes what might be called a calculus of value, according to which every entity carries a specific "degree of existence" and "degree of excellence," with the overall value of each entity determined as the arithmetical product of these two numerical figures. Yet he never follows up this far-reaching proposal with a discussion of its ramifications. One wonders: Is one "excellent" human being worth as much as two or three who are not "excellent"? Do the concerns of a community, possessing more "existence" than any individual, take precedence over those of an individual? How should human beings treat those entities that rank below themselves in "existence" but still possess some measure of intrinsic worth? That such crucial questions remain unanswered is suprising, in light of Edwards's wonted logical thoroughness. One can only conclude that his interest lay not in comparing creatures with one another but in pointing to the God whose nature is immeasurably beyond the finite ladder-steps of the created chain of being.[40]

Connected with Edwards's doctrine of being is his highly distinctive notion of "consent," according to which each and every being subsists as a being-related-to-something.[41] As he says in one of his most enigmatic utterances: "For being, if we examine it narrowly, is nothing else but proportion."[42] Consent finds its paradigmatic instance within the very being of God, that is, in the society of persons of the Holy Trinity. Edwards interprets God's consent to Godself in Augustinian fashion by taking the Holy Spirit to be the subsistent bond of love connecting Father and Son.[43] Looking at the matter of consent from a slightly different angle, it was God's consent to Godself or self-regard that formed the basis for the divine act of creation. For God necessarily has highest regard for that which is most worthy.[44] The Trinity and the creation are thus the two great divine "communications," flowing from two great exercises of consent by God, the one *ad intra* and the other *ad extra*. Every creaturely consent is a miniature echo of the Trinity, the perfect archetype of harmonious diversity, and also an echo of creation, the perfect model of disinterested regard for highest worth.

God and Knowing

Turning from Edwards's ontology to his idealism, we move immediately into better-charted terrain.[45] Scholars have devoted more attention to idealism than perhaps any other feature of his philosophical thinking.[46] Yet the connection between his idealism and his theological interests has not been fully appreciated. Edwards's idealism was in part a reaction to the threat of a mechanistic and materialistic universe, as most alarmingly illustrated in the writings of Hobbes, the bête noire of the eighteenth-century Christian philosophers. One of the earliest entries in Edwards's personal notebook indicates his opposition to Hobbes: "As we have shown and demonstrated (contrary to the opinion of Hobbes, that nothing is substance but matter) that no matter is substance but only God, who is a spirit."[47] The speediest way for Edwards to cut the Gordian knot of atheistic materialism was to deny the very existence of independent matter, and with it the independent efficacy of material causation. "There is no such thing as mechanism," Edwards writes, "if that word is taken to be that whereby bodies act each upon other [*sic*], purely and properly by themselves."[48] Idealism reflected a theocentric strategy of turning the tables on materialism, making God as immaterial into the central and defining reality and rendering matter a merely derivative phenomenon of consciousness.

Edwards's theocentric impulse becomes yet more apparent in his further claim, related to his idealism, that God alone is truly "substance."[49] To him "substance" denotes something complete in itself, self-contained, and self-sufficient, and thus any understanding of creatures as themselves substances presents a direct challenge to his theocentric vision of a world in every respect derived from and dependent upon God. In claiming God as sole substance, Edwards is not postulating a static divine essence, of which all seeming finite realities are modifications (à la Spinoza),[50] but a more dynamic conception of God as an incessantly active though inherently stable source of finite reality. He qualifies his identification of God as sole substance when he writes: "God is as it were the only substance, or rather, the perfection and steadfastness of his knowledge, wisdom, power and will."[51]

Strictly speaking, it is not so much that God is sole substance (which might indeed be interpreted pantheistically) but that God's consciousness constitutes the ground of all reality, as he explains in a crucial passage of *The Mind*:

> And indeed, the secret lies here: that which truly is the substance of all bodies is the infinitely exact and precise and perfectly stable idea in God's mind, together with his stable will that the same shall gradually be communicated to us, and to other minds, according to certain fixed and exact established methods and laws: or in somewhat different language, the infinitely exact and precise divine idea, together with an answerable, perfectly exact, precise and stable will with respect to correspondent communications to created minds, and effects on their minds.[52]

This theocentric idealism differs from an anthropocentric idealism (such as Kantianism) by locating an imperturbable basis for all acts of knowing outside of the human mind itself, in the terra firma of the divine being. Because the world as it is could not conceivably differ from the world as it appears to God, Edwards's idealism is quite consistent with an objective approach to epistemology. It does not dissolve the world into a phenomenalistic haze, because the ideas in God's mind are taken as regulative of, indeed, efficacious of, correct creaturely perceptions.[53] From the theocentric perspective one might ask: What firmer foundation for reality could there be than the ideas of God? As Aquinas wrote, "The knowledge of God is the cause of things."[54] Herein lies the clue to Edwards's unique blend of idealism and empiricism.[55] The data of sense experience are reliable and trustworthy, in spite of the fact that the *objects* of sense experience are taken to be ideal rather than material, because these ideal objects have an unshakable ontological ground in an all-encompassing divine mind. Only because Edwards's epistemology is radically God-centered does he succeed in his peculiar combination of empiricism and idealism.

Another aspect of Edwards's idealism lay in his high valuation of consciousness and his attendant conviction that all things exist for the sake of consciousness. For him even the immanent glory of God was as good as nonexistent without some manifestation to consciousness, "For goodness has no existence but with relation to perception."[56] Yet this distinctive emphasis on consciousness had a theological origin. Wallace Anderson explains that Edwards early in life "was convinced that the primary and essential element in religion consists in cognition—a unique consciousness and knowledge of God," and that "he became convinced that religion, taken in this sense, is the very purpose of the entire creation."[57] *End of Creation*, though written just prior to his death, voiced his lifelong convictions. There he characterized the knowledge of God among elect creatures as the most "worthy" element of the entire universe, the bull's-eye as it were of God's intention in creating the world.[58] Yet the idealism of *The Mind*, just as much as the argument of *End of Creation*, found its roots in his conception of the knowledge of God.

Idealism was simply the extension of Edwards's theological conviction that God's glory, to be truly glorious, must reverberate in the hearts and minds of his creatures. In effect he treated the knowledge of God's glory as the paradigm case for all acts of knowing. Beginning with the notion that God's glory must be known and appreciated for it to have any significance, he generalized this notion into the sweeping principle that "nothing has any existence anywhere else than in consciousness."[59] The concept of God as known, as manifest, as visibly glorious, proved so decisive a factor in Edwards's thinking that it gave birth to idealist metaphysics.

God, Beauty, and Causality

More briefly, I will touch on the theocentric tendencies in Edwards's aesthetics and his approach to causality. Without question beauty is a central and constitutive category in his thinking, and here again he shows himself chiefly concerned with God.[60] His writings include no discussion whatever of manmade beauties, or the nature of the fine arts. These things did not concern him, and this conspicuous omission should make us reluctant to consider Edwards an aesthetician in the ordinary sense. Even his occasional rhapsodies regarding the beauties of nature function chiefly as a foil to a deeper reflection on the divine beauty. "Primary beauty," to use Edwards's terminology, is immeasurably higher than mere "secondary beauty," the beauty of outward and material things.[61] As Norman Fiering claims, "For Edwards all that is ordinarily meant by 'beauty' was to be understood only as a *symbolic* counterpart to a higher kind of correspondence, that of wills."[62] Primary beauty remains primary in his aesthetic thinking, and secondary beauty holds interest for him because it mirrors the primary beauty of spiritual realities. Edwards regards divine beauty as a truly *distinguishing* feature of God: "God is God, and distinguished from all other beings, and exalted above 'em, chiefly by his divine beauty, which is infinitely diverse from all other beauty."[63] Just as with Edwards's characterization of God as supreme Being, the conception of God as supreme Beauty serves not to reduce or limit God in any way but rather to accentuate the divine uniqueness and transcendence.

With respect to causality Edwards tends toward occasionalism, attributing all events to divine agency and denying that created agents are properly capable of producing effects on one another. Creatures, that is, are not the *causes* of observed effects but merely provide the *occasions* for God to act.[64] This move is a part of Edwards's broader strategy to secure the world again for divine involvement by overthrowing the eighteenth-century notion of a self-contained mechanistic universe. His occasionalism is thus of a piece with his idealism and is equally radical, because it addresses the problems posed by such notions as material substances or efficacious created causes through simply eliminating these conceptions altogether.

Edwards is entirely uncompromising in denying the causal self-sufficiency of the creature, and nowhere is this position more patent than in the argument of *Original Sin*, where he writes:

> God's upholding created existence, or causing its existence, is altogether equivalent to an *immediate production out of nothing*, at each moment, because its existence at this moment is not merely in part from God, but wholly from him; and not in any part, or degree from its antecedent existence.[65]

Even Edwards's most loyal partisans had trouble with this passage, since it effectively denied any real involvement of creatures in the causal process. It presented one of his most tendentious arguments, yet it effectively illustrates his dialectical audacity. Not with halfhearted measures but with a bold philosophical counterstroke he met the mechanistic and materialistic threat to God's involvement in mundane reality.

A couple of conclusions follow from the foregoing analysis of Edwards's philosophy, one related to Edwards's thought in general, and the other related to the use of metaphysics within Christian theology. The intimate connection between Edwards's metaphysics and his theocentrism establishes a link between the metaphysical writings and the more purely theological works. It should be clear that the early philosophical speculations of *The Mind* are not a separate canon within the canon, an island among his other writings. Nor do they represent an abortive project that Edwards undertook in his immaturity and abandoned in his maturity.[66] Instead they are a reflection of the most permanent and enduring elements of Edwards's thought and exhibit his pervasive concern with the reality, centrality, and supremacy of God.

Edwards's *The Mind* serves as a challenge to the customary Neoorthodox or Barthian objections against the theological use of metaphysics.[67] One thinks of Karl Barth's famous characterization of *analogia entis*, or the theological use of ontology, as "the invention of Antichrist"![68] His stridency derived from the assumption that metaphysics in practice becomes a tool wielded by sinners against God, to subjugate God to anthropocentric presuppositions. Metaphysics for Barth thus robs God of the glory.[69] Yet this criticism does not stick to Edwards. As I have shown, he applied his philosophical acumen to exploring and explaining the radical transcendence and utter incommensurability of God. The case of Edwards might provoke a reappraisal of the claim that metaphysics in principle blunts the sharp edges of distinctive Christian claims concerning God. Edwards's "Being in general" is no remote or empty abstraction but is the living God of Scripture. In his case, the God of philosophy and the God of theology were one and the same.[70]

3

Contemplation

The Spirituality of
the *Personal Narrative* and *Diary*

In a review of publications in the field of American religious history during the 1980s, Martin Marty noted the "astonishingly few titles to be noticed" under the rubric of "spirituality."[1] This scholarly lacuna in what Marty otherwise refers to as "a decade of achievement" is difficult to explain in light of the recent boom in academic books on spirituality in Christendom and in world religions generally. Two imposing English-language book series, together comprising more than a hundred volumes, attest to both the depth and breadth of the current revival of scholarship in the field of spirituality.[2] Since the recent literature on spirituality is finely attuned to historical, social, and cultural contexts, it holds the promise of augmenting and enriching the perspective of American religious historians.

To a large extent, this recent neglect of spirituality in American religion applies to Edwards. Almost everyone who knows of Edwards knows of his piety. But though the secondary studies make perfunctory references to Edwards's "devotion," "faith," or "mysticism," the precise character of his spirituality and its bearing on his well-known intellectual and ecclesiastical achievements has remained unclear—despite the availability of ample materials for a study of his spirituality. Two primary sources, the *Personal Narrative* and *Diary*, though both relatively brief (about 6,500 and 16,000 words, respectively), provide a wealth of insight into Edwards's early life and document his shifting interpretation of his own spiritual experience.[3] Another boon in interpreting Edwards's spirituality is Charles Hambrick-Stowe's *The Practice of Piety: Puritan Devotional Disciplines in Seventeenth-Century New England* (1982), a wide-ranging work that gave greater scrutiny than previous studies to the concrete practices of spiritual life in New England Puritanism.[4] Though Hambrick-Stowe's research stopped at 1700 and thus did not include Edwards, his retrieval of the more contemplative and less active dimension of American Puritanism provides a useful starting point for a study of Edwards's spirituality.

The phrase "Edwards's spirituality" can be interpreted variously. It might be equated with his ideal of the Christian life. If it is taken in this fashion, the investigator appropriately turns to Edwards's statements on true religion in his sermons and in such treatises as *Religious Affections*. One might compile the spiritual advice he gave out piecemeal in his correspondence. One could also make note of specific individuals whom Edwards set forth as spiritual exemplars—most notably David Brainerd, whose *Diary* Edwards published with incisive commentary.[5] My study of Edwards's spirituality is, however, differently conceived and more narrowly circumscribed: to ascertain the kind of spiritual experience depicted in Edwards's autobiographical writings and to juxtapose that depiction with his inherited Puritan tradition of spiritual experience and spiritual autobiography.[6]

The *Diary* and *Personal Narrative* indicate that Edwards's spirituality is fundamentally contemplative rather than active. In recounting his life story, he fails to mention any works of love toward fellow humans. To a remarkable degree, his spiritual development occurred in independence of family, church, or friends. Moreover, a longing for contemplative solitude permeated his early years and was linked with an ascetic discipline of "temperate" eating. While his reliance on ascetic and meditative practices was not unusual for a Puritan, there was something unique in his sweeping conception of the entire Christian life as a viewing or apprehending of God. For him, spirituality *was* contemplation. He also distinguished himself from the mainstream New England tradition by shifting attention away from the self and toward the self's perceptions of God. In the period between the writing of the *Diary* and the *Personal Narrative*, Edwards reconceived the spiritual life in such a way as to downplay self-scrutiny in favor of a disinterested viewing of God in Godself. It seems that Edwards's experience of God was less significant to him for what it revealed about himself (i.e., that he was "saved") than for what it revealed about God (i.e., that God was "excellent"). As Edwards wrote: "The sweetest joys and delights I have experienced, have not been those that have arisen from a hope of my own good estate; but in a direct view of the glorious things of the gospel."[7] Thus, by minimizing both preparatory penance and gracious assurance, Edwards fashioned a spirituality that was less anthropocentric and more theocentric than that of his Puritan forebears.[8]

In what follows, a brief sketch of Puritan spirituality will serve as background to Edwards's *Diary* and *Personal Narrative*. After an analysis of the texts, the discussion will turn to the bearing of Edwards's contemplative spirituality on our image of the man and his work.[9]

The Character of Puritan Spirituality

The term "spirituality," in its Christian application, can be defined as the personal assimilation of salvation or of God's grace by the believer.[10] An age-old distinction is drawn between the "active life" (*vita activa*) and the "contemplative life" (*vita contemplativa*) and between two corresponding types of believer, traditionally symbolized by Martha and Mary in Luke's gospel.[11] The contrast between the two is relative rather than absolute, since almost all practicing Christians engage in certain contemplative practices at one time or another. Thus Charles Hambrick-Stowe interprets the difference as a matter of degree: "The contemplative is distinguished from the common practicing believer by the regularity, protractedness, and continuing intensity of the exercises."[12] For our purposes, contemplative spirituality may be characterized as a form of practice that seeks to cultivate an ever-deepening awareness of divine truth and reality, and the love of God for God's own sake. It is typically linked with solitude and silence, and the discipline of the body, as aids to focusing the mind and heart on God.[13] Active spirituality, by contrast, is a form of practice that consists in outgoing acts of love toward fellow human beings, and it is usually connected with a systematic effort at organizing one's life so as to facilitate such works of love.

The received viewpoint has been that Puritan Christians were activists. They understood the Christian life in dynamic terms, as a struggle of God's chosen few against the world, the flesh, and the devil. Their spirituality was very much at home in the world and was more likely to find expression in the marketplace, school, or kitchen than in the privacy of the prayer closet. The sense of an all-encompassing divine providence led them to concern themselves with God's work in the world at large rather than exclusively in their individual lives. Because of their outgoing and gregarious approach to life, the highest expression of Puritan spirituality was corporate and family worship rather than solitary prayer.

Union with God was not the goal but the beginning of the spiritual life, and the all-important matter for the Puritans was to discern correctly whether one did or did not belong to Christ.[14] Hypocrisy was the great and damning sin, and for this reason, mere outward conformity to some rule was no consolation at all. It was all too easy to confuse some natural state—intellectual conviction, emotional stirrings, or pangs of conscience—with genuine and supernatural grace. A chasm separated nature from grace. Hence Puritanism was a Spirit-centered movement that stressed the believer's immediate relationship with God rather than the mediation of grace through the ministry, sacraments, or institutional church. Puritans were hostile to "technique" in the spiritual life, in part because they believed themselves to be dependent on the inscrutable and unmanipulatable will of God.

In an effort to transcend hypocrisy, Puritanism became preoccupied with the search for "signs" that would unmistakably indicate the presence of grace within a particular person. This engendered a tendency toward endless self-scrutiny. By means of ruthless introspection one could strip away the successive onionskins of vain and self-flattering hopes and at last discern a core of sincere and unhypocritical faith.[15] Even more important to the Puritans than self-scrutiny alone was the "morphology of conversion," described by Edmund Morgan as a scheme of experience in which "each stage could be be distinguished from the next, so that a man could check his eternal condition by a set of temporal and recogniz able signs."[16] While the details of the morphology varied from one Puritan teacher to another, the unquestioned assumption was that the sinner would only receive grace after becoming aware of his or her spiritual impotence and utter helplessness before God. Therefore "humiliation" or even "terror" had to precede "conversion" or "grace."[17]

So much for the standard portrayal of Puritan spirituality. Hambrick-Stowe offers another picture, in which the Puritans were no less contemplative than active: "Puritanism was as affective as it was rational, and Puritans were as wont to withdraw into contemplative solitude as they were to be active in the marketplace."[18] Salvation for the Puritans, he argues, was never a given or a fully achieved state but always a journey and a goal. While *theologically* it may be true that union with God was realized at the beginning of the Christian life, *experientially* this union became a conscious fact only through a lengthy process of spiritual development. Conversion was only one event in the Puritan life-pilgrimage, and many scholars have overemphasized it. Hambrick-Stowe suggests that a "dynamic two-part cycle of emptying and filling" characterized the whole of Puritan spirituality, not merely the transition accomplished in conversion.[19]

Meditation regularly accompanied the Puritans' reading of the Bible and other books. The focus of this meditation was not limited to penitence over sins; it also sought to enlarge the believer's grasp of spiritual realities through focussing her or his mind on Christ, the saints, and the glories to come. Basic to the Puritans' practice of spirituality was "technique"—manuals of devotion, written prayers, private fasts, times and methods of meditation. The Puritans opposed the Catholic or specifically Tridentine teaching that the "means of grace" have efficacy in and of themselves, but they never neglected or despised the means as a result. While the Puritan minister was expected to pray in the pulpit without written helps, extemporaneously, both preacher and layperson were free to use books of written prayers in their private devotions. The Puritans' practice of diary-keeping was an aid to self-knowledge, much like the Catholic practice of going to the confessional. For the Puritans, moreover, writing was itself a means of grace.

Puritan spirituality, in sum, left more room than is commonly supposed for the solitary seeker after God. Hambrick-Stowe concludes that while "contemplatives" were probably a minority in New England Puritanism, they were the culmination of a pervasive spirituality in which the entire population participated.

The *Diary* and *Personal Narrative*

My examination of the *Diary* and *Personal Narrative* will center on the question: What indications does one find in the texts that Edwards was a contemplative? The conclusion will hinge on a related question: What revisions in our general picture of Edwards result from identifying him as a contemplative?

While both Edwards's *Diary* and *Personal Narrative* are revealing, they are revealing in different ways. As one would expect, the *Diary* is a raw transcript of lived experience, with all its ambiguities, hesitations, and vicissitudes. Here we see Edwards trying to make up his mind regarding his experiences. The *Personal Narrative*, on the other hand, was written perhaps a decade and a half later and is a highly stylized and meticulously crafted piece that presents a self-consistent account.[20] Richard Lovelace showed that seventeenth-century Puritans intended their autobiographies to serve a practical purpose in instructing and edifying their readers and that consequently they reshaped their material to suit their ends. This observation holds true for Edwards as well. The *Personal Narrative*, though clearly dependent on the *Diary* and occasionally following it verbatim, exhibits a unity and clarity not apparent in the earlier work. It bears the imprint of Edwards's theological efforts in the intervening years to distinguish between natural and gracious experience, a process that culminated in the publication of *Religious Affections* in 1746. The *Personal Narrative*, as Daniel Shea notes, is essentially didactic: "By narrative example he will teach what is false and what is true in religious experience, giving another form to the argument he carried on elsewhere; and he hopes actually to affect his readers by both the content and the presentation of his exemplary experience."[21] While the discussion will draw on both the *Diary* and *Personal Narrative*, it will rely on the latter as Edwards's considered judgment on the meaning of his earlier experiences.

Edwards departed from the conventions of Puritan autobiography in the way he treated his conversion in the *Personal Narrative*. While the text includes a conversion, coinciding with his first experience of the "new sense of things," it does not really fit the genre of the Puritan conversion narrative. He alloted very little space to the period prior to the new sense and so did not bring out a contrast between the "before" and the "after" of conversion. In addition, he did not single out his conversion experience as an indication of grace. On the contrary, he states expressly—and astonishingly!—that "it never came into my thought that there was any thing spiritual or of a saving nature, in this."[22] His focus was sanctification rather than justification. The first experience of the new sense held significance simply as the commencement of his progress toward holiness.

Edwards's most noteworthy departure from convention, however, was his rejection of the Puritan morphology of conversion that made humiliation for sin a necessary prelude to consolation and assurance. In the *Personal Narrative*, Edwards's experiences of deep penitence for sin came long after his conversion, and in fact toward the very end of the recorded period. He became aware quite early on that his experiences did not conform to the received theory. The *Diary* for 1722 expressed the worry "I do not remember that I experienced regeneration, exactly in those steps, in which divines say it is generally wrought." He specifically mentioned the lack of a full "preparatory work."[23] Yet he soon stopped trying to fit experience to doctrine and instead altered his doctrine. *Personal Narrative* implicitly, and *Religious Affections* explicitly, repudiated the old morphology by making the *nature* of one's spiritual experiences rather than their *order* the discriminating factor in determining whether or not they were gracious. For all these reasons, Edwards's *Personal Narrative* is not a Puritan conversion narrative; instead, it is a treatise on the Christian life in autobiographical form, forming a kind of phenomenology of the believer's vision or perception of God.[24]

At first glance, the Edwards of the *Diary* and *Personal Narrative* appears to be a Puritan of the classical conception. He depicts his spiritual life as struggle and strain: "It was my continual strife day and night, and constant inquiry, how I should *be* more holy, and *live* more holily."[25] Edwards's exercises in self-scrutiny were entirely in keeping with his inherited tradition—the restless conscience of early New England. He committed himself to introspection: "Whenever I do any conspicuously evil action, [I intend] to trace it back, till I come to the original cause." He even resolved to examine his dreams for the light they might shed on his motives.[26] The *Diary* contains frequent references to a "weekly account" that seems to have been a tabulation of duties performed, with higher numerical figures indicating greater fidelity to his self-imposed regimen. Edwards's spiritual account-keeping shows how far he went toward systematizing his spiritual life, although he later came to believe that he had previously acted "with too great a dependence on my own strength."[27] Given these considerations, Edwards's spirituality might seem active and outgoing, works-oriented and yet introspective.

A closer scrutiny of the *Diary* and *Personal Narrative*, however, calls into question the notion of Edwards as activist. In recounting for himself and his readers what he believed to be important about his life, Edwards left out a great deal. Conspicuously missing from the texts is any depiction of his social and physical context. Even by the standard of Puritan autobiographies, which often limited themselves to "God and the soul," Edwards's autobiographical writings represent an extreme case. From the *Personal Narrative* alone, one would never know that Edwards had a mother, hometown, siblings, intellectual interests, and friends (other than the Smiths)! He never identifies himself as a Congregationalist minister. He mentions his father twice but gives no comment on their relationship.[28] Not only is the context for action missing, but so are the actions themselves. Nothing happens—at least in the external realm. The *Personal Narrative* has no real plotline; it is less a genuine story than a depiction of successive states of experience. If outgoing acts of love and service to fellow humans are the mark of an activist spirituality, then Edwards's *Diary* and *Personal Narrative* wholly fail the test.

Terminology and word frequency confirm this point. The vocabulary of *Personal Narrative* is extraordinarily rich in words describing subjective states: "sense" (22 times), "affection"-"affect" (16 times), "contemplation" or "meditation" (15 times), "view" (10 times), and "conviction" (6 times). Words describing the quality of these subjective states also occur quite frequently: "sweet"-"sweetness"-"sweetly" (38 times!) and "delight"-"delightful" (24 times). Even more striking than the nouns for subjective states are the words "appearance"-"appear" (33 times) and the synonym "seem" (27 times). Coupled with a subject and object, the verbs "appear" and "seem" dominate the narrative in their nearly sixty occurrences. The unifying theme of *Personal Narrative* is how things "appear" to Edwards.[29]

One of the classical features of contemplative spirituality evident in *Personal Narrative* is the quest for solitude with God.[30] The opening paragraph recounts the founding of a quasi-monastic community of praying schoolboys who, under Edwards's guidance, built a "booth in a swamp" for prayer. Though this "booth" was in a "very retired spot," it was still not remote enough for Edwards's liking, and he adds, "I had particular secret places of my own in the woods, where I used to retire by myself." The eremitic impulse thrust him deeper into the Connecticut countryside. Ola Winslow comments: "The significant detail in this episode for the understanding of Jonathan Edwards is that praying with his companions did not satisfy him . . . hence, unknown to his companions, he had his own place of secret prayer."[31] It is striking how much solitude there is in the *Personal Narrative*—in Edwards's fantasies of "being alone in the mountains, or some solitary wilderness, far from all mankind, sweetly conversing with Christ," in his "often walking alone in the woods and solitary places, for meditation, soliloquy, and prayer," and in his retirement to "a solitary place, on the banks of Hudson's river."[32] In Edwards's youthful encomium to the thirteen-year-old girl whom he was later to marry—the closest thing to a love letter in all his writings—he notes that she "loves to be alone, walking in the fields and groves, and seems to have some one invisible always conversing with her."[33]

It is common for contemplatives to feel exasperation over practical affairs that distract them from God. Faced by the pressures of everyday life, Edwards exhibited just this sort of frustration. After he became a tutor at Yale College in 1724, his first *Diary* entry is a lament:

This week has been a very remarkable week with me, with respect to despondencies, fears, perplexities, multitudes of cares, and distraction of mind: it being the week I came hither to New-Haven, in order to entrance upon the office of tutor of the college. I have now abundant reason to be convinced of the troublesomeness and vexation of the world, and that it will never be another kind of world.[34]

In the *Personal Narrative*, Edwards's spiritual experience follows a steadily rising curve after the beginning of his "new sense" until he returned to Yale. The account of his declension is brief and blunt: "After I went to New Haven I sunk in religion; my mind being diverted from my eager pursuits after holiness by some affairs that greatly perplexed and distracted my thoughts."[35] A cause-and-effect relationship is implied: the distractions of college teaching brought on a spiritual decline. In neither the *Diary* nor the *Personal Narrative* does Edwards describe the "affairs" that distracted him. The essential thing for him was simply that they distracted him from pursuing God. Elsewhere in his *Diary* Edwards says that he found all manner of "change or alteration" to be spiritually detrimental— "journeys, change of place, change of business, change of studies, and change of other circumstances."[36] He desired stability, so as to engage in his spiritual exercises without hindrance.

Not only was solitude crucial to Edwards's spirituality but so was ascetic discipline. His general attitude to the body was Platonic in the sense that he sharply distinguished the soul and the body, held that the soul as superior ought to rule the body, and insisted that religious practice diminishes the influence of the body over the soul.[37] One searches his writings in vain for any passage in which he expressed an unalloyed delight in any sort of physical activity.[38] He regarded "temperance," or an abstemious approach to eating and drinking, as a form of "mortification" that gave "deep wounds to the body of sin; hard blows, which make him stagger and reel."[39] One *Diary* entry shows that Edwards believed his sparse diet was an aid in concentrating his mind: "By a sparingness in diet, and eating as much as may be what is light and easy of digestion, I shall doubtless be able to think more clearly." Two of the early "Resolutions" related to eating and drinking, and quite a few of the later *Diary* entries. Indeed, Edwards's concern for "temperate" eating and drinking bordered on obsession. He was wary of meals that offered a wide variety of foods, because he thought they might lure him into eating more than usual without realizing it. He once considered the possibility that self-denial at the table might be injuring his health but judged that only the *certainty* that he was harming himself would justify eating more. While eating he sometimes feared he would later grow "faint"—an indication of just how little food he was consuming at the time. To a disturbing extent, he vacillated and dithered over his eating policies in the effort to find an arrangement that could satisfy both stomach and conscience.[40]

The youthful Edwards showed the sort of social separation or dislocation common in contemplative spirituality. "No lifelong friendship dates from his college days," says Winslow, and "there is no record even of transient intimacies."[41] In the *Diary* he comes across as a high-spirited and independent person often piqued at the inadequacies of others. He refers often to his own "fretful-ness." He repeatedly debates over whether and when to reprove others, and the sin that he most frequently attributes to himself is "evil speaking" or censori-ousness. Evidently Edwards's standards for others were as high and exacting as those he held for himself: "I could bear the thoughts of no other companions but such as were holy." In what seems to be the only specific reference to church attendance in the *Diary*, Edwards says that he became "impatient at the church meeting."[42] With the significant exception of the Smith family in New York, whose company he relished and whose absence he later mourned, Edwards's relations with other human beings in his early life seem to have afforded him little edification or pleasure. It was the adoptive family of the Smiths in New York, rather than the natural family of the Edwardses back in East Windsor, that received credit in the *Personal Narrative* for fostering his spiritual devel-opment.

Edwards's censoriousness was most keenly aroused by his own family and his parents in particular. Though in his *Diary* he expressed himself guardedly on family matters, the references to "fretfulness" often occur in direct conjunction with references to his parents. Not surprisingly, the irritation reached a higher pitch after he returned to live with them in May 1723, following his brief pastorate in New York. Later in the month, he tried in his *Diary* to convince himself—the effort itself is telling!—of the "great obligations I am under to love and honour my parents." Some weeks later, he concluded that "it is a very hard matter to speak evil of another without sin."[43] This statement leads one to wonder: Was the younger Edwards an insufferable little zealot, convinced that he knew what was right and wrong with everyone around him? Perhaps Edwards's age should be taken into account; many nineteen-year-olds conceive an exaggerated inde-pendence vis-à-vis their parents. Yet even when we balance out the youthful *Diary* with the mature *Personal Narrative*, it becomes clear that Edwards's spirituality is neither familial nor social but solitary.[44] In Augustine's *Confessions*, every new phase of the author's spiritual development involved other human beings: Mon-ica, the Manicheans, the mistress, and so on. In the *Personal Narrative*, by con-trast, other human beings are conspicuous by their absence.

The surest evidence of Edwards's identity as a contemplative is his repeated reference in the *Personal Narrative* to his practice of "contemplation" (13 times) and "meditation" (2 times). The final *Diary* entry intimates an intensive practice: "To set apart days of meditation on particular topics, as . . . the greatness of my sins . . . the great future things promised."[45] While we have no text like Loyola's *Spiritual Exercises* that describes the method and scope of his meditations, it is plausible to suppose that the diligent Edwards explored many avenues and ap-proaches. One *Diary* entry clearly indicates that his meditative practice included the writing down of his reflections, and it is possible that many of his miscella-neous writings originated in this way.[46]

An overlooked contemplative feature of the *Personal Narrative* is Edwards's brief but telling reference to the Song of Songs, indicating his acquaintance with the Canticles mysticism and its erotic interpretation of God's relation to the soul. The paragraph in question is shot through with images of seclusion and intimacy. Edwards takes an individualistic rather than ecclesial line of interpretation: God's lover is not the church but the solitary believer, namely, Edwards. This section includes one of three references in the *Personal Narrative* to Edwards's desire to be "swallowed up in God" and culminates in an exclamation over the "sweet burning" or "ardor of soul that I know not how to express."[47]

Edwards as a Contemplative

Scholars generally have seen Jonathan Edwards as a Christian thinker, not as a practitioner of the Christian life. Yet the biographical evidence indicates that Edwards's exercises of piety were just as pronounced and as regular a feature of his life as were his intellectual explorations. Praying was as indispensable to him as thinking was. If among his writings only the *Personal Narrative* had survived destruction and all the rest had perished by fire, Edwards would perhaps enjoy a reputation as an outstanding spiritual figure in early America. The character of his spirituality was both theocentric and contemplative. It was theocentric in that it revolved around God and the service of God for God's own sake rather than the self and the self's fulfillment. Consequently, it carried a moderately ascetic flavor and tended toward self-abnegation. It was contemplative in that it implied that the human person is to serve and please God by pondering God's character and works. The theocentric aspect of Edwards's spirituality agrees entirely with his metaphysical thought, as presented in chapter 2; the contemplative aspect comports with Edwards's theory of spiritual perception, as expounded in chapter 1.

In its contemplative aspect, Edwards's spirituality followed definite precedents in the New England Puritan tradition, as shown in the preceding discussion. Yet in its theocentric aspect, his spirituality represented a departure from that tradition, which was explicitly preoccupied with the self in a way that he was not. Describing the changing conceptions of conversion from the Reformation to the nineteenth century, Jerald Brauer writes: "If it is viewed from the perspective of the magisterial reformation worked out by Luther and Calvin, Puritanism can be seen as a gradual subjectivizing of the Reformation faith."[48] Charles Cohen quips: "Puritans may have thought of themselves as sinkholes of corruption, but sinkholes deserving extended discussion."[49] Even the vocabulary of Puritanism reflected interest in the self. A study of seventeenth-century Puritan vocabulary showed no less than forty-two compound words beginning with the prefix "self-" that were in current usage.[50] While Edwards's spirituality does not wholly lack

Puritanism's dark fascination with the self, it is basically outward-looking rather than introspective.

In various religious traditions, the contemplative individual is peripheral to the larger society. For religious cultures such as medieval Europe or Buddhist Sri Lanka, the sister or monk who has entered the contemplative life has passed into a society beyond society. By leaving parents and family, the contemplative is, so to speak, without antecedents; by remaining celibate, without offspring and family responsibilities; by refraining from mundane occupations and concerns, without economic ties. The marks of the contemplative include physical isolation and social separation—factors conspicuous in the *Diary* and *Personal Narrative*. Of course Edwards was not a monk; yet he pursued a solitary and contemplative life to the extent that was compatible with his responsibilities as husband, father, and pastor. Winslow says: "He was a man consecrated to religious life before he was a husband, father, neighbor, or townsman; and he made few compromises."[51]

An irony of Edwards's solitary spirituality is that the notion of community in various forms was integral to his philosophical and theological reflections.[52] The language of "heavenly love" he used in *Personal Narrative* to describe his fellowship with the Smiths recurs frequently in the sermons on *Charity and Its Fruits* and in the *Miscellanies* on heaven. The mature Edwards, moreover, had diverse connections and relations with others: Sarah his wife (with whom he shared an "uncommon union"),[53] his parishioners, his disciples Samuel Hopkins and Joseph Bellamy, and such Scottish admirers and correspondents as John Erskine and others. In his *Humble Attempt* Edwards emerged as a clerical statesman, spearheading an international effort in concerted prayer. A recent study by Gerald R. McDermott argues that Edwards's writings contain the outlines of a "public theology" treating the civil community and the individual Christian's relation to it.[54] Despite all these connections, however, Edwards's life and ministry were rooted in a contemplative practice that drew him away from others and toward solitude with God. Presuming that Samuel Hopkins was correct, or nearly so, in his estimate that Edwards spent thirteen hours every day in his study,[55] then it appears that the pastor's study replaced the Connecticut forests of his youth as Edwards's chosen location for contemplative retreat.

A good deal of commentary on the *Personal Narrative* has stressed Edwards's "new sense" of God's glory. The noun "sense" has attracted attention, while the verb "appear" has gone unnoticed. Yet an interesting feature of the verb, besides its sheer numerical frequency, is that it requires a subject and an indirect object (e.g., "God appeared to me"). Someone or something "appears," and someone is "appeared to"; an object is implied alongside the subject. What Edwards expressed with the word "appears" was not so much an emotion as an apprehension, not something that welled up from the depths of the self but something that derived instead from external reality.[56] The metaphor of sight underscored the thing seen as much as the seer.

Ultimately Edwards's ideal of the Christian life exalted the perception of God above all else. Seeing God was not a means to anything else but an end in itself. Seeing God was more important than acting for God. Seeing God took precedence even over being saved, as he writes in *Personal Narrative*:

> The sweetest joys and delights I have experienced, have not been those that have arisen from a hope of my own good estate; but in a direct view of the glorious things of the gospel. When I enjoy this sweetness, it seems to carry me above the thoughts of my own estate; it seems at such times a loss that I cannot bear, to take off my eye from the glorious pleasant object I behold without me, to turn my eye in upon myself, and my own good estate.[57]

Complete absorption in God, rapt enjoyment of the divine "sweetness," and forgetfulness of one's self—here in a nutshell is Edwards's spiritual ideal.

If one is to lose oneself in the vision of God, then it might follow that one is also to lose oneself in the service of God. Some of Edwards's followers, and especially Samuel Hopkins, pushed the aspect of self-abnegation much further than Edwards ever did, insisting that the true saint must be "willing to be damned for the glory of God."[58] While Edwards never endorsed this line of thought and explicitly rejected it in his *Miscellanies*,[59] he nonetheless helped prepare for it through his radical notion of contemplation as a delight in God solely for God's own sake. Edwards's commendation of David Brainerd, whose heroic efforts in missionizing the Native Americans brought him to a premature death, also reinforced an ideal of total self-renunciation for the sake of God.[60]

The driving motivation for the contemplative life was not the sufferings and disappointments of the present life but rather the attractive prospect of seeing God. As Edwards wrote in his *Miscellanies*: "True weanedness from the world don't consist in being beat off from the world by the affliction of it, but a being drawn off by the sight of something better."[61] The vision of God was literally endless, as one sees in the conclusion to *End of Creation*; in heaven the saints move everlastingly closer to God, while they everlastingly fall short of perfect union with God.[62] The vision of God was increasingly desired and desirable to the saints, as noted in *Religious Affections*; the invariable mark of genuine spiritual experience is a desire for more of the same.[63] Thus the entire life of faith was, in effect, a growth in contemplation.

Since Edwards was unquestionably a religious thinker of high caliber as well as a contemplative, one naturally looks for a silver thread joining praxis and theory, experience and reflection. A clue comes in Edwards's persistent use of optical or ocular language throughout his writings in constitutive metaphors that govern the way he thinks about spiritual experience. Salvation means "seeing" God. Unregenerate people are "blind" to God. God is supremely "beautiful." The glory of God "shines upon" the elect in heaven, and is "reflected back" to God.

The *Personal Narrative*, as already noted, relentlessly repeats the words "appear" and "seem." Edwards here is depicting how he "sees" things, and especially how he "sees" God. Thus contemplative practice and theological reflection converged in Edwards's comprehensive notion of the vision of God, a vision he regarded as the goal of Christian living and Christian thinking. God is to be seen, and in being seen is to be appreciated.[64]

4

Valuation

Ethics and Divinity in *End of Creation*

The Background of British Moral Philosophy

Toward the end of the seventeenth century, English theology became preoccupied with ethics and the ethical implications of the Christian faith. This moralizing of Christianity was evident in John Locke's *The Reasonableness of Christianity* (1695), a text prophetic of tendencies in English thought during the subsequent century.[1] Concerning Jesus and his disciples, Locke asserted that "righteousness, or obedience to the law of God, was their great business" and that "there is not, I think, any of the duties of morality, which he has not, somewhere or other, by himself and his apostles, inculcated over and over again to his followers."[2] Increasingly, educated persons valued Christianity because it provided otherworldly sanctions (i.e., heaven and hell) as inducements to everyday virtues. The deist Anthony Collins, when asked why he sent his servants to church, answered: "I do it that they may neither rob nor murder me."[3] This curt reply is only an exaggerated expression of a common sentiment. Archbishop John Tillotson's sermons, which were widely studied, praised, and imitated in the early part of the century, conveyed the same point, that Christianity has its prime significance in upholding standards of good conduct.

Paralleling this growing stress on Christianity's ethical aspect was the emergence of "moral philosophy" as a discipline distinct from theology. Thomas Hobbes's controversial book *Leviathan* (1651), with its egoistic interpretation of human behavior and reduction of right and wrong to the sovereign's will, found few defenders or adherents, but it was a profound stimulus to ethical theorizing in the English-speaking world. Various social factors also promoted the development of moral philosophy. Englishmen of the late seventeenth century, who had experienced the turbulence of the Civil War and the excesses of religious enthusiasm, were eager to establish a basis for ethical discussion that was only loosely connected with church dogma. Just as theological ethics gave way to moral philosophy, so in political theory the divine right of kings was succeeded by the social contract theory in its various forms. Western thinkers were reluctant to allow distinctively theological beliefs to serve as ultimate sanctions for private or public morality. Underlying this theoretical shift, Leslie Stephen detected a dimmed perception of God: "Men who live under a visible monarch do not speculate as to the origin of the sentiment which makes them obey his laws. Their loyalty and the fear of his power are sufficient reasons."[4] Yet when God no longer speaks from Sinai, promising blessing and threatening ruin, then one needs a moral philosophy to account for why we should embrace virtue and shun vice.

On the western shore of the Atlantic, the moral philosophies of Samuel Clarke, Lord Shaftesbury, and Francis Hutcheson were supplanting the older Puritan theology at Harvard and Yale Colleges.[5] Although the continuing influence of Calvinism retarded the growth of the new thinking, New England in the early eighteenth century underwent a complex cultural shift described as "Angliciza-tion" by Harry S. Stout and as "the Moderate Enlightenment" by Henry F. May.[6] A growing spirit of liberalism and toleration muted the shriller notes of the old-time Calvinism. The new attitude to religion was characterized by moderation and the avoidance of extremes. By the time that Jonathan Edwards composed his major theological treatises in the 1750s—*Freedom of the Will*, *Original Sin*, and *Two Dissertations*—the New England zeitgeist posed a formidable challenge to Calvinist orthodoxy.

Jonathan Edwards developed a complex response to New England's "reason-able religion," which both assimilated key elements of the new thought and yet preserved much of the Puritan legacy. His strategy was not merely to repristinate Puritanism or to return to the past. Instead he entered into a creative engagement with the leading thinkers of his day in order to reconstruct historic Protestantism on an entirely new basis, corresponding to the empirical and ethical bent of post-Lockean English thought. As chapter 2 showed with respect to metaphysics, Ed-wards's work was fundamentally an apology for the reality, priority, and centrality of God. Along similar lines, Norman Fiering found in Edwards's ethical thought a reversal of the secularizing trend that was transforming theology into moral philosophy:

> Moral philosophers had begun the process of converting into secular and naturalistic terms crucial parts of the Christian heritage. Edwards in a sense reversed the ongoing process by assimilating the moral philosophy of his time and converting it back into the language of religious thought and experience. . . . His purpose, contrary to that of the philosophe, was to turn the best thought of his time to the advantage of God.[7]

Within Edwards's corpus, the most important study of ethics is contained in the posthumously published *Two Dissertations* (1765), comprising *End of Creation* and *True Virtue*. Taken together, these treatises argue that the love of God is the necessary context for all truly moral actions, and that morality finds its proper and sole fulfillment in authentic religion.[8] Edwards thus rejected the optimistic "moral sense" hypothesis of Shaftesbury and Hutcheson, according to which all persons, believer and unbeliever alike, possess an inherent tendency toward benevolence. In *Original Sin* Edwards reaffirmed the Calvinistic doctrine of innate depravity. In *Freedom of the Will* he contended that human choices are determined by "motives" and that the unbeliever consistently chooses what is not truly good. In *True Virtue* he took issue with those writers who "don't wholly exclude a regard to the *Deity* out of their schemes of morality, but yet mention it so slightly, that they leave me room to suspect they esteem it . . . a subordinate part of true morality." He countered that "if true virtue consists partly in a respect to God, then doubtless it consists *chiefly* in it."[9] Against the tendency of his times, Edwards insisted that genuine morality requires genuine religion, and that the love of humanity is specious apart from the love of God.[10]

Puzzlingly, scholars have lavished attention on *True Virtue* while neglecting its companion piece, *End of Creation*. The major writers on Edwards speak glowingly of the profundity and importance of *End of Creation* but then omit it from serious consideration in their interpretations. Biographer Ola Winslow comments that "the whole of his intellectual history is epitomized in these hundred pages," while Perry Miller finds that it exhibits "Edwards at his very greatest," and theological historian Arthur Cushman McGiffert calls the essay "one of the most significant and prophetic in the whole range of modern theological literature."[11] Yet if *End of Creation* is among the most brilliant theological writings of its era, it is also among the most neglected. Despite a voluminous secondary literature on Edwards's writings, only a couple of articles, and no books have been devoted specifically to *End of Creation*.[12] As far as scholarly analysis is concerned, one might speak of *End of Creation* as a "new" eighteenth-century text.

In this chapter I will make three distinct though interrelated claims regarding *End of Creation*. First, I will argue that this work, together with *True Virtue*, was part of an apologetic effort in response to eighteenth-century moral philosophy. A full understanding of the *Two Dissertations* thus requires some background in British ethical thought during the period, especially the "moral sense" philosophy of Shaftesbury and Hutcheson. The treatises were apologetic in that they attempted to make Christian beliefs intelligible and credible to the unconvinced outsider, in this case the semi-Christian, semi-secularized European intellectual of the era. The fundamental claims of *End of Creation* and *True Virtue* were Calvinistic commonplaces—the inseparability of religion and ethics, and the glory of God as the purpose of creation—yet Edwards's manner of arguing for these claims was quite innovative.

Second, I will show that Edwards's basic strategy in the *Two Dissertations* consisted in the divinizing of ethics and the ethicizing of the divine. In *True Virtue* he sought to make ethics inseparable from God, and in *End of Creation* he sought to make God inseparable from ethics. The former took its start in ethical theory and then incorporated God; the latter began with God and then incorporated ethical theory. My focus will be on *End of Creation* and its implicit argument that God is fully ethical according to the criteria of eighteenth-century moral philosophy. In the course of my argument, I will show that *End of Creation* may be understood in cultural terms, as well as in philosophical and theological terms, as a tacit effort to understand God on the analogy of a well-bred aristocrat or enlightened monarch. God's relation to creatures, for Edwards, shows a marked resemblance to the bearing and demeanor of the "superior man" of Aristotle's *Nichomachean Ethics*. In order to ethicize God, Edwards had to anthropomorphize God.

Third, I will argue that Edwards's ontological system of values in *End of Creation* engenders serious problems with respect to God's relation to the world, the freedom of God in creating, and the particularity of divine grace. Yet I will attempt to show that *End of Creation*, despite some basic conundrums, offers an internally consistent perspective on God and ethics, although it rests on principles that Edwards presupposes but does not establish within the treatise. Specifically, his argument assumes, but does not justify, a Calvinistic particularism that directs God's redemptive grace to the elect rather than to humanity as a whole.

An Analysis of *End of Creation*

End of Creation is an intricately written and almost forbiddingly dense treatise. Karl Dietrich Pfisterer compared it to a "mathematical formula" so concise that it yields "expected and unexpected deductions."[13] Moreover, as already noted, *End of Creation* has been little studied. For both these reasons, my treatment of *End of Creation* will commence with an interpretive summary of the text. Following this summary, in the final two sections of this chapter, I will consider the ethicizing of God and some of the attendant issues.

End of Creation was published posthumously in 1765 along with *True Virtue*, as the first of a two-part work.[14] The decision of Edwards's literary executors to publish the treatises conjointly suggests that he intended these texts to be read and understood in close conjunction. Internal evidence in the treatises further demonstrates a connection, for *True Virtue* twice refers back to *End of Creation* as "the former treatise" and "the preceding discourse."[15] Since *End of Creation* never refers explicitly to *True Virtue*, the relation between the two is asymmetrical, and Paul Ramsey concludes that Edwards "intended *End of Creation* to be read first, and presupposed its argument and conclusion in all that he says in *True Virtue*."[16]

One of the conceptual links between *End of Creation* and *True Virtue* lies in a crucial idea that might be termed the "principle of proportionate regard." To quote Edwards's own words: "For 'tis fit that the regard of the Creator should be proportioned to the worthiness of objects, as well as the regard of creatures."[17]

Numerous other passages attest to the pervasiveness of the principle in Edwards's writings.[18] It is noteworthy that Edwards applies this principle to the Creator as well as creatures. God, no less than human beings, is ethically bound to take into account and respect the inherent worth of each entity. The principle of proportionate regard gives Edwards permission to indulge in what might otherwise seem empty speculation regarding God's intentions in creating.

Edwards's ethics in the *Two Dissertations* is based on ontology. He identifies God as "Being in general" and the highest ethical principle as "benevolence to Being in general."[19] Such frequently recurring terms as "worth," "worthy," "worthiness," "value," "fit," and "fitness," show that moral agency rests on inherent values. Much like Augustine and Aquinas before him, Edwards views the universe as possessing a well-defined moral topography that dictates what sort of response is appropriate in each circumstance.[20] The precise application of the principle of proportionate regard requires the calculus of values, mentioned in chapter 2, whereby the worthiness of any given object is reckoned as the mathematical product of its "degree of existence" times its "degree of excellence."[21]

The principle of proportionate regard forms the backbone of the *Two Dissertations*. The general thesis of *End of Creation*—that God creates the world for God's own sake—is but a specific deduction or application of the principle. Because God in acting has highest regard for what is most worthy, God must create the world for God's own sake. Furthermore, proportionate regard underlies *True Virtue* no less than *End of Creation*. Just as God in creating is bound to give highest regard to what is highest in "worth," so it is with creatures as well, who are morally bound to the principle of "benevolence to Being in general." The two works are like mirror images of one another: *End of Creation* applies the principle of proportionate regard to God and God's actions, while *True Virtue* applies it to creatures and creatures' actions.

The internal layout of *End of Creation* testifies to Edwards's efforts at organizing his argument. Nonetheless, a discernible sprawl of ideas from chapter to chapter and from section to section indicates that his attempts at organization were not wholly successful, perhaps because his chosen topic resisted systematization. The preparatory notebooks or *Miscellanies* that Edwards kept throughout his adult life show the gradual development of his thinking on God's "end in creation." They indicate that the longer he pondered God's end in creating, the more his thinking on the topic ramified and diversified.[22] *End of Creation*, in its published form, is less a single course of argument than a set of pathways to a common destination.[23]

Following a brief introduction, devoted to the "Explanation Of Terms," *End of Creation* divides into two chapters, which further subdivide into four and seven sections, respectively. The first chapter treats "What Reason Teaches Concerning This Affair"; the second chapter considers "What Is To Be Learned From Holy Scriptures."[24] From the introduction onward, Edwards assumes that both human and divine agencies are necessarily telic or goal-directed. Any entity that does not act toward specific ends cannot be considered as an intelligent and voluntary agent. He proceeds to differentiate the various kinds of ends, which may be classified in accordance with two sets of paired terms, "chief ends" versus "inferior ends," and "ultimate ends" versus "subordinate ends." The first pair of terms establishes a hierarchy of *valuation* among ends by distinguishing those ends that are more valued ("chief ends") and less valued ("inferior ends"). The second pair establishes a hierarchy of *subordination* by distinguishing those ends that are sought for their own sake ("ultimate ends") and those sought for the sake of another end ("subordinate ends").

The distinction between "subordinate" and "ultimate" ends is critical for the argument of *End of Creation*, in that Edwards is struggling to find a way of affirming that God's "ultimate end" in creating is God's own self, yet still maintain that human welfare is equally an "ultimate end" in God's creating. Faced with the choice between a emergent Enlightenment tradition that made God "subordinate" to human welfare, and a Calvinist tradition that made human welfare "subordinate" to God's self-glorification, Edwards rejects both positions and seeks a third alternative. He does so by identifying divine glory with human welfare, so that the problem of subordination—of determining which end is more "ultimate" than the other—simply disappears.[25] God's glory *is* humanity's happiness, and vice versa, as he writes: "Nor ought God's glory and the creature's good to be spoken of as if they were properly and entirely distinct. . . . God in seeking his glory, therein seeks the good of his creatures."[26]

The first section of chapter 1 lays the foundation for Edwards's insistence that God creates the world out of self-regard. Reason, as well as Scripture, implies that "God is infinitely, eternally, unchangeably, and independently glorious and happy."[27] The doctrine of *creatio ex nihilo* itself, according to Edwards, indicates that God is independent of creatures. After expressing his principle of proportionate regard, according to which God will create with regard to what is "in itself most valuable," he insists that God's own self is the end of God's act of creating.[28] Yet an ambiguity emerges: What exactly is meant in asserting that God is the "end" of creating? The rest of *End of Creation* addresses this question, for Edwards's thesis requires that God's self be attainable as an "end" of God's acting.

The second section approaches God's end in creating from the angle of what is "fit," "proper," "amiable," "desirable," or "valuable" for God. Edwards contends that it is not "fit" that God's internal glory should lack any external manifestation.[29] Pressing the point, he suggests that each divine attribute be interpreted as "a sufficiency to certain acts and effects" or a capacity for producing "correspondent effects." "If the world had not been created, these attributes never would have had any exercise."[30] Extending his point still further, he insists that it is not enough for the divine attributes to be manifested, but the manifestations must be seen and known and appreciated by intelligent onlookers.[31] One might say that God seeks a cheering section, a squad of enthusiastic spectators rather than listless bystanders!

Edwards's argument takes a new direction at the end of section 2, shifting its basis from the principle of proportionate regard to an inherent "disposition" in God to "communicate" or "emanate." Whereas "proportionate regard" represented God as carefully deliberating and calculating the results of his actions, Edwards's "emanation" makes it seem that God's goodness simply overflows to create a world. He states his point summarily: "Therefore to speak strictly according to truth, we may suppose that a disposition in God, as an original property of his nature, to an emanation of his own infinite fullness, was what excited him to create the world."[32] In the same passage, Edwards uses images of God as an overflowing "fountain" and as refulgent "light." His most remarkable analogy is that between a tree growing outward into buds, leaves, and fruits and God's self-extension into a world.[33] Edwards seems to be aware that the reader might interpret emanation, and the impersonal images of light, fountain, and tree, as implying a blindly necessitated or even pantheistic deity. Hence his phrasing is unusually circumspect: "Such an emanation of good is, in some sense, a multiplication of it," and "so far as the communication or external stream may be looked upon as anything besides the fountain, so far may it be looked on as an increase of good."[34] The verbal qualifications—"in some sense," "so far as"—gloss over the critical question of whether the "emanation" does or does not represent an increase in the divine goodness.[35]

Edwards in fact wishes to have his cake and eat it too, to have an emanation that does and does not increase the reservoir of divine goodness. The paradox arises because of his equal insistence on God as self-sufficient and as self-communicative. In upholding God's self-sufficiency and God's self-regard as the motive for creating, he argues that even the production of the entire universe did not augment God's already infinite blessedness and glory. Otherwise God might *need* something outside of Godself. Followed to its logical terminus, this line of thinking leads to an emanation that is self-contained and does not go outside of Godself, as in Edwards's analogy between God and the tree sending forth its branches. Yet in upholding God's self-communication and God's goodness as the motive for creating, he argues that the production of the universe did in fact *increase* God's glory. Otherwise God would have no conceivable reason to create, since nothing would be gained as the outcome. These two lines of reasoning, with the corresponding conceptions of God as complete in Godself or as completed through creation, introduce a fundamental tension that *End of Creation* never quite resolves.

The third section explains how God "manifests a supreme and ultimate regard to himself in all his works."[36] In one sense, the third section serves as a counterpoise to the strong accent on divine self-communication in the second section by returning to the theme of divine self-sufficiency outlined in the first section.

In another sense, the third section unites and transcends the first two sections by explaining how God's self-regard is able to generate an external impulse toward self-communication. The reason for an external impulse in God is not obvious, since a supremely self-regarding God might also be supremely self-preoccupied. (One recalls Aristotle's notion of God as "thought thinking itself.") Edwards reasons that self-regard includes within itself a regard for the regard of others: "He that loves and approves any being or thing, he naturally loves and approves the love and approbation of that thing."[37] Thus even the strictest self-regard is compatible with a regard for others.

The fourth section comprises Edwards's responses to four proposed objections to the argument: (1) that it compromises "God's absolute independence"; (2) that it implies that "God does everything from a selfish spirit"; (3) that it is unworthy for God to act "out of regard to the notice . . . of worms of the dust"; (4) that it "derogates from the *freeness* of his goodness."[38] The chosen objections suggest that Edwards feels susceptible to criticism from antithetical directions: first from the more philosophical or perhaps deistic opponent concerned with upholding divine self-sufficiency (objections 1 and 3) and second from the more Biblically minded or evangelical opponent concerned with maintaining the divine self-communication in all its freedom and graciousness (objections 2 and 4). Edwards's responses recapitulate his earlier positions. The gist is that God's supreme self-regard is consistent with a regard for creatures, and a regard for creatures is consistent with God's supreme self-regard.

The second chapter, containing Edwards's Biblical exegesis, illustrates many points elaborated in the first chapter.[39] Here Edwards investigates such Biblical terms as "name," "honor," "praise," and "glory of God," which are spoken of in Scripture as the reason for God's actions. Perhaps the most significant feature of the second chapter is its concluding section, in which Edwards shifts his focus from origination to consummation, from creation to redemption. God's final purpose for creatures—or rather the *elect* creatures—consists in an unceasing temporal progression in which the creatures' participation in God is everlastingly advancing but never complete. As in the mathematical notion of the asymptote, the creatures' advance toward God never reaches its terminus.[40] Glorification is literally endless.

The Ethicizing and Anthropomorphizing of God

A striking feature of *End of Creation* is its use of a human-divine analogy for understanding God's intentions and actions. Perry Miller commented on the treatise's "courageous—or, some may say presumptuous—invasion of the Godhead by that pattern of reality Edwards had learned on earth. As far as language could go, he would say how and why God actually operates."[41] The first few paragraphs are a notable instance of theological anthropomorphism, as Edwards sets the context for understanding God by considering "a man that goes on a journey to obtain a medicine to cure him" and "a man that loves honey" and so "puts it into his mouth for the sake of the pleasure of the taste."[42] The style is surprisingly familiar and homely for a doctrinal treatise, and for a Calvinist in particular the tone borders on the irreverent. Prima facie, *End of Creation* does not portray the inscrutable God of Calvinism, who eternally elects some merely for his own good pleasure and whose purposes and actions can be known only after the fact. It is true that the Puritans exhibited a greater confidence in their ability to explain God than their doctrine of election, taken separately, would lead one to believe. Nonetheless, Edwards's *End of Creation* represents a high degree of anthropomorphism.

It seems that Edwards in order to ethicize God had no choice but to anthropomorphize God. Since ethics is a matter of ordinary human experience, the assertion that God is ethical requires the use of images and concepts derived from everyday life. Although Edwards agreed with Christian orthodoxy generally that our idea of God is based finally on revelation rather than reason alone,[43] the *Two Dissertations* were an apologetic enterprise that sought to establish God's moral status within the thought-forms of his day. An appeal to revelation alone would have been insufficient for his purposes. The only way for Edwards to vindicate God as ethical in the eighteenth-century context was to portray God as more human and more humane than his Puritan predecessors had done.

In its ethicizing of God, *End of Creation* drew from both the "intellectualist school" and the "sentimentalist school" of eighteenth-century British moral philosophy, but more decidedly from the latter.[44] The intellectualist school, represented by Samuel Clarke, John Balguy, and Richard Price, emphasized the objective aspect of ethics, as pertaining to the eternal and immutable relations of things. "There is no congruity or proportion ... no fitness and agreement in the application of similar and equal geometrical figures one to another," wrote Samuel Clarke, as plain as the "fitness" of God's receiving honor from his creatures.[45] Edwards sounds most like Clarke and the intellectualist school in his mathematical computation of "worthiness" based on the principle of proportionate regard.[46]

In contrast, the sentimentalist school of Lord Shaftesbury and Francis Hutcheson focussed on the subjective aspect of ethics. According to L. A. Selby-Bigge, these authors were distinguished by "psychological analysis" or a "method of holding fast to the content of experience, and resisting all attempts to explain it away."[47] They wished to describe moral experience from the inside, carefully categorizing and appraising the varied instincts of ethical life. In particular, they identified a "moral sense" or impulse toward "benevolence" as a basic constituent of human nature. Hutcheson, in *An Inquiry Concerning the Original of Our Ideas of Virtue or Moral Good* (1725), argued that "Benevolence" was "in some degree extended to all mankind, where there is no interfering Interest," and he compared this "universal Benevolence" to "that Principle of Gravitation, which perhaps extends to all Bodies in the Universe."[48]

Edwards's anthropomorphizing of God owes much to Shaftesbury and Hutcheson, inasmuch as *End of Creation* portrays God psychologically. The text is studded with such words as "appetite," "gratify," and "desire," and in his introduction he identifies an agent's "last end" with "an immediate gratification of any appetite or inclination of nature."[49] It is not only that God has purposes to accomplish through various actions, but also that God may fittingly be spoken of, in very human terms, as "gratified" and "pleased" in the accomplishment of these purposes. Furthermore, Edwards's God in *End of Creation* perfectly matches the ethical desiderata of the sentimentalist school because God is supremely "gratified" in the well-being of others. As Hutcheson said: "The DEITY is call'd good, in a moral Sense, when we apprehend that his whole Providence tends to the universal Happiness of his Creatures." For an "infinitely good Being . . . could never employ his assumed Authority to counteract the universal Good."[50] Edwards's God is truly virtuous, because God is "gratified" at the sight of his creatures' happiness.

The moral sense theory of Shaftesbury and Hutcheson gave Edwards a powerful tool in *End of Creation*. It helped him to anthropomorphize God through portraying God as the subject of humanlike desires and fulfillments and to ethicize God by highlighting the "universal benevolence" disclosed in God's creation of the world.[51] At the same time, Edwards's use of moral sense theory was quite selective, since he repudiated the crucial idea that human beings possess an inherent and virtuous benevolence. For Edwards it was not human beings but God who fully and adequately exemplified the moral virtue of benevolence.

Edwards also drew on British moral philosophy in *End of Creation* in negotiating the competing claims of individual and community, of creature and Creator. Because of Hobbes and Bernard Mandeville, the moral status of self-love had become a lively issue in eighteenth-century ethical discussions. Mandeville's *The Fable of the Bees* (1705–29) implied rather cynically that supposedly beneficent actions were reducible to sheer selfishness. The question was whether self-love could be morally justified. The thinkers of the sentimentalist school answered in the affirmative, arguing that because benevolence extends to the "universal system" of persons, it necessarily authorizes a person's regard for self. Shaftesbury taught that the affection toward "self-good" may be either commendable or culpable, depending on whether it is "moderate" or "immoderate," consistent with or inconsistent with the good of the species or the whole. Hutcheson extended and clarified Shaftesbury's position, reasoning that "every moral Agent justly considers himself as a Part of this rational System, which may be useful to the Whole; so that he may be, in part, an Object of his own Benevolence."[52] The result was a moral vindication of self-love.

This background of ethical debate illumines Edwards's position in *End of Creation*, where a crucial issue lay in the relationship between God's self-regard and God's concern for others, or divine self-sufficiency and divine self-communication. Mirroring the argument of the sentimentalists on the compatibility of self-love and concern for others, Edwards asserted that God in seeking God's own glory also seeks the good of creatures. Because Edwards identified God with "Being in general" in the *Two Dissertations*, God in effect occupied the same ethical position as did the "universal system" in Shaftesbury and Hutcheson. In a sense, Edwards's vindication of self-regard in *End of Creation* was even more emphatic than that of the moral sense thinkers, who in principle admitted that a creature's self-love could be excessive and disproportionate. Because of God's unique ontological status, as that "Being in general" on whom all entities depend and in whom all are included, there could not even in principle be any conflict between God's self-regard and the creature's good. Thus, through his reliance on British moral philosophy, Edwards was able to emphasize God's self-regard in *End of Creation* without diminishing his stress on God's gracious regard for creatures.

A final way that Edwards borrowed from eighteenth-century culture in *End of Creation* was in his implicit representation of God as a well-bred gentleman or enlightened monarch. As I have already argued, Edwards was anthropomorphizing God. But to what human being could God more fittingly be compared than an enlightened ruler, who knew his place and his dignity and yet cared for his people's welfare? Edwards's self-regarding deity shows affinities to Shaftesbury's notion of the astute gentleman who fulfilled his appointed social role. Since Shaftesbury was himself a member of the British nobility, it is not surprising that his ethic centered on personal virtue and considered good actions to be those things that a good man does. In order to *do* good, one had to *be* good.[53] The moral sense teaching could be seen as a generalization of this aristocratic attitude, combining an appropriate self-regard or amour-propre with the principle of noblesse oblige. The well-bred gentleman felt that his lofty social status obligated him to care for those less fortunate than himself. Thus the aristocratic ethic effectively combined a heightened sense of self with a concomitant awareness of the needs of others, and so served as an effective vehicle for Edwards's representation of God as self-regarding and yet beneficent.

God's aristocratic preoccupation with honor becomes evident in a telling passage in *End of Creation*, where Edwards draws an analogy between God and a "truly great man": "It is considered as below a truly great man to be much influenced in his conduct by a desire of popular applause. The notice and admiration of a gazing multitude would be esteemed but a low end, to be aimed at by a prince or philosopher, in any great and noble enterprise." Yet he balances this statement with the comment that it is "not beneath a man of greatest dignity and wisdom to value the wise and just esteem of others, however inferior to him." Entirely to disregard popular esteem, "instead of being an expression of greatness of mind, would show an haughty and mean spirit."[54] Here the ideal of the "truly great man" serves as an ethical standard, or at least as an appropriate analogy, for God. This passage represents God as the kind of "great-souled" or "superior man" set forth in Aristotle's *Nichomachean Ethics*. Edwards's reference in the passage cited to "greatness of mind" almost certainly refers back to Aristotle's *megalopsuchia*, variously translated from Greek into English as "great-souled," "proud," or "superior."

Whether or not Edwards was directly or indirectly influenced by the *Nichomachean Ethics* (which was widely studied in his era), the God of *End of Creation* is strikingly reminiscent of Aristotle's vignette of the "superior man." The "superior man" shows a measured self-regard, which is neither excessive and "vain" nor deficient and "poor-spirited." "The man who claims less than his due is poor-spirited," says Aristotle, "for the better a man is, the more he deserves, so that he who deserves most is the best"—a statement that reminds one of Edwards's principle of proportionate regard. Furthermore, the "superior man" is concerned with public honors, but in a discriminating manner. "It goes without saying that he concerns himself with honor," yet "honor . . . proffered for trifling reasons he will not consider for a moment."[55] Analogously, Edwards argued that a "truly great man" is not subject to the whims of popular approval yet does not ignore well-deserved and well-founded praise. Aristotle's aristocratic ethic, with a few minor modifications, merges into the eighteenth-century ideal of the enlightened despot, who regards his own well-being as indistinguishable from that of his people. The aristocrat who becomes monarch is bound by the same moral principle as before: noblesse oblige. His high position is not an excuse for self-indulgence but rather an opportunity for beneficence. The God of *End of Creation* resembles an enlightened despot in the sense that God possesses unlimited power but uses it for the sake of others.

Enlightenment Universalism and Calvinist Particularism

Considered in its entirety, Edwards's representation of God in *End of Creation* raises fundamental questions, some of which he anticipated in the course of his argument: Is God truly gracious, if God acts strictly for God's own sake? If God's saving mercy does not extend universally to all intelligent creatures, then is God still ethically praiseworthy and virtuous? Moreover, does the principle of proportionate regard vitiate the principle of grace, by implying that God loves the worthy rather than the unworthy? Finally, is God free in creating the world, if this act flowed from a "emanative disposition" in God that demanded fulfillment?

Some of the problems exhibited by *End of Creation* are endemic to the entire doctrine of divine creation. Historically, Christian orthodoxy insisted that God's creating was reasoned and deliberate rather than accidental, and yet also free in the sense that God was not obligated to create a world. The paradox of creation was captured succinctly in a specimen of eighteenth-century verse:

> In himself compendiously blest, . . .
> Is one unmov'd self-center'd Point of Rest,
> Why, then, if full of bliss that ne'er could cloy,
> Would he do ought but still enjoy?
> Why not indulge his self-sufficing state,
> Live to himself at large, calm and secure,
>   A wise eternal Epicure?[56]

The classical teaching on God showed opposing tendencies. Orthodoxy stressed that God was perfectly happy and blessed and self-sufficient, quite apart from creation. Yet this tenet led to a problem: If God's reservoir of glory was eternally full, then what did the creation of the world add to it? Might not God's decision to create suggest an initial incompleteness in God? But there were problems on the other side as well: If one reasoned (along with the Neoplatonists) that God's reservoir of glory and goodness overflowed or emanated because of its sheer superabundance, then did this principle not compromise God's freedom in acting and make God subject to an inner compulsion to create? Neither an incomplete God nor an unfree God was acceptable to traditional theologians, though one or the other would seem to be logically mandated. In approaching *End of Creation*, one should remember that Edwards was tackling an issue that Christian orthodoxy has perhaps never successfully resolved.[57]

A number of difficulties in *End of Creation* derive from Edwards's reliance on the principle of proportionate regard. Because God is infinite in "worthiness," and creatures are merely finite, the proper application of proportionate regard is unclear. One might argue that God's infinitude eclipses all finite entities, and that God therefore ought to love only Godself. God's act of creating would then become inexplicable. A related objection appeared during the late-eighteenth- and early-nineteenth-century debates over *True Virtue*. Critics said that the principle of "benevolence to Being in general" limited virtue to loving God and left no room for loving the creature.[58] Alexander Allen criticized Edwards on this score: "The great wrong which Edwards did, which haunts us as an evil dream throughout his writings, was to assert God at the expense of humanity."[59] When all is said in *End of Creation*, it is hard to see how God's proportionate regard includes a concern for mere mortals. Moreover, there is a moral as well as a metaphysical issue, since humans are not only finite but sinful. The morally depraved are not obvious objects for God's proportionate regard. Yet biblical and Christian love in its very nature is a love for the unworthy. Proportionate regard, if consistently applied to redemption as well as creation, would vitiate Edwards's evangelical teaching on unmerited grace.

Oddly enough, if it seems that proportionate regard might from one angle eliminate grace altogether, from another angle it appears to extend grace universally, so as to bring everyone to blessedness.[60] God is bound to regard each and every entity according to its measure of "existence" and "excellence." In principle, it would seem that God cannot ignore or pass over any existent but is obliged to love them all. Only something altogether nonexistent possesses no "existence" or "excellence," and hence merits no consideration at all. Hutcheson wrote that "we conclude the Deity benevolent in the most universal impartial manner,"[61] and this conclusion would seem ultimately to be that of Edwards's line of reasoning as well. For this reason, the Calvinistic distinction between the elect and the reprobate, the saved and the damned, does not readily find a place in *End of Creation*. The text in fact maintains an eerie silence regarding hell and damnation; its concluding section is written as though there were a single, eternal destiny for all humanity. Yet Edwards's writings as a whole leave no doubt that he adhered to traditional beliefs regarding the afterlife. Up to the end of his life, including the period during which he composed his *Two Dissertations*, he continued to hold to orthodox teachings on eschatology, heaven, and hell.[62]

One must conclude that *End of Creation* presupposes principles of Calvinist particularism that are neither expounded nor justified in the course of argument. The closing section of the treatise, with its repeated references to "the creature," is really not speaking about the creature per se but the elect human, chosen by God to share in God's eternal life and glory. Edwards's worldview was church-centered, for "the elect creatures . . . must be looked upon as the end of all the rest of the creation."[63] The saints were the goal that God aimed for in creating the universe. Elect humans stood for Edwards in a representative relationship to the rest of creation; they fulfilled in actuality what God willed in principle for all creatures.[64] Even the damned unwittingly served to increase the good attained by God and the saints in heaven by giving to God an opportunity for self-manifestation and to the saints a spectacle of God's justice and power.[65] In this phase of his thinking, Edwards was decidedly out of step with the eighteenth-century cultural context and its ideal of universal benevolence.[66]

It is instructive to contrast Edwards at this point with his contemporary John Wesley (both were born in 1703), whose theology was better attuned to the zeitgeist.[67] Wesley's Arminianism abolished Calvinist particularity and removed the stumbling block of unconditional election. He insisted on God's will to save all. Since God's love was universal and unselective, so was the believer's to be as well. The Christian life, as Wesley said, was a matter of "universal, disinterested love" that had no regard to proximity, sect, party, or nation. Although Wesley's *A Plain Account of Genuine Christianity* (1753) recalls aspects of Edwards's *True Virtue*, its ethical position was more explicitly humanitarian. The Christian "loves every soul that God has made, every child of man, of whatever place or nation," and this love is "generous and disinterested, springing from no view of advantage to himself, from no regard to profit or praise."[68] For Wesley, both God and the virtuous human loved all rational creatures in disinterested fashion, without making distinctions on the basis of individual worth. Thus Wesley's deity, to a greater degree than Edwards's, conformed to Hutcheson's moral ideal of "universal impartial benevolence."

To return to my initial theme, namely, the moralizing of Christianity, a scrutiny of *End of Creation* has shown that Edwards's ethicizing and anthropomorphizing of God fell within sharply defined limits. God was virtuous in terms of eighteenth-century categories yet also transcended them in fundamental ways. In the last analysis, Edwards's God failed the test of "universal impartial benevolence" suggested by Hutcheson and endorsed by innumerable Enlightenment thinkers. God was selective, conferring grace on some and withholding it from others. Despite the enculturation of Edwards's deity in terms of British moral philosophy, as a God of benevolence, of aristocratic demeanor and enlightened rule, his God was simply not confined by the contemporary standards of reasonableness. Like his Puritan predecessors, Edwards worshipped the mighty Jehovah, who thundered with his voice and performed mighty deeds that we cannot comprehend. Much in God remained mysterious, and even scandalous to natural reason. If this conclusion is paradoxical, then the paradox resides in Jonathan Edwards himself, who was at once a reasonable man of the Enlightenment age and a Calvinist of the deepest hue.

5

Narration

Drama and Discernment in
History of Redemption

Hᴉꜱᴛᴏʀʏ," ᴀᴄᴄᴏʀᴅɪɴɢ ᴛᴏ Edward Gibbon, "is, indeed, little more than the register of the crimes, follies and misfortunes of mankind." Another eminent representative of the Enlightenment, Voltaire, said that "history is just the portrayal of crimes and misfortunes" and often is "no more than accepted fiction."[1] Such cynicism regarding history, expressed here by two of the leading secular minds of the eighteenth century, followed from a sense that human affairs are too muddled and multifarious to fit into any comprehensive scheme.[2] Prima facie, there seems no reason to assume that history shows a grand plan rather than a disconnected series of unrelated episodes. An attempt to ascertain the meaning of history as a whole inevitably evokes the question: Who or what imposes a pattern on the human past? In describing history as "accepted fiction," Voltaire intimated that the pattern of the past arises from the historian's own ingenuity or bias. Past events have no inherent meaning, only the significance that human beings read into them.

An alternative to Voltaire's view of history as irrational is the notion of impersonal law governing world events. Thus the ancient Greeks commonly thought of history in terms of historical cycles, a theory reiterated in modern times by Oswald Spengler and others.[3] According to this hypothesis, civilizations rise and fall according to rigid and ineluctable laws. The development of each society through time may be charted with reference to the point it occupies along a circular path. The cyclic theory, in both its Greek and Spenglerian versions, is deeply pessimistic. It asserts that the evils of the world will ceaselessly return and denies that anything radically new or better can ever emerge. The future is akin both to the present and to the past. A different kind of impersonal law in history is the familiar modern notion of progress, which gained increasing influence in the seventeenth and eighteenth centuries and dominated the Western mind during much of the nineteenth century. The idea of linear progress—interpreted by many writers as a secularized version of Christian eschatology—leads ultimately to an optimistic vision of history, in contrast to the pessimism of the cyclical viewpoint.[4] It implies that the evils of the world can and will gradually disappear and affirms that history continuously advances into a newer and better state of affairs for humankind. Despite the differences between the cyclical and the progressive theories, both rest on the assumption that there are inherent principles or powers at work in human affairs guaranteeing the direction of history and enabling the informed individual to predict the future.

Edwards's *A History of the Work of Redemption* falls within a very different tradition of historical reflection than either the cynicism of Voltaire, the cyclical pessimism of the Greeks and Spengler, or the progressive optimism of the typical nineteenth-century thinker.[5] It is a Christian "universal chronicle," based on the biblical narratives yet incorporating church history as well, in the fashion of Augustine's *City of God*. Because of its universality, *History of Redemption* belongs to a different genre than Cotton Mather's *Magnalia Christi Americana* (1702). It is not a national or folk history, nor a filiopietistic exercise in commemorating the founders, but an effort to delineate the entire story of God's dealings with humanity in global and cosmic perspective. *History of Redemption* shows the two distinctive characteristics of the "universal chronicle," as noted by C. A. Patrides: it begins with creation, and it treats the entire known world. By the year 1100, Western Europe possessed some sixty of these chronicles, though many were quite unoriginal and simply imitated their predecessors, especially Augustine.[6] An outstanding work within the genre was the *Discourse on Universal History* (1681) by the great French clergyman Bishop Jacques-Bénigne Bossuet. Written about a half century prior to Edwards's work, Bossuet's history showed considerable learning and literary artistry.[7] Yet one feature that sets the *History of Redemption* apart from Bossuet's history and most other "universal chronicles" is its strong infusion of eschatology. It traces the course of world affairs all the way to the consummation. It not only reconstructs the past and describes the present but extrapolates the future. *History of Redemption* is as much about the future, as Edwards envisioned it, as it is about the past and the present.

Scholars have differed greatly over the value and significance of *History of Redemption*. Some have seen it as the most resolutely traditional of Edwards's major works, while others have insisted that it contains the seeds of later American progressivism and optimism. Perry Miller voiced strong yet oddly dissonant claims on behalf of the book. "If one stops with the surface narrative," wrote Miller, then the work "sounds like a story book for fundamentalists." "Measured against modern scholarship," he added, "it is an absurd book, where it is not pathetic." Nonetheless, Miller asserts that Edwards "attained to the revolutionary insight . . . that what man sees as the truth of history is what he wills to prevail." In its summons not merely to gather data but to *interpret* the data of history, *History of Redemption* "becomes a pioneer work in American historiography."[8] In his extensive introduction to *History of Redemption*, John F. Wilson dismisses Miller's claim, noting that the challenge of historical interpretation is an age-old issue in Christian thought and was not new to Edwards or to the eighteenth century.[9]

Subsequent to Miller, hardly anyone supported Miller's reading of *History of Redemption* as a "pioneer work" in terms of method. On the contrary, a number of writers insisted that Edwards's book does not really count as history at all. Peter Gay described *History of Redemption* as "thoroughly traditional" and commented: "In the modern sense, in the sense of Voltaire and Hume, almost none of Edwards' history is history—it is Calvinist doctrine exemplified in a distinct succession of transcendent moments." More harshly still, Gay called the work "reactionary" and "fundamentalist." Rather than moving forward with the times and adopting the secular and nonprovidential historiography of the emergent Enlightenment, "Edwards serenely reaffirmed the faith of his fathers."[10] Without repeating Gay's polemical barbs, Wilson essentially concurred with Gay's conclusion that *History of Redemption* is not a work of history in the modern sense of the term. Wilson wrote: "I deemphasize the importance conventionally given to the word *history* in the title, arguing instead that that work is primarily theological." Wilson commonly referred to the text as "the Redemption Discourse," and insisted that the book "had controlling theological premises and was intended to eventuate in religious practice or conversion." Edwards understood "the human saga as the production of a play that God had authored."[11] The emphasis in Edwards's "history" was not on the free and contingent interplay of human agents but on the dominating direction given to the world by God.[12]

A longstanding issue in the interpretation of *History of Redemption* has been the role of eschatology. In his 1937 classic *The Kingdom of God in America*, H. Richard Niebuhr intimated that Edwards's interest in *History of Redemption* had shifted from "the eternal kingdom" to "the kingdom coming upon earth," and that this shift linked him with the later progressivist tendencies in American thought.[13] An influential 1959 essay by C. C. Goen attributed to Edwards a strikingly original "postmillennial" viewpoint and argued that "Edwards' proposal of an imminent millennium within ordinary history was a definitive factor in the religious background of the idea of progress."[14] Alan Heimert pursued much the same line of interpretation as Niebuhr and Goen.[15] Goen suggested that Edwards's expectation of God's coming reign decisively shaped his attitude toward the present. His world teetered on the brink of glory. While Stephen Stein's more recent study of Edwards's eschatology underscores the influence of Moses Lowman and other writers on Edwards[16] and thus casts doubt on the appropriateness of Goen's description of Edwards's viewpoint as a "radical innovation," Goen's article nonetheless makes a strong and convincing case for the priority of eschatology in interpreting *History of Redemption*. John F. Wilson corroborates the importance of eschatology, saying that Edwards "makes the temporal process a function of a far grander whole. In crucial respects eternity is actually brought within time . . . and time is endowed with significance by being taken up into eternity."[17]

Another pivotal issue in *History of Redemption* concerns the integration and coherence of the narrative. Perry Miller observed that "the real thesis of the *History of Redemption* is the unity of history."[18] While this general point has not been contested and should be obvious enough from the text, the basis of historical unity in Edwards has been variously explained. Miller himself suggested that the basic plotline for *History of Redemption* was taken from Edwards's experience with his parish and then projected onto history at large: "The book definitely embodies Edwards' time and place; it is the history of Northampton writ large. It is a cosmic rationalization of the communal revival."[19] Gerhard Hoffman, in one of the few studies of Edwards published in German, concluded that Edwards conceived of redemptive history as a "history of piety" (*Frömmigkeitsgeschichte*) mediated by the periodic "outpouring" of the Holy Spirit on God's people.[20] William Scheick, in distinction to Miller and Hoffman, viewed redemptive history as analogous to the experience of the individual believer, rather than the church at large. He expounded the ingenious hypothesis that history for Edwards "merely manifests in large the experiences of the individual soul undergoing the regenerative process."[21] In support of his assertion, Scheick cited a passage from Edwards's notebook on typology: "The gradual progress we make from childhood to manhood is a type of the gradual progress of the saints in grace."[22] An attractive feature of theories that interpret *History of Redemption* in the light of individual or corporate religious experience is that they provide a link between Edwards's theology of revival and his theology of history.

John F. Wilson presents an alternative explanation for the coherence and unity of *History of Redemption*, namely, Edwards's typological exegesis.[23] "The basic terms by means of which he achieves unity," writes Wilson, are "a reliance upon, and appropriation of, the figural tradition of interpreting the Old Testament and the New."[24] From the early church onward, Christian writers used typological interpretation to establish connections between the two testaments. Christ served as the linchpin of typological exegesis, the supreme "antitype" foreshadowed by widely varied elements within the text—persons, places, stones, animals, plants, sacrifices, weather formations, agricultural phenomena, and so forth. In attempting to decode each passage in the Hebrew Bible and refer it to the as-yet-future coming of Christ, typological interpretation showed a strong unifying tendency. Whatever the surface meaning of the text, its hidden meaning pertained to Jesus.[25] The recent republication of Edwards's key texts on typology—*Images of Divine Things*, *Types*, and *Types of the Messiah*—underscores his application of typology to the natural world and the centrality of Christ in his vision of nature and of history alike.[26] "I believe that the whole universe," he asserted, "heaven and earth, air and seas, and the divine constitution and history of the holy Scriptures, be full of images of divine things, as full as a language is of words."[27] Throughout *History of Redemption* Edwards explicitly appealed to typology, using varied terminology—"images," "types," "representing," "signifying," and "shadowing forth."[28] His use of typology reflected a sense that the entire world is teeming with signs and symbols of divinity.

My argument in this chapter will build on the existing literature but will significantly qualify Goen's and Heimert's judgment that *History of Redemption* presents an essentially optimistic, progressivist, and rationalized vision of history. According to that interpretation, Edwards believed that he could discern the past, present, and future course of redemptive history and that this course moved consistently onward and upward. Heimert went so far as to speak of Edwards's "ultimate hubris—his assumption that in all America he alone understood the destination of history, and even the precise blueprint for its fulfillment."[29] This position is not wholly false but is one-sided. Edwards's keen sense of the sufferings of the church tempered his optimism, his frequent depictions of historical decline modified his progressivism, and his recognition of the radical limitations of the human perspective on history sharply curtailed his tendency toward rationalism. Edwards's analogy of the "river" of divine providence provides a corrective to the impression of him as a smug prognosticator and glib triumphalist. The river analogy also highlights the neglected issue of *perspective* within the narrative, and the extent to which the meaning of history depends on the breadth and scope which one brings to the interpretation of individual events.

Plotting the Course of History

For Edwards all of history coheres within a single pattern. The general thesis that he states at the beginning of *History of Redemption* lays emphasis on the continuity and comprehensiveness of God's activity in history: "The Work of Redemption is a work that God carries on from the fall of man to the end of the world."[30] Edwards explains that the work of redemption is the greatest of all God's works and that all that God does, including creation, is done for the sake of redemption. "The whole scheme of divine providence" may be regarded as "reducible to that one great Work of Redemption."[31] The salient analogies in *History of Redemption* underscore the unity, coherence, and gradual progress of God's plan. The work of redemption may be compared to the erection of "an house or temple," in which "one part after another" is set in place "till at length the topstone is laid."[32] Using a different analogy, Edwards writes that the work of redemption in history is "very much after the same manner as the carrying on of the same work . . . in a particular soul from the time of its conversion till it is perfected and crowned in glory." There are "ups and downs," yet "in the general grace is growing."[33] Among his other analogies for the work of redemption are the elaborate preparations made before the arrival of an "extraordinary person" as one's guest,[34] a "mighty wheel" that turns away from God and returns once more, "the manifold wheels of a most curious machine,"[35] and a "large and long river" having many tributaries that join together into a single stream.[36]

To understand the development of history and to grasp its essential unity, Edwards sought to identify its underlying forces. For him the impetus of history derives from the conflict of good and evil—Cain versus Abel, the Israelites versus the pagans, the church versus its persecutors.[37] Strife between the righteous and the wicked is the driving force of world history. He begins *History of Redemption* with the theme of suffering, and he plays the opening chord, so to speak, in a minor key. The text from Isaiah 51:8 is intended "to comfort the church under her sufferings and the persecutions of her enemies."[38] True religion is shown to be such by virtue of the opposition it arouses: "Contraries are well argued one from another; we may well and safely argue that a thing is good according to the degree of opposition in which it stands to evil." History shows the "baseless cruelty" suffered by the people of God.[39] Behind the various events and circumstances of religious persecution is the invisible power of Satan, animating and activating the human agencies of evil. The text of *History of Redemption* is studded with dozens of references to the devil.[40] Since one of the dominant characteristics of apocalyptic literature is the sharp demarcation of good and evil and their cataclysmic conflict with one another, one concludes that Edwards portrayed all of history, and not merely its consummation, in apocalyptic terms.[41]

In every age and generation the church faces opposition, and Edwards states sweepingly that "every true Christian has the spirit of a martyr."[42] Among the prominent persecutors of the church are the ancient pagans and "Antichrist," which Edwards identifies with Roman Catholicism.[43] *History of Redemption* more or less equates the triumph of Christians over their enemies with the triumph of God himself. The overthrow of paganism by Christianity moved him to celebrate: "The gospel sun . . . now rose and began to enlighten the heathen world, after they had continued in gross heathenish darkness for so many ages."[44] Yet the overthrow of Antichrist was to be an even more glorious event than the ancients' desertion of their pagan deities and temples. "The kingdom of Antichrist" was "the masterpiece of all the contrivances of the devil against the kingdom of Christ," and so its downfall signals the end of "the darkest and most dismal day" and the beginning of the "glorious time" of the church.[45] Edwards viewed Antichrist as an "apostate" rather than "heathen" power.[46] It posed an extreme danger for the saints because of its insidious imposture of true religion, as "a contrivance of the devil to turn the ministry of the Christian church into a ministry of the devil."[47] The reign of Antichrist commenced sometime subsequent to Constantine's rule in the early fourth century, and Edwards speculated that Antichrist would continue in power until 1260 years were completed.[48] Edwards did not claim to know with certainty when Antichrist would be decisively routed, yet he expected it to happen in the not too distant future.[49]

The prominent place of Antichrist in the narrative shows us, in the words of Stephen Stein, "Edwards's . . . religiously sanctioned prejudice and anti-Catholicism."[50] Edwards follows the so-called "trail of blood" ecclesiology common to earlier Protestant historians and marytrologists. Throughout the centuries of Roman Catholic persecution, "God was pleased to maintain an uninterrupted succession of witnesses through the whole time in Germany and France, Britain, and other countries," which included such groups as the Waldensians.[51] Also singled out for unfavorable mention in *History of Redemption* in addition to pagans and Catholics are Jews, Muslims, Native Americans, Anabaptists, Enthusiasts, Quakers, Socinians, Arminians, Arians, and Deists![52] Of all the religious groups mentioned by Edwards only mainstream Protestants escape general censure, and even they are upbraided for their spiritual coldness and defection from orthodoxy. The true believers seem to be a tiny huddle surrounded by a hostile mob; thus Edwards's conception of the church shows the sectarian tendency common to apocalyptic writing.

While history discloses a consistent and predictable conflict between the church and the nonchurch, its pattern of development is complex and convoluted. Edwards attempts to uphold two seemingly incompatible premises, namely, that God's work of redemption moves continually in cycles of advance and decline, and that redemption edges ever closer to its completion in the "glorious times."[53] Time and again, persecution nearly destroys the church, yet throughout history it continues to grow stronger and more influential. The path of redemptive history is both cyclic and linear at the same time. Traced out in three dimensions, it resembles the movement of a corkscrew's tip, which when viewed from the end turns incessantly in circles but when seen from the side makes steady progress in a single direction. Depending on the particular passage one is reading, Edwards portrays either an up-and-down cycle or a stepwise advance. Sometimes he dramatizes the desperate plight of God's people in times past and their precarious position on the verge of utter ruin. He notes "how often the church has been approaching to the brink of ruin, and the case seemed to [be] lost, and all hope gone."[54] Yet just as often he speaks of the steady progress of God's kingdom: "Thus we see how the light of the gospel which began to dawn immediately after the fall, and gradually grew and increased through all the ages of the Old Testament . . . is now come to the light of perfect day."[55] I will refer to these two tendencies in *History of Redemption* as the "contrast motif" and the "preparation motif," respectively.

These two motifs show opposing conceptions of God's activity in history and therefore are difficult to reconcile. The contrast motif suggests that God manifests and glorifies himself through an eleventh-hour appearance to save his people from certain destruction. As in the old-fashioned melodramas in which the heroine is roped to the railroad track and the audience waits with bated breath for her rescue just as the train rounds the final curve, so Edwards heightens the tension in his narrative by emphasizing how desperate the situation appears to be just prior to God's intervention. The more hopeless the circumstance, the more glorious is the moment of deliverance. "Goliath must have on all his splendid armor when the stripling David comes against him with a sling and a stone for the greater glory of David's victory."[56] In reference to the persecutions of the early Christians, Edwards writes: "Thus it was the darkest time with the Christian church just before the break of day. They were brought to the greatest extremity just before God appeared for their glorious deliverance, as the bondage of the Israelites."[57] In Edwards's recounting, all of history demonstrates that the darkest hour for God's people comes just before the dawn: the oppression of the Jews under the pagan kingdoms was a prelude to the coming of the Messiah, the persecutions of the first Christians led to the conversion of the Emperor Constantine, the slaying of God's witnesses in the Middle Ages gave way to the Protestant Reformation.

This contrast motif does not square well with the notion of progress in redemptive history. It seems to be cyclic in such a way as to exclude any advancement. If God's people are almost annihilated again and again, then it would seem that every generation that survives the impending holocaust will have to rebuild from the rubble all over again, like a family forced to reconstruct its home from the foundation after each devastating new storm strikes it down.[58] How could one speak of "progress" under circumstances such as these? One finds in *History of Redemption* that Edwards uses the analogy of the sun's rising in two different and apparently incompatible ways. In keeping with the contrast motif, he speaks of the "darkest time" as coming "just before the break of day." Again and again, the people of God find themselves at the moment of deepest darkness, just before sunrise. Yet in other passages he compares the course of redemptive history to the circuit of the sun—from nighttime, to dawning, to morning, and finally to noontime brightness. We come at length to "the light of perfect day." If the church repeatedly returns to the moment of darkness before the dawn, then there can be no steady and unbroken advance from darkness to dawn to noon.

Despite his up-and-down cycles, Edwards nonetheless conceived of redemptive history as a movement from A to B, so that each successive era stood closer, and was more akin, to the glorious consummation than the era that immediately preceded it.[59] One of the *Miscellanies* reveals his powerful sense of advancement and novelty in history:

> God is continually causing revolutions. Providence makes a continual progress, and continually is bringing forth things new in the state of the world, and very different from what ever were before. He removes one that He may establish another. And perfection will not be obtained till the last revolution, when God's design will be fully reached.[60]

All events of history are part of "God's great design" and push relentlessly toward "the great event," that is, the end of the world. Likewise, he writes in *History of Redemption* that "the light of the gospel, which first began to dawn and glimmer immediately after the fall, gradually increases the nearer we come to Christ's time."[61] Edwards uses the term "gradual" in keeping with its Latin etymological meaning of "occurring in steps or stages." Each of the various stages of history serves as a preparation for that which comes after it, and thus one may speak of a preparation motif. To return to my analogy of rebuilding, one might say that after each new storm strikes the edifice, the builders erect it with stronger materials and make it larger and more impressive each time. Thus there is both an up-and-down cycle and a forward progress over time.

In one key passage in *History of Redemption*, Edwards distinguishes "four successive great events" that are sequential phases of "Christ's coming in his kingdom." The first is the appearance of Jesus in the first century; the second is the destruction of the heathen Roman empire in the time of Constantine; the third is the overthrow of Antichrist; and the fourth and last is the coming of Christ to judge the world. Before each of these "comings" of Christ there is a period of spiritual degeneracy and great wickedness, and "by each of them God delivers his church . . . with a glorious advancement of the state of the church."[62] The four comings of Christ stand as milestones along the road toward the church's "glorious times." Much discussion regarding Edwards's eschatology has hinged on the distinction between "premillennialism" and "postmillennialism"— the former involving a millennium or golden age on earth inaugurated by Christ's glorious return, the latter a millennium inaugurated by the church's own efforts and culminated by Christ's return.[63] Yet Christ's "four comings" in *History of Redemption* complicate the picture to such an extent that the distinction between premillennialism and postmillennialism loses most of its pertinence. The millennium does not arrive at once in full force, but *creeps in* through a process of gradual and successive inauguration. Several intermediate stages—each one a semimillennium of sorts—elapse between the church's suffering state and its final deliverance and glorification. Because of this pattern of successive inauguration, it becomes extraordinarily difficult to interpret the course of history. Each new phase of the church's revival and progress could be either the dawning of the full and final millennial glory or just a temporary upsurge to be followed by another plunge into suffering and darkness.

The difficulty of tracing the course of history is shown in Edwards's ambiguous interpretation of his own time.[64] Toward the end of *History of Redemption*, Edwards concludes his summary of past redemptive history and takes up the task of forecasting the near future, beyond the time of writing in the 1730s. He is especially concerned to ascertain when Antichrist will be destroyed. Edwards writes: "We have all reason from the Scripture to conclude that just before this work of God begins [i.e., the overthrow of Antichrist] it will be a very dark time with respect to the interests of religion in the world. It has been so before those glorious revivals of religion that have been hitherto." Almost immediately he adds that "it is now a very dark time with respect to the interests of religion" and that "whether the times shall be any darker still, or how much darker before the beginning of this glorious work of God, we can't tell."[65] Here the darkness of the present time may serve as a basis for hope: things are so bad that they must soon get better. On the other hand, Edwards muses that the darkness might not yet have reached its limit, and deeper darkness may lie ahead. Conversely, spiritual light at the present time may mean that greater light lies just ahead or else that the light will soon go out. The cycles of history have unpredictable lengths and combine with one another in complicated ways. Edwards can infer an imminent millennium from either a dreary present or a splendid one!

By far the most controversial aspect in Edwards's interpretation of history was his suggestion in *Some Thoughts on the Revival* (1743), in the aftermath of the Great Awakening, that the millennium might soon commence, and might do so in America. The celebrated passage begins as follows:

> 'Tis not unlikely that this work of God's Spirit, that is so extraordinary and wonderful, is the dawning, or at least the prelude, of that glorious work of God, so often foretold in Scripture, which in the progress and issue of it, shall renew the world of mankind. If we consider how long since the things foretold, as what should precede this great event, have been accomplished; and how long this event has been expected by the church of God, and thought to be nigh by the most eminent men of God in the church; and withal consider what the state of things now is, and has for a considerable time been, in the church of God and world of mankind, we can't reasonably think otherwise, than that the beginning of this great work of God must be near. And there are many things that make it probable that this work will begin in America.[66]

This brief passage became a cause célèbre among Edwards's detractors, including Charles Chauncey in particular, and Stephen Stein notes that "within a short time after it was printed, he became defensive about his remarks on the millennium, insisting that they had been misunderstood."[67] The quoted passage, to be sure, contains a number of important qualifying phrases: the Great Awakening is only a "dawning" or "prelude" of the "glorious work," the renewing of humanity will come only as "the progress and issue" of the "glorious work," and the whole opinion is said to be merely probable or "not unlikely."

In a letter to a Scottish acquaintance, Edwards bitterly complained that his true sentiments regarding the millennium had been intentionally misrepresented:

> It has been slanderously reported and printed concerning me, that I have often said that the millennium was already begun, and that it began at Northampton . . . but the report is very diverse from what I have ever said. Indeed, I have often said, as I say now, that I looked upon the late won-

derful revivals of religion as forerunners of those glorious times so often
prophesied in the Scripture . . . but there are many that know that I have
from time to time added, that there would probably be many sore conflicts
and terrible convulsions, and many changes, revivings and intermissions,
and returns of dark clouds, and threatening appearances, before this work
shall have subdued the world, and Christ's kingdom shall be everywhere
established and settled in peace.[68]

If one reads the key paragraphs in *Some Thoughts* and the letter to Scotland in
isolation from the rest of Edwards's corpus, then the letter may come across as
a recantation of sorts. Yet setting these statements alongside the argument of
History of Redemption, one finds that they cohere with one another. Given the
complexity of the historical process, Edwards could simultaneously affirm that it
was "not unlikely" that the Great Awakening was a "prelude" of the "glorious
work of God" yet that it was also probably to be succeeded by "returns of dark
clouds and threatening appearances." Since *History of Redemption* was published
posthumously, Edwards's contemporaries would not have understood his complex conception of history in which alternating waves of light and darkness lead
eventually to millennial glory.

Discerning the Pattern of History

The discussion thus far has highlighted the complexity of history's course and
the consequent need for discernment on the part of the would-be intepreter.
Edwards himself frequently stressed this point in *History of Redemption*. He writes
that "in order to see how a design is carried [to] an end, we must first know
what the design is." If one does not know the "design" of God, then history "will
all look like confusion, like a number of jumbled events coming to pass without
any order or method, like the tossing of the waves of the sea."[69] In understanding
God's work in history, the whole has epistemological priority over the part; that
is, one cannot interpret the part without having at least a bare outline or sketch
of the whole in one's mind. The broader patterns within history can only be
grasped with the help of special guidance, and this must come to us from God.
Only God is "high enough up" to see the entire course of world history and "far
enough ahead" to see how individual events contribute to history's culmination.
Human beings understand the course and direction of history insofar as they
participate in God's panoramic vision of the whole.

For Edwards the Scriptures provide the key to seeing the design of redemptive
history. He writes in *History of Redemption* that "the Scriptures are that which
God designed as the proper means to bring the world to the knowledge of himself,
rather than human reason or anything else."[70] Yet it is not enough merely to
acknowledge the Bible, for one must understand "the drift of the Holy Ghost in

it," and "most persons are to blame for their inattentive, unobservant way of reading the Scriptures." All too often, readers of the Bible approach the stories of Abraham, Isaac, Jacob, and others "as if they were only histories of the private concerns of such and such particular persons," and so "the infinitely great things contained or pointed at in them are passed over and never taken notice of."[71] Thus redemptive history involves a profound hermeneutical problem. It is not possible to discover the pattern apart from God's revelation in Holy Scripture, and even after receiving this revelation it is quite possible to read the biblical text yet miss the tendency and direction of God's activity in the world.[72]

Edwards's image of the "river" of providence summarizes all the major aspects of his historical vision I have touched on thus far: the ultimate unity of history, the contribution of the parts of history to the whole, God as the final goal of the historical process, the apparent reverses that ultimately contribute to history's advance, and, not least of all, the severe limitations of perspective that hamper the human observer.

> God's providence may not unfitly be compared to a large and long river, having innumerable branches beginning in different regions, and at a great distance one from another, and all conspiring to one common issue. After their very diverse and contrary courses which they hold for a while, yet all gathering more and more together the nearer they come to their common end, and all at length discharging themselves at one mouth into the same ocean. The different streams of this river are ready to look like mere jumble and confusion to us because of the limitedness of our sight, whereby we can't see from one branch to another and can't see the whole at once, so as to see how all are united in one. A man that sees but one or two streams at a time can't tell what their course tends to. Their course seems very crooked, and the different streams seem to run for a while different and contrary ways. And if we view things at a distance, there seem to be innumerable obstacles and impediments in the way to hinder their ever uniting and coming to the ocean, as rocks and mountains and the like. But yet if we trace them they all unite at last and all come to the same issue, disgorging themselves into one and the same great ocean. Not one of the streams fail of coming hither at last.[73]

This analogy is essentially *optical*, based on a panoramic or synoptic vision of history. As the previous chapters have shown, Edwards regularly speaks of "seeing" God or spiritual things. In this passage, however, there is a somewhat different application of the visual analogy. The postulated observer is not standing on earth looking up into heaven but lifted up in heaven glancing down toward the earth. The object of vision is not God, but the vantage point is God's. Human beings become aware of God's design in history and the pattern of the whole inasmuch as they are, so to speak, raised off the ground and enabled to see the world through the eyes of God. Never mind that the events of history fade away, the past is gone, the future is not yet, and only the present is visible to us. Edwards's river requires a point of view that people caught in time's flow cannot fully attain—a vision of the whole of history sub specie aeternitatis, under the aspect of eternity.

The river analogy exemplifies Edwards's characteristically aesthetic approach to the problem of evil. The streams of divine providence seem to have "very diverse and contrary courses . . . because of the limitedness of our sight, whereby we can't . . . see the whole at once." What seems to be disharmonious when taken in isolation appears harmonious when viewed in the perspective of the whole. As early as the first entry in *The Mind*, Edwards held to a notion of "proportion" that resolved partial discord into universal concord: "Particular disproportions sometimes greatly add to the general beauty, and must necessarily be, in order to a more universal proportion."[74] In *True Virtue*, he develops the same basic notion when he distinguishes "particular beauty" from "general beauty" and defines the latter as "that by which a thing appears beautiful when viewed most perfectly, comprehensively and universally, with regard to all its tendencies, and its connections with everything it stands related to."[75] The river analogy is simply an application of Edwards's aesthetic principle that true beauty is "general beauty" or what appears to be beautiful within the context of the whole. In substance, his position is remarkably akin to what John Hick calls "the aesthetic theme" in Augustine, namely, "his affirmation of faith that, seen in its totality from the ultimate standpoint of the Creator, the universe is wholly good; for even the evil within it is made to contribute to the complex perfection of the whole."[76] Whether Edwards's conception of a cosmic harmony that incorporates evil within it does justice to the evilness of evil is debatable.

The analogy of the river helps to explain one of the puzzling themes in Edwards's writings, namely, his near obsession with "the saints in heaven." In the later *Miscellanies* one finds an inordinate number of entries devoted to showing that the saints are acquainted with earthly affairs and "are spectators of God's providences relating to his church here below." Edwards reasons that the "beatifical vision" of the blessed consists not in the sight of God in isolation from the world but rather in "beholding the manifestations that he makes of himself in the work of redemption." Those in heaven have a much better view than those on earth, for "the saints in heaven will be under advantages to see much more . . . than the saints on earth."[77] The vision of God's doings in the world leads the departed saints to a growing knowledge and appreciation of God, hence to ever greater degrees of blessedness. As Edwards argues in *End of Creation*, the knowledge of God is the very purpose for which the world was created, and it will go on increasing throughout eternity.[78] Thus Edwards's preoccupation with the departed saints can be taken as a reflection of his concern for seeing history from God's point of view.

Several conclusions follow from my examination of *History of Redemption* in this chapter. Edwards considers God's perspective to be the only finally valid one for viewing history, and he sees the human perspective as radically limited, fragmented, and deficient. Even when informed and enlightened by Scripture, the interpreter of history cannot escape obscurity and ambiguity. Hence the project of construing or constructing history as a whole was doomed to merely partial success, even in terms of the assumptions Edwards himself set forth in *History of Redemption*. Strictly speaking, he was neither a rationalist who presumed to know exactly what God is doing in the world nor a triumphalist who viewed every event in history as somehow contributing to the final glory. These observations qualify the prevailing interpretation of Edwards set forth by Goen and Heimert.[79] The question of *perspective* is critical, for it is only from God's vantage point that the course of history is quite clear and unambiguous.

The oscillating pattern of darkness and light, or suffering followed by deliverance, can be interpreted in different ways—as the cosmic amplification of the cycle of revival and relapse shown in the New England awakenings, or perhaps as the individual penitent's experience of desolation and consolation writ large and applied to history as a whole. While I would not altogether discount these explanations, I believe that they overlook an obvious and pervasive influence on Edwards, namely, the biblical texts that were the basis for much of his recounting of history.[80] In effect, *History of Redemption* projects onto history as a whole the pattern of Jesus' career—suffering and death, followed by resurrection. A number of passages in the text link Edwards's historical vision with his understanding of the cross of Christ. He writes: "The glorious power of God appears in conquering his many and mighty enemies by ... a poor, weak, despised man. He conquers them and triumphs over them in their own weapon, the cross of Christ." The circumstances of Jesus' coming, at a point in time where the Jewish people were "very low" and the pagan nations were "exalted to the greatest height," demonstrates that God "took a contrary method from that which human wisdom would have taken." "With a small number in their greatest weakness, he conquered his enemies in their greatest glory. Thus Christ triumphed over principalities and powers in his cross."[81] For a biblically inspired thinker such as Edwards, the paradigm of darkness changed into light lies in the story of Good Friday and Easter.

Although Edwards was quite optimistic regarding the future prospects of the church and the ultimate realization of God's kingdom on earth, he lingered over the theme of suffering. History shows no straightforward, linear advance into glory but follows a tortuous and obscure path of gains and losses, afflictions and deliverances, promised yet deferred fulfillments. It discloses a strange and unlikely pattern of suffering and failure transformed into deliverance and triumph, yet changed back again into suffering all over again. God is able to see and to interpret the whole, together with the saints in heaven. We who dwell in the midst of history, however, suffer from a severely limited perspective. We cannot declare definitively whether the present darkness is a prelude to deeper darkness or else the presage of a new dawn, whether the present light will shine ever brighter or else be extinguished all over again.

Despite these perplexities, Edwards did not lapse into skepticism regarding the intelligibility of history. He would not have concurred with the sentiment of Voltaire that "history is just the portrayal of crimes and misfortunes." The human past was indeed filled with suffering, but this suffering was not without significance. Pains and difficulties served to prepare God's people for their ultimate glorification. Even more important for Edwards, in distinction to Gibbon and Voltaire, the outcome of history was entirely assured and known prophetically in advance. In the terms of the river analogy, God was the "ocean" into which all the streams of history finally flowed. Each tiny tributary had its ultimate destination in the ocean of divinity.[82] If one viewed events from the standpoint of the biblically revealed ending, then one gained an imperfect but nonetheless valuable insight into the course and progress of history. To use a twentieth-century analogy, history was like a mystery novel in which the conclusion explains everything that precedes. Someone who glances at the last few pages has little difficulty in tracing the plotline through all the earlier chapters. Seeing God's work in *History of Redemption* was a matter of viewing history from the perspective of the ending, where God and the departed saints already dwell.

6

Persuasion

Edwards as a Christian Apologist

Dᴜʀɪɴɢ ᴛʜᴇ ᴇɪɢʜᴛᴇᴇɴᴛʜ century, Christianity was something to be defended and Western theology entered an era of apologetics. Jonathan Edwards was no exception. To grasp the significance of his Christian apology, however, one must view it in relation to the cultural context and see his apology as a response to specific questions regarding and objections to faith. Hence this chapter will begin with extended excursuses, first into the intellectual situation of early modernity insofar as it impinged upon belief in God, and second into the various apologetic strategies used by leading eighteenth-century thinkers to address this situation. In differing ways, all the thinkers analyzed and compared in this chapter—Paley, Butler, Schleiermacher, and Edwards—were responding to a growing tendency in eighteenth-century thought to marginalize God and remove God from significant involvement in nature, history, and human affairs. In general the eighteenth-century Christian apologists have not fared well with historians. Yet contrary to the impression conveyed by Paul Hazard and others that these writers were unimaginative blunderbusses and that all the really interesting ideas were conceived in the minds of freethinkers and deists,[1] one finds on examination that the leading apologists showed both penetration and originality. In many respects their apologetic responses were at least as creative and diverse as the English deism and German "Neology" that provoked them to write.[2]

One distinctive in the treament of Edwards as apologist here is the full use of and reliance upon the *Miscellanies*, a vast corpus of nearly fourteen hundred notebook entries that remained in manuscript for two centuries until it was first fully transcribed by Thomas Schafer in the 1950s. In 1793, Edwards's son, together with a Scottish editor, transcribed and published a number of the *Miscellanies* on apologetic subjects, clearly with a view to rebutting the radical deism that circulated around the time of the French Revolution. This collection, entitled *Miscellaneous Observations on Important Theological Subjects*, was soon incorporated into the nineteenth-century editions of Edwards's writings.[3] In part because of the tendentious selection of entries and in part because of the inaccurate transcriptions, which conflated separate sections into longer passages and often sought to "improve" Edwards's written style, this collection fails to give a complete or accurate impression of Edwards as an apologist. Harvey Gates Townsend's partial transcription in *The Philosophy of Jonathan Edwards* (1955) was also inaccurate, and it simply omitted Edwards's exegetical comments. Only with the 1994 publication of the first part of the *Miscellanies* in the Yale edition has there been a reliable published text.[4] From the 1950s through the early 1990s, only those few who journeyed to the Beinecke Rare Book Library at Yale University had access to Thomas Schafer's typescript transcriptions of the whole *Miscellanies* collection.[5] One long-term effect produced by the restricted access to the *Miscellanies* has been to conceal the volume and variety of Edwards's apologetic writings. This chapter is an attempt to redress this deficiency in the literature on Edwards.[6]

Locating God in the Modern Age

An eminent historian of modern theology, B. A. Gerrish, describes the early modern period in Western culture as "the retreat of God." Slowly, by small and almost imperceptible degrees, God moved out of the world and became, intellectually speaking, an unnecessary hypothesis. By the middle to late eighteenth century, it seemed to educated Europeans that almost everything that could be explained could be explained without reference to God. It would be "not so very far from the truth," writes Gerrish, "if we said that the story begins with a God who does everything, moves on to a God who acts occasionally, and ends with a superannuated God who need not exist at all."[7] The gradual diminishment of God's place and role in the cosmos and human affairs led at last to the questions: *Where* is God after all? And *what* is left for the Almighty to do? God became superfluous.

The Christian thinker of the early eighteenth century faced the hitherto unprecedented dilemma of finding a place for God in a world in which God did not readily fit in. Many of the locations or functions previously assigned to God had become untenable by the year 1700. During the early 1600s, God was commonly linked with "innate ideas" naturally implanted in the human mind. God was thought to be literally inescapable for each person, since the very structure of mental and moral awareness included within it a sense of the supreme Being.[8] This situation changed decisively with Locke. His epochal book *An Essay Concerning Human Understanding* (1690) delivered the coup de grâce to "innate ideas," which never quite recovered from the blow. The *Essay* brought a problem for religion, since it now appeared that the "idea" of God was not innately implanted in the human mind, yet God was clearly also not an object of direct sense experience. Thus Locke's empiricism created grave difficulties in accounting for God as an idea in human minds. The ultimate skeptical implications of the empiricist approach became apparent in David Hume's posthumously published *Dialogues Concerning Natural Religion* (1779).

For most premodern thinkers, God was present to the physical universe no less obviously than to the human mind. God was the "first mover" whose action was indispensable to the functioning of the cosmos. Yet the attempt to situate God in the physical universe began to falter as the seventeenth and eighteenth centuries progressed. In the Aristotelian physics and Ptolemaic cosmology that prevailed prior to the advent of Copernicus, Galileo, and Newton, material bodies were thought to remain in motion only as long as some external force acted upon them. The continuing movement of the planets implied a continuing impetus from without. The divine *primum mobile* communicated its motion to the starry sphere at a regular rate and then this motion was in turn transferred, with some loss by friction, to the spheres of the outer and inner planets. One might say that God's finger moved Venus and Mars.

Newton's first Law of motion reversed the Aristotelian principle, so that moving bodies were understood to continue in motion *unless* externally acted upon. With this change in physical theory, God's presence to the physical universe was rendered scientifically superfluous to a degree that would have been inconceivable to thinkers of earlier times. Though Newton himself insisted that God is needed to maintain the universe in working order, later scientists gradually found that the functions assigned to God by Newton could be adequately explained through natural causation alone. The famous quip of the physicist Laplace to Napoleon regarding God—"I have no need of that hypothesis"—was simply the final stage of a lengthy process that detheologized and dedivinized the physical universe.[9]

Some of the eighteenth-century difficulties in finding a place for God were remote repercussions of the Protestant Reformation of some two centuries earlier. The sacramental and ecclesiastical system of the later medieval church had located God quite tangibly in the realm of everyday experience. God was present on the altar, in the consecrated bread and wine. God was humanly embodied in the priest. God guided the church through the hierarchy of the church, especially by the pope as the *vicarius Christi* or representative of Christ on earth. In all these ways, God was concretely and specifically present to the world. Yet the Reformers brought to Catholicism a hermeneutics of suspicion that tacitly questioned or directly challenged the tangible identification of God with pope, church, and sacraments.[10] Protestantism, of course, highlighted the Bible and insisted on its inspiration, yet the growth of biblical criticism in the seventeenth and eighteenth centuries complicated the appeal to the Bible as "the word of God."[11] Theologians who attempted to uphold the inspiration and veracity of the Bible often conveyed the impression of a God who spoke, not a God who speaks. When not linked with a dynamic conception of religious experience, the appeal to the Bible as an inspired text shifted the locus of God's activity to the ancient past. Even if God parted the Red Sea and inspired Isaiah, what was God doing today? A simple assertion of biblical inspiration did not provide a definite place for God in the eighteenth century.

The appeal to religious experience was a perennial possibility for Christian thinkers, and the church had always had its mystics and spiritual mistresses and masters. Yet by year 1700, a reliance on religious experience as a test of truth was quite unacceptable to mainstream European intellectuals. The bloody religious conflicts of the preceding century and a half had demonstrated the perils of "enthusiasm," and few notions in the early eighteenth century were more un-popular than the idea that God communicates truths by hidden means to a favored few. Locke's attack on enthusiasm was one of the most celebrated and influential chapters of his *Essay*.[12] Bishop Butler's words to John Wesley are em-blematic of the era: "Sir, the pretending to extraordinary revelations and gifts of the Holy Ghost is a horrid thing, a very horrid thing."[13]

Compounding even further the problem for Christian thinkers was the rise of English deism around the year 1700. Ernst Cassirer speaks of "the extraordinary effect which English deism had on the whole intellectual life of the eighteenth century," and he attributes this effect not to the brilliance or originality of the leading deists but to their "honest desire for truth" and "moral seriousness" in criticizing existing beliefs and practices.[14] Recent studies of eighteenth-century deism emphasize the diversity of the movement and the difficulty of drawing a clear dividing line between the orthodox and the heterodox.[15] However, speaking broadly, the deists

> had begun by defending the pre-eminence of Christianity on the ground that it and it alone corresponded with the true nature of religion; but, gradually becoming more conscious of their divergence from historic Christianity, they transformed themselves into the champions of natural, as opposed to revealed, religion.[16]

Interpreting the deists in this way—as insiders who gradually became outsiders—one sees why their arguments presented such a dilemma for orthodoxy. The challenge came not from without but from within. Because orthodox thinkers shared with the deists many of the same principles and presuppositions, it was exceedingly difficult for them to differentiate themselves from their opponents.

To the question of God's location and function the deists gave unambiguous answers: God is beyond the world in a transcendent realm, all alone. Long ago, God created the world and established its natural laws and moral regulations, but now God leaves it to function just as originally determined. The logic of the deists' position fit well with the broad cultural phenomenon of the retreat of God, and yet it decisively undercut the fundamental Christian belief in a specific, redemptive act of God in history. "For us men and for our salvation," says the ancient creed, Christ "came down from heaven, and . . . was made man."[17] Fol-lowing the rise of deism, the challenge for Christian thinkers was not merely to find a place for God in a post-Lockean, post-Newtonian intellectual world, but to do so while also refuting the deistic notion of a God who established the world and then withdrew from it. To recapitulate: God's location and function in the world had become a dubious matter in the early 1700s when Jonathan Edwards came of age and composed his works.

If the word "apologist" is defined in the classical sense as the defense lawyer who seeks to overturn the accusations against a client, then most of the leading Christian thinkers of the eighteenth century (and more recently) can be viewed as apologists for the faith.[18] The nonbeliever, especially the educated nonbeliever, was much on their mind. They wrote and spoke with a keen awareness of the outsiders who did not share or only minimally shared their convictions. Schleiermacher's "cultured despisers of religion" have been the intended audience of many distinguished theological works. Almost the entire course of modern theology in the West, from the deist controversy until quite recently, may be seen as a constantly shifting set of apologetic attempts to interpret the faith so as to make it understandable and credible to those who did not profess it. Consequently it is better not to separate apology from theology but to view them as interpenetrating and as mutually conditioning. Paul Tillich wrote that "systematic theology is 'answering theology'," and therefore "apologetics . . . is an omnipresent element and not a special section of systematic theology."[19] This observation on the omnipresence of apologetics seems especially applicable to the early 1700s.[20]

As a propaedeutic to my analysis of Jonathan Edwards, I will first examine three figures who exemplify some major tendencies within eighteenth-century apologetics: William Paley (1743–1805), Joseph Butler (1692–1752), and Friedrich Schleiermacher (1768–1834). Despite their differing situations, these thinkers both drew on and reacted against a common background of English deism and German Neology. Paley exemplified an evidentialist argument, Butler an analogical argument, and Schleiermacher a romanticist argument on behalf of Christianity. They represent three different responses to the retreat of God, and provide points of reference for understanding Edwards's position as a Christian apologist. Since Paley and Schleiermacher lived and wrote subsequent to Edwards, and Butler's impact on Edwards was marginal at best, my analysis of these other apologists is not intended as a study of historical influences. It is instead a heuristic device that enables me to uncover aspects of Edwards's apology that might otherwise pass unnoticed.

It quickly becomes apparent when Edwards is juxtaposed with Paley, Butler, and Schleiermacher that his apologetic position is more encompassing than any of theirs yet shows affinities with all of them. For the purposes of analysis, it is helpful to distinguish two different kinds of apology for Christianity in Edwards's writings—explicit and implicit. The "explicit apology" is most akin to Paley's and is focused on the rational demonstration of God's existence and the corroboration of historical evidences for miracles and fulfilled prophecy. The "implicit apology" is something distinctive to Edwards. He interpreted the world as a thoroughgoing unity in which God functioned as the unifying principle. His implicit apology was an exceptionally ambitious endeavor, since he sought to use every conceivable form of reasoning—metaphysical, moral, experiental, and historical—in a many-sided effort to establish the centrality and supremacy of God.

Three Apologists: Paley, Butler, and Schleiermacher

The intent of the evidentialist argument was to prove that there were specific events in history—especially miracles and fulfilled prophecy—that so luminously showed God's reality and power that no reasonable person could dispute it. The approach is termed evidentialist inasmuch as the actual thrust of argument was devoted less to discussing and analyzing the alleged supernatural events than to weighing the evidence for and against their facticity or historicity. The operating assumption was that if the biblical miracles really occurred, then the Christian religion is true. Various Christian authors of the eighteenth century could be classified as evidentialist, yet none more classically exemplified this apologetic tradition than William Paley, whose *A View of the Evidences of Christianity* (1794) both summed up the British apologetic arguments of the previous century and set the pattern for nineteenth-century theological conservatives.[21] Despite the sharp criticisms of Paley, voiced especially by the English Romantics, his contemporaries regarded him highly, and D. L. LeMahieu writes: "In the eyes of most churchmen and Christian intellectuals, Paley rebutted Hume just as surely as Butler had routed the deists earlier in the century."[22]

Paley structured the whole of the *Evidences* around his appeal to miracles. He begins with a brief reflection, "Of the Antecedent Probability of Miracles," rebutting David Hume's celebrated argument against miracles.[23] The longest section of the *Evidences*, "Of the Direct Historical Evidence for Christianity," is largely an argument for the historicity of the miracles of Jesus and of the early church as attested by the apostles. Paley devotes considerable ingenuity to demonstrating the credibility of the apostles and the unlikelihood that their testimony to the miracles was either intentionally deceptive or inadvertently erroneous. Later he discusses the morality of the gospel message, the remarkable spread of Christianity, and the originality of Christ's character, yet he relegates these to a brief section, "Of the Auxiliary Evidences of Christianity." A concise discussion of biblical prophecy is also included.

The opening argument against Hume provides a philosophical foundation for the book. Paley contends that the only evidence counting against a particular alleged miracle is evidence pertaining to the particular miracle in question, and not the kind of generalized philosophical reflection that Hume presented. As many have observed, Hume in his argument against miracles inconsistently in-

vokes the sort of uniform and law-governed causal order that he rejects elsewhere
in his writings. LeMahieu notes "the ironic fact that in the miracle controversy
it was Paley, and not Hume, who was more the authentic empiricist."[24] Paley
professes to follow the factual evidence wherever it might lead. His starting point
is not that the alleged Christian miracles actually happened but simply that "in
miracles adduced in support of revelation, there is not any such antecedent im-
probability as no testimony can surmount."[25] In his response to Hume, Paley
changed the terrain on which the argument was conducted, and "the battleground
thus shifted from a dispute over logic to a specific discussion of evidence."[26] The
question was no longer "Can miracles happen?" but rather "Is there adequate
evidence for us to believe that such-and-such a miracle actually happened?"[27]

For Paley, the gospel of Jesus is at core "a miraculous story," and the apostles
lived and died to bear witness to the miracles. The miracles are the proper foundation of the apostles' own belief in Jesus: "That this particular person, Jesus of
Nazareth, ought to be received as the Messiah, or as a messenger from God, they
neither had, nor could have, any thing but miracles to stand upon." Paley does
not think that any alleged revelation can be credible apart from miracles: "Now
in what way can a revelation be made but by miracles? In none which we are
able to conceive." Yet the miracles alleged in the New Testament had to be *proved*
as actual events, and a sizeable portion of *Evidences* is given over to the defense
of the apostles' credibility. If these men had been deceivers, argues Paley, it is
inconceivable that they should have "passed their lives in labours, dangers, and
sufferings," for "with a consciousness at the bottom of hollowness and falsehood,
the fatigue and restraint would become insupportable." The testimony of the
earliest Christians is all the more credible because of their adverse circumstances.
The first preachers "had to contend with prejudice, backed by power." Responding to yet another of Hume's arguments, Paley provides a counterargument
against alleged pagan miracles. The gist of it is that no "satisfactory evidence"
exists that any other persons, pretending to be witnesses of miracles, suffered for
the sake of their testimony in the way that the apostles did.[28] In sum, the apostles'
faith in Jesus rested on the actual occurrence of the miracles, and the faith of
later believers rests on the validity and veracity of the apostles' testimony to the
miracles.

Obviously, Paley's argument requires that the texts of the New Testament
accurately reflect the testimony of the apostles. Aware of this difficulty, Paley
buttresses his position with various arguments to show that "what the gospels
contain, is the same as what the apostles preached." He demonstrates the "high
probability" that the New Testament documents "actually came from the persons
whose names they bear," as evidenced by the huge number of ancient Greek
manuscripts and by the fact that these texts were widely and accurately cited by
patristic authors and that the canon of the New Testament was largely a matter
of consensus in the first centuries.[29]

Paley's other arguments in *Evidences* may be mentioned briefly. The early spread of Christianity, despite great opposition, confirms the truth of the new faith. The Christians did not call for a mere reformation of paganism, but for something unheard of—the abandonment of old gods for a new God. While the expansion of Islam outwardly resembles the spread of Christianity, these two are radically dissimilar, according to Paley. Muhammed gained adherents by military conquest and by appealing to base and ignoble instincts—for many wives, for a sensual paradise after death, and so on. Jesus, in contrast, won his followers by the simple force of truth. "For what are we comparing? A Galilean peasant accompanied by a few fishermen, with a conqueror at the head of his army."[30] Throughout its history, according to Paley, Christianity has exercised a positive moral influence among each people that professed it.[31] He concludes his *Evidences* by acknowledging the difficulties and obscurities in his argument and portraying them as actually beneficial to faith. "Irresistible evidence" for Christianity would "produce *obedience* by a force little short of mechanical constraint."[32] Finally, in common with other eighteenth-century writers, Paley stressed the moral aspect of the Christian religion: "If I were to describe in a very few words the scope of Christianity, as a *revelation*, I should say, that it was to influence the conduct of human life, by establishing the proof of a future state of reward and punishment."[33]

Evidences exhibits a forensic style and owes much to Thomas Sherlock's *The Trial of the Witnesses* (1727), an immensely popular book based on the imaginative supposition of the apostles being put on trial for fraud and found not guilty. Paley himself argues like an Old Bailey lawyer, laying out the items of evidence one by one, trying to build up a convincing case by amassing many particulars. In accordance with his legal mentality, his reasoning was atomistic rather than holistic, and to clinch his case he typically relied on what he regarded as the indubitability of very small bits of evidence. With regard to the New Testament writings, for instance, Paley comments "that each of these books contains enough to prove the truth of the religion; that, if any one of them therefore be genuine, it is sufficient."[34] This piecemeal and sometimes picayune approach to Christianity struck the Romantics as objectionable.

Paley's evidentialist argument was successful in providing a clear and unambiguous place for God's action in the world, namely, in the miraculous events that decisively show God's presence, power, and purpose. Yet this perspective had many liabilities. In Paley's argument, it mattered little what kind of miracle occurred, as long as it was supernatural. Christ might heal the sick, or, let us say, levitate. A miracle is a miracle is a miracle as far as Paley was concerned. Regarding the resurrection of Jesus from the dead, he commented: "It is not that, as a miracle, the resurrection ought to be accounted a more decisive proof of supernatural agency than other miracles are." Instead the resurrection had importance for Paley's argument because "it is completely certain that the apostles . . . asserted the fact."[35] With this lack of discrimination of lesser and greater Paley opened the door to a kind of intellectual and theological formalism.

Modern theologians have often criticized Paley and his ilk for promoting a "God of the gaps," that is, a deity that intervenes to perform miracles but then retreats from the world the rest of the time. Appeals to God occur only in interpreting matters that remain inexplicable to scientific reason.[36] This "God of the gaps" is uninvolved in the vast preponderance of events that take place in the world, hence is largely deistic. The general viewpoint connected with the "God of the gaps," sometimes called rational supernaturalism, is basically compatible with the Enlightenment's notion of a self-governing and self-sustaining world, since only miracles serve as exceptions to a deistic view of God and a secular view of the world. While Paley never directly denied God's abiding presence and activity in the world, his overweening emphasis on the miraculous conveyed this impression to many readers.

A quite different strategy appears in Bishop Butler's celebrated *Analogy of Religion* (1736), a book widely regarded as the definitive orthodox rebuttal of English deism and one of the most important works of Christian apologetics ever written.[37] Some judge that Butler struck a "mortal blow" against deism.[38] While Paley more or less embraced the Enlightenment's worldview, miracles excepted, Butler began from a different set of premises. He attempted to demonstrate the existence and activity of God by establishing a systematic set of correspondences between two distinct realms, natural and supernatural. He offered no proof that God is a moral being and exercises dominion over humans as the Creator; this much, Butler argued, even the deists conceded.[39] Instead he sought to prove that biblical teachings—for example, the reality of a future life, the final judgment by God, and the mediatorship of Jesus—are reasonable because they are extensions or extrapolations of principles embodied in everyday experience. The force of the analogical argument according to Butler was a matter not of isolated points (as in Paley) but of the "accumulated evidence" or "the whole general analogy considered together."[40]

A distinguishing feature of Butler's argument was his appeal to probability rather than certainty. He writes: "Probable evidence is essentially distinguished from demonstrative by this, that it admits of degrees; and of all variety of them, from the highest moral certainty, to the very lowest presumption." While to the "infinite Intelligence" of God all things are equally open, obvious, and certain, to us "probability is the very guide of life."[41] So cautious was Butler in his reasoning and so ready to acknowledge the arguments against orthodoxy that some Christian readers have seen the Anglican bishop as a virtual skeptic, nearer to Hume's agnosticism than the church's faith. Yet Butler was scrupulous not to assign any argument more certainty (or less ambiguity) than he thought it actually merited. The strength of his argument came from the weaving of small strands into a single cord. One of Butler's legacies to Christian apologetics was his insistence on the importance and utility of probable evidence, and his influence is obvious in such later works as John Henry Newman's *A Grammar of Assent* (1870). In light of life's uncertainties, we often have no choice but to act on the basis of probabilities. According to Butler, each person is morally bound to do what he or she thinks is best, even if it is merely probable and not at all certain.[42]

In keeping with his cautious bent of mind, Butler insists that the finite human intellect cannot determine a priori what sort of world God did make, or should have made.[43] The "small parts" of the divine scheme that come within our view do not furnish us with an appropriate notion of the whole. Humans can grasp the general aim of God's government over the world but cannot particularize this knowledge so as to understand the whys and wherefores of each little happening. Butler adopts an almost Stoic tone of detachment when he speaks of the relation of the individual person to a "much larger plan of things." The best we can do in understanding the world is to reason by analogy "from that part of the divine government over intelligent creatures which comes under our view, to that larger and more general government over them which is beyond it."[44]

The analogy between the natural and supernatural phases of God's moral government has various aspects, but perhaps the most crucial for Butler is that between natural and supernatural punishments. It happens in everyday life, for instance, that "natural punishments . . . follow, or are inflicted in consequence of actions which procure many present advantages; for instance, sickness and untimely death are the consequence of intemperance." Moreover, the consequences of wrongful action are often long delayed, but then "after such delay these . . . come, not by degrees, but suddenly, with violence." For "if the husbandman lets his seedtime pass without sowing, the whole year is lost to him beyond recovery." The very "constitution and course of nature" serves "as a declaration of the Author of Nature, for virtue, and against vice." God's government over us in our natural experience, Butler concludes, is as "strict and proper" as the government exercised by parents over children and masters over servants.[45] Thus the "punishments" of the natural realm stand in analogy to the future, supernatural punishments threatened in Scripture, and they make it appropriate for us to believe in and to anticipate the latter. Like Paley, Butler shares the Enlightenment assumption that Christianity has its prime significance in providing supernatural sanctions for moral behavior. He writes: "Religion teaches us, that the character of virtue or piety must be a necessary qualification for a future state of security and happiness . . . and that the present state was intended to be a school of discipline for improving ourselves."[46] Butler's ethic is essentially prudential, that is, each person is to do right and shun wrong in order to gain rewards and escape punishments.

Only occasionally does Butler speak of miracles in the *Analogy*, and then he defends them with the peculiar argument that no stronger presumption exists against miracles than against ordinary events: "There is presumption of millions to one against the story of Caesar, or of any other man." The analogy of nature likewise removes any presumption against "a Mediator between God and men," since "we find all living creatures are brought into the world, and . . . preserved, by the instrumentality of others." Because one cannot say in advance how God might wish to communicate with humanity, we have no sound reason for rejecting the notion of special revelation and instruction from God. With regard to the unequal distribution of revelation—one of the deists' most potent objections to orthodoxy—Butler responds by noting that inequities and disparities exist in the sphere of natural experience as well. Health, wealth, and other natural advantages are bestowed "with the most promiscuous variety among creatures of the same species."[47] Even with regard to the apparent unfairness of human life, the supernatural once again is in analogy with the natural.[48]

The *Analogy* pursued a steep and difficult path, and ultimately Butler found more admirers than imitators. Few subsequent writers chose to perpetuate the fine nuances and qualifications of his arguments. The commonest criticism of the *Analogy*, notes Leslie Stephen, was that "it is an attempt to meet difficulties, by suggesting equal or greater difficulties," and he adds that "it should, therefore, lead to scepticism rather than to conviction."[49] Butler concluded that there are a natural order and a supernatural order of divine providence, analogous to one another but both fraught with puzzles and ambiguities. If one starts from presuppositions alien to Butler's, one might easily follow his reasoning to a conclusion like Hume's, that the world does not evidence the existence of God or divine providence. In effect, Butler charged the deists with a twofold error in demanding greater certainty and clarity in the case for Christianity than could possibly be attained, and in presenting the case for deism as stronger than in fact it was. Yet the question raised by this form of argument, as Basil Mitchell notes, was "whether the degree of agnosticism which he allows . . . is not, nevertheless, so great as to weaken his entire case beyond the point at which it remains a 'living option.' "[50] Butler's deity often seems hypothetical rather than actual.

One strength of Butler's apology as compared with Paley's was its broader construal of God's presence and activity as not confined to miracles but woven through the very texture of the world. Since miracles played only a minor role in Butler's apology, his position was less vulnerable than Paley's to a piecemeal assault.[51] Butler's God was the moral governor who created and maintains the natural and supernatural realms in their mutual correspondence. Thus he located God primarily in relation to the larger structures and patterns of the moral universe. Yet, in part for this very reason, that Butler's God was more attuned to the cosmic order than to the human individual, some have found the *Analogy* religiously dissatisfying. God is remote, there is little place for spiritual joy or delight, and duty is the last word. Leslie Stephen writes that "the God whom Butler worships is, in fact, the human conscience deified," and "removing the colouring of theological dogma, his doctrine thus becomes a lofty stoicism."[52]

The spiritual sterility that many readers found in Butler and Paley spurred the rise of romantic religion. Romanticism was a reaction against the narrowness of the earlier eighteenth century, especially its reliance on reason at the expense of feeling or sentiment.[53] With respect to Christian apologetics, the net effect of romanticism was to call into question the use of rational argumentation to defend the faith. Samuel Taylor Coleridge insisted that the "mode of defending Christianity, adopted by Grotius first; and latterly, among many others, by Dr. Paley" had actually increased the number of infidels. "Never could it [i.e., the growth of unbelief] have been so great, if thinking men had been habitually led to look into their own souls, instead of always looking out." Arguments based on mere sense experience were likely to lead one away from religion. The world, said Coleridge, was not some "lifeless Machine whirled about by the dust of its own Grinding," as taught in "the Mechanico-corpuscular Philososophy," and "it was one of the great purposes of Christianity . . . to rouse and emancipate the Soul from this debasing Slavery to outward Senses." In his conclusion to *Aids to Reflection* (1825), and in allusion to Paley, Coleridge wrote: "*Evidences* of Christianity! I am weary of the Word. Make a man feel the *want* of it; rouse him, if you can, to the self-knowledge of his *need* of it; and you may safely trust it to its own Evidence."[54]

The impact of romanticism on Christian thought became apparent in Friedrich Schleiermacher's *On Religion: Speeches to Its Cultured Despisers* (1799).[55] While this work is usually regarded as a seminal text for the development of modern theology, it is also one of the great Christian apologies, as suggested by its title's reference to the "cultured despisers" and by the circumstances of its composition. While serving as chaplain in a Berlin hospital, Schleiermacher became acquainted with members of the German literary avant-garde, including Friedrich Schlegel and Henriette Herz. Schleiermacher's cultured friends had wholly rejected traditional religion and wondered why the brilliant young minister still clung to it. At a surprise party for his twenty-ninth birthday they urged him to write on religion, and their promptings brought him to compose the *Speeches*.[56]

The basic thrust of the *Speeches* is to establish the autonomy of "religion" understood as a fundamental sphere of human life distinct from that of reason and morality.[57] Religion for the young Schleiermacher is not in essence a knowing or a doing, but rather a "feeling" (*Gefühl*) or "intuition" (*Anschauung*). Thus he repudiates the common Enlightenment strategies of vindicating religion by showing it to be reasonable or demonstrating that it provides incentives for moral behavior. Religion is instead "a revelation of the Infinite in the finite, God being seen in it and it in God." The devout mind sees all things in relation to their transcendent basis: "The contemplation of the pious is the immediate consciousness of the universal existence of all finite things, in and through the Infinite, and of all temporal things in and through the Eternal."[58]

Schleiermacher has much to say regarding "the Universe." His apology for religion comprises a certain view of the world: "The Universe is ceaselessly active and at every moment is revealing itself to us," so we are "to take up into our lives and to submit to be swayed by . . . each of these influences."[59] Religion is thus a passive and receptive response to a ceaselessly active universe. Moreover, the world exists to the pious mind as a profound unity: "The sum total of religion is to feel that, in its highest unity, all that moves us in feeling is one; to feel that aught single and particular is only possible by means of this unity."[60] Mysticism, in its negative connotation, is a disparagement or annulment of the finite for the sake of the infinite; religion, on the contrary, is an intuition of the infinite in and through the finite.[61] To be religious is to see all things in relation to God and God in relation to all things.[62] One is reminded of the poetry of Schleiermacher's contemporary William Blake: "To see a World in a Grain of Sand, / And a Heaven in a Wild Flower, / Hold Infinity in the palm of your hand, / And Eternity in an hour."[63]

Schleiermacher's *Speeches* expounded a revolutionary new understanding of God's presence and activity in the world.[64] God was immanent and pervasive, not removed from the world as in deism nor limited to certain holy events as in the "God of the gaps." The change was most obvious in his discussion of "miracle," no longer understood as a special category of events in the physical universe but rather as a specifically religious mode of apprehending the world. "Miracle," he wrote, "is simply the religious name for event. Every event, even the most natural and usual, becomes a miracle, as soon as the religious view of it can be the dominant."[65] The more religious one is, the more one sees the miraculous everywhere. For Schleiermacher, no less than Paley, it was "miracle" that established the validity of religion. Yet the "miracle" in question was a transformed perception. Unlike Paley, the young Schleiermacher was not especially concerned with sacred events of long past, inscribed in ancient texts. For him we had to find God for ourselves and not rely on the testimony or the experiences of others. Secondhand religion was never genuine. Religious feelings "must be indubitably your own feelings, and not mere stale descriptions of the feelings of others, which could at best issue in a wretched imitation."[66]

In repudiating Paley's sort of apology, Schleiermacher expanded God's location in the world. Now God was at the center of life rather than the periphery, contemporaneous rather than fixed in the past, active here and now. Yet this broadened conception of God's presence and activity had its disadvantages. First, Schleiermacher sharply distinguished religion from knowledge, as explained in chapter 1. Inasmuch as religion was something other than knowledge, it no longer found support in the rational arguments employed by the theologians. Thus a secular person who did not perceive events as "miracles" might regard Schleiermacher's religious perspective as irrelevant to mundane life and perhaps as an expression of wishful thinking. Second, the dramatic expansion of God's presence and activity in Schleiermacher was not unlike the elimination of God's presence and activity. In functional terms, a God who does everything is much like a God who does nothing—the old *deus otiosus* of the deists. As Gerrish explains, "To talk of God's *acts* (in the plural) is to relapse into anthropomorphism . . . to imagine God as one personal agent among others in space and time." On the other hand, "Schleiermacher has no hesitation in speaking of the divine *activity*," so that "every natural event is . . . grounded in the eternal activity of God."[67] The question raised by Schleiermacher's later critics, and most notably Karl Barth, is whether the position set forth in the *Speeches* does not lead toward secularization and a loss of any place for God.[68]

Edwards's Explicit Apology

The preceding discussion has prepared for an examination of Edwards's Christian apology as set forth in the *Miscellanies*. Although he was an apologist for particular doctrines (e.g., the Calvinist tenets defended in *Freedom of the Will* and *Original Sin*), Edwards also presented a general case for Christianity, which will be the focus here. With the phrase "explicit apology" I refer to those texts and arguments in which Edwards was directly engaged with the salient debates of his time regarding the credibility of Christianity, such as the respective roles of revelation and reason, arguments for the existence of God, historical evidences for Christianity, and so forth. Douglas Elwood acknowledged such an explicit apology in Edwards when he commented, or rather lamented, "it must be admitted that there are places where Edwards sounds like any other eighteenth-century apologist."[69] Scholars have given little attention to Edwards's explicit apology not only because the crucial texts were tucked away in the unpublished *Miscellanies* but also because this aspect of Edwards seemed rather conventional and pedestrian.[70] Yet, as I will argue in the conclusion to this chapter and to the book as a whole, the explicit apology is critical for understanding Edwards's approach to Christianity and for grasping the comprehensiveness and the distinctiveness of his religious outlook.

Edwards felt that he was living in an era of spiritual declension. He stigmatizes his age as "distinguished from all other ages of the Christian church for deadness in the practice of religion and for practical licentiousness and so of the absence of the Spirit of God."[71] He judges that the deists were actually worse off than the "heathen" that never received the Holy Scriptures, since people who have heard and rejected the gospel are more "absurd, brutish and monstrous in their notions and practices" than those who never heard it. The ancient pagans humbly submitted to the received traditions about the gods (which were not valueless), yet the deists haughtily rejected the authority of the Christian revelation. Generally Edwards does not name his intellectual adversaries, yet a later entry in the *Miscellanies* includes an antideistic broadside that singles out and condemns John

Toland, Lord Shaftesbury, Thomas Chubb, David Hume, and Lord Bolingbroke—a veritable who's who of British freethinkers. This text and others indicate that Edwards formulated his explicit apology for Christianity in response to deism.[72]

Edwards's most sweeping argument against deism was his assertion of the insufficiency of natural reason and the consequent necessity of revelation.[73] Nothing definite can be known of God apart from special revelation. "Were it not for divine revelation," writes Edwards, "I am persuaded that there is no one doctrine of that which we call natural religion [but] would, notwithstanding all philosophy and learning, forever be involved in darkness, doubts, endless disputes and dreadful confusion." If there had been no revelation, then "the world would be full of disputes about the very being of God." No one would ever know if God is singular or plural, personal or impersonal. "Ten thousand schemes there would be about it."[74] Edwards points out that the philosophers of ancient Greece and Rome, for all their brilliance and persistence and candor in pursuing the investigation of God or the gods, never came to a consensus. In time, "the infinite contradictions and uncertainties among the ancient philosophers produced the sects of the sceptics."[75] Not even the "ingenious Chinese" (whom Edwards regarded highly) came to a settled knowledge of God through their natural reason. Thus history plainly shows the insufficiency of natural reason as a substitute for revelation.

As a churchman and pastor, Edwards sought to provide the requisite knowledge for people to lead lives in service to God. Yet apart from revelation, there would be confusion over practice as well as theory. If no one were certain about God's nature, then no one would know what God expects from humanity, whether God forgives, or if there is a life beyond. Only special revelation informs us of the truths that are essential to the practice of religion.[76] One of Edwards's stock arguments against the deists is that they practice no "public worship" among themselves and so provide no viable alternative to the worship of the Christian church.[77] Along the same line, he notes that without a public promulgation of God's will to his creatures, the "moral government" of God would fail, just as a kingdom would degenerate into chaos if the king never informed his subjects of the laws of the land.[78]

Fundamentally, the deists erred because they failed to distinguish between an a priori deduction of religious truths and an a posteriori vindication. "It is one thing to see that a truth is exceeding agreeable to reason, after we have been told it and have had it explained to us," writes Edwards, "and another to find it out and prove it of ourselves."[79] In religious matters no less than secular, familiarity breeds contempt: "We are ready to despise that which we are so used to . . . as the children of Israel despised manna."[80] All that was true in deism had been borrowed, or rather stolen, from orthodox Christianity. Edwards held much the same view of Islam. This religion contained many truths adopted from the Bible, yet Muhammed inconsistently rejected the biblical testimony to Jesus' divinity.

Muslims, like the deists, bit the hand that fed them.[81] Both groups were guilty of ingratitude.

Edwards's strictures against deism contain a puzzle, since he clearly relies on reason while he asserts its insufficiency. As much by his actual practice of reasoning as by his overt statements, he exhibited a tremendous rational confidence. Douglas Elwood correctly says: "He admits suspended judgment at difficult points, but he never makes an irrational appeal to authority."[82] John Gerstner concurs, noting that "he tended to explain rationally what most other Reformed theologians were inclined to leave in 'mystery.' "[83] He showed none of the fear and distrust of philosophy that one senses in the writings of Luther, Pascal, Kierkegaard, and Barth. The answer to this puzzle lies in Edwards's sharp distinction between regenerate and unregenerate reason. A thinker who reasoned from biblical principles was wholly different from one who argued from natural reason alone. There was vast scope for the exercise of reason, but only after reason had embraced the truths of revelation by faith. Edwards fit into the Augustinian or Anselmian pattern of "faith seeking understanding," hence there was no contradiction in his reliance on reason combined with his assertion that reason is no substitute for revelation.

The classical arguments for God's existence—ontological, cosmological, teleological, and moral—play a noticeable role in Edwards's *Miscellanies*. His early essay "Of Being" presents a kind of ontological argument. The inconceivability of nonexistence or nothingness demonstrates the existence of a necessary being or God. Edwards reasserted this point many times: "God is a necessary being, because it's a contradiction to suppose him not to be."[84] A related argument, connected with Edwards's idealism, was that God or "Being in general" must not only exist but also be conscious, "for how doth one's mind refuse to believe, that there should be being from all eternity without its being conscious to itself that it was."[85] Furthermore, if God were not conscious of the universe, then large segments of the universe would be unobserved by any intelligent beings, hence would be as good as nonexistent.

Edwards's cosmological argument for God derives from his strict notion of universal causality, as presupposed in *Freedom of the Will*. " 'Tis acknowledged by all to be self-evident, that nothing can begin to be without a cause."[86] Both the existence of the world and the world's specific mode of existence require a cause of some kind. There must be a reason why some bodies are in motion and others are not. Perhaps Edwards's boldest argument for God is based on the sheer fact of the world's continuance from moment to moment. " 'Tis certain with me that . . . the existence of things every moment ceases and is every moment renewed," writes Edwards, and so "we see the same proof of a God as . . . if we had seen [him] create the world."[87] This occasionalist understanding of causality is reminiscent of Edwards's position in *Original Sin*, as discussed earlier in chapter 2.[88]

The presence of design and unity in the world is also a demonstration of God's existence. "The world is evidently so created and governed as to answer but one design in all the different parts of it and in all ages."[89] The same laws of nature hold sway in all parts of the universe and at all times. Edwards often draws an analogy between the world and a body that is unified in its parts and its self-organization: "There is just the same sort of knowledge of the existence of a universal mind in the world from the actions of the world . . . as there is of the existence of a particular mind in an human body from the observations of the actions of that, in gesture, look and voice." If we do not discern the presence of this "universal mind," then the problem lies in the limitation and partiality of our human vantage point: "There wants nothing but a comprehensive view, to take in the various actions in the world and look on them at one glance."[90] Just as in *History of Redemption*, there is a consistent pattern to the whole, but we may not be in a position to see it. Most often, Edwards bases his teleological argument on the large-scale design of the world, but occasionally he appeals to specific features of particular creatures. He writes that "the contrivance of the organs of speech is peculiarly wonderful," and elsewhere he reasons that human souls prove God's existence as "pieces of workmanship" more intricate than any manmade machines.[91]

One finds the rudiments of a moral argument for God in Edwards's assertion of an "inward testimony . . . of the being of God" implied in the common awareness that "when we have done good or evil, we naturally expect from some superior being reward or punishment."[92] He even says that "the being of God may be argued from the desirableness and need of it," for the world can scarcely be so defective as to lack a universal governor to relieve the miseries and correct the injustices of human life. In connection with this view of God as moral ruler, dispensing rewards and punishments, Edwards was concerned to establish the reality of life after death. Many notebook entries are devoted to "immortality" or the "future state." In common with other Christian writers of the eighteenth century, Edwards was convinced that a clear and definite expectation of future rewards and punishments from God was needed to keep people from becoming "negligent, dull and careless" about religion.[93]

An argument for future rewards and punishments followed from God's end in creating the world and from humans' end as rational, volitional creatures. Edwards held the anthropocentric view that God made the world for the sake of humans, and so "the world had as good have been without us, as for us to be a few minutes and then be annihilated."[94] God's great purpose in making the world would fail without the continued existence of human beings. Along similar lines, he reasoned that "God made intelligent beings for the taking delight in his works," yet the disproportion between the happiness of the present time and the heavenly "sight of God's excellency" is as great as that between a pea and a mountain.[95] Only if some human beings attain eternal life with God will God's purpose in creating the world be fulfilled. Only on this same condition will there be a fulfillment of the God-given human capacity for happiness in God. Heaven for Edwards is a place of abundant, almost soul-shattering delight. In a manner reminiscent of Aquinas, he reasons that "God provides some proper good for the satisfaction of the appetites and desires of every living thing"; therefore, the same principle applies to "the desires of virtue and love to God."[96] The present life has many hindrances to the enjoyment of God. Only in heaven will these encumbrances be taken away and human beings be free to enjoy God eternally, singlemindedly, and undistractedly. Heavenly love will know no limits of intensity or of duration, and it is only reasonable to think that God intends such a state to exist.[97]

Like most Christian apologists, Edwards insisted on the divine inspiration and veracity of the Bible. In accordance with the Reformed tradition and such earlier figures as Calvin, Edwards saw the Bible as self-authenticating and asserted that its teachings and very words strike the mind as God-given. Despite its lack of "rhetorical ornaments," the Bible "shines brighter with the amiable simplicity of truth."[98] At points the very phraseology of the Bible is so exceedingly expressive that human wisdom alone could not have contrived it, as in the "strange system of visions" in the Book of Revelation.[99] Another confirmation of the divine origin of the Scriptures is that "wondrous universal harmony . . . in the aim and drift" of the writings.[100] Yet this self-authenticating power of Scripture is not recognized by all readers, because one must have a receptive frame of mind to perceive it. A person may be "greatly affected" by a particular text on one occasion, yet may later find the same text to be "insipid, mean, impertinent, and inconsistent."[101] In addition to the Bible's self-authentication, Edwards appealed to external attestation and historical verification. He argues that if the biblical writings had been written many years after and many miles distant from the recorded events, then one would expect numerous and obvious discrepancies in the texts. " 'Tis proof that Scripture [is true], that the geography is consistent."[102] A very long notebook entry discusses the canon of the New Testament writings and the substantial agreement among the early Christians on which books were inspired.[103]

Much like Paley, Edwards presented historical evidence to confirm the truth of Christianity. Some arguments were based on the Old Testament and the distinctiveness of the Jews. Their worship, as exhibited in the Psalms, plainly shows that they alone worshipped the true God and worshipped him truly.[104] Among all nations of antiquity, the Jews alone abandoned polytheism and the worship of idols. Though the gods of the Greeks and Romans have long since passed away, the God of Abraham is still worshipped by multitudes. The practice of circumcision is in itself an argument for the divine origin of Israelite religion, since this ceremony is "the most unlikely to [be] of human institution," and seems "so much to discountenance the pleasure of lasciviousness."[105] The very survival of the Jewish people, despite the repeated attempts to destroy them, attests to God's providence and makes them a "standing evidence" for God.[106]

A handful of *Miscellanies* entries develop an apology based on miracles, which Edwards defines as events "wrought by the immediate power of God" that have often "interrupted" the "laws and course of nature."[107] There is a strong presumption in favor of Jesus' miracles, since he publicly performed many of them, and "if the matters of fact had been false, they would have been denied by Jesus' contemporaries."[108] Christ's miracles were indications that "the whole course of nature" was "subject to his command," thus they establish his divinity.[109] God would never have allowed a religious impostor to perform the great feats that Jesus performed, as for instance when he raised Lazarus from the dead. Miracles confirm the words of the person who accomplishes them.[110] Above all other miracles, the resurrection of Jesus confirms his teaching and his divinity. One notebook entry argues that Jesus was truly dead after his crucifixion and was not merely in a deathlike "swoon."[111] Jesus' prophecies of the future, no less than his miracles, are evidential. His accurate prediction of Jerusalem's destruction confirms him as God's spokesman. Yet, in distinction from the earlier Hebrew prophets, he did not speak in the name and by the authority of another—"Thus saith the Lord"—but he spoke in his own name and by his own authority—"Verily, verily, I say unto you." Once again, his deeds and words prove his divinity.[112]

For Edwards, the experiences of the apostles and the early church corroborate the truth of Christianity. Anticipating Paley's later arguments, Edwards reasons that the dramatic change in the attitude of the apostles, from fear and dismay to boldness and confidence, shows the truth of Jesus' resurrection and his continuing presence among them.[113] Moreover, the spread of Christianity in the Roman Empire without the aid of human power, wealth, or learning is itself a kind of miracle that shows the presence and power of God. Nothing as remarkable ever happened before or since.[114] The cessation of miracles after the apostolic age does not mean that God no longer acts among his people, for "God now communicates himself to his church in a much more excellent and glorious way than that by miracles . . . by the communications of his Spirit of holiness to the hearts of his people."[115] Despite the evidential value of the biblical miracles, Edwards does not consider them apart from an inward and equally miraculous work of the Spirit in the hearts of believers.

Many of the later *Miscellanies* deal with "heathen traditions" that anticipate or parallel the teachings of Christianity. In these still unpublished texts, Edwards is more tolerant and liberal in his attitude toward non-Christian religions than one might expect from his published writings. One suspects that Jonathan Edwards, Jr., and the other custodians of Edwards's legacy had no desire to advertise these opinions and so omitted the relevant texts from the published collection of *Miscellaneous Observations*. In one of the more striking entries, Edwards inquired whether "heathen philosophers" did not have "some degree of inspiration of the Spirit of God." He goes on to say: "Inspiration is not so high an honour and privilege as some are ready to think. It is no peculiar privilege of God's special favourites." Essentially Edwards held that "inspiration" is a matter of degree and is not an all-or-nothing affair: "Why might not Socrates and Plato and some others of the wise men of Greece have some degree of inspiration as well as the wise men from the East who came to see Christ when an infant[?]"[116] In expressing such sentiments, Edwards stood in a line of liberal Christian thought stretching from Origen and Clement of Alexandria to Erasmus and Zwingli among the Reformers and many of the Renaissance humanists.

While Calvin anticipated Edwards by asserting that the Spirit of God may have inspired some of the pagans without bringing them to salvation,[117] Edwards in these later *Miscellanies* is indebted to such works as Hugo Grotius's *The Truth of the Christian Religion* (1622), Theophilus Gale's *The Court of the Gentiles* (1669–82), and Andrew Michael (Chevalier) Ramsay's *The Travels of Cyrus* (1727). He copied lengthy extracts of these writings into his notebooks and developed a whole series of *Miscellanies* regarding "heathen traditions" on such subjects as the Messiah, evil spirits, the Trinity, the incarnation of deities, original sin, infused grace, Christian duties, spiritual worship, the Sabbath, immortality, the future judgment, the resurrection of the body, and the final conflagration.[118] In essence, Edwards held to divine revelation through ancestral traditions. What the heathen possessed was not a natural theology but a revealed theology: God inspired individuals to speak religious truths, and then these truths were transmitted as a part of the people's common lore.[119] Thus Edwards was able to maintain his antideistic position that all true knowledge of God comes through revelation yet also to explain the existence of religious traditions analogous to Christianity among peoples who were geographically disconnected from Christendom. As indicated by the number of entries, Edwards's concern for "heathen traditions" was a chief preoccupation of his later years, and he may well have intended to discuss this issue in the magnum opus that he did not live to write.

A final aspect of Edwards's explicit apology is his appeal to "fitness," "proportion," "propriety," or "congruity"—words he used to express the inherent suitability and appropriateness of God's works and ways. This language of "fitness" corresponded to Edwards's assumption that the doctrines of the Christian faith could not be deduced a priori or proven in advance as "reasonable" yet could be vindicated after the fact as suitable to the character of God and the condition of humanity. In this Augustinian approach, revelation had priority over reason, yet reason had an important role in explicating and expounding the truths given by revelation. For Edwards, the moral government of God over humanity, the Incarnation and rule of Christ, the atoning death of Jesus, the final judgment, and even the eternity of hell's torments were all exceedingly "fitting." Concerning the Incarnation, he writes that "if God takes any care of human affairs," then "it seems exceeding proper" that "God should send some person to be a common instructor, savior and redeemer of mankind."[120] Given the age-long strife within the race, it is "most worthy and becoming" for God to send Christ as a peacemaker.[121] The crucifixion of Jesus is also "fitting," for "it seems exceedingly congruous, that he should give to the creature the highest sort of evidence or expression of love."[122] Thus the many particular elements and aspects of Christ's work "were done the most wisely and fitly that can be imagined."[123]

Edwards applies the principle of "fitness" to salvation as well as to the person and work of Christ. The "very light of nature," he writes shows that there must be an "accepting" of Christ, through faith, on the part of the offender.[124] It is fitting also that the "universal law by which mankind are to be governed should be a written law."[125] Edwards's view of hell, expounded in innumerable sermons and notebook entries, should be seen in relation to "fitness." Essentially, his point is that eternal torment is a suitable punishment for sin against God, since the gravity of anyone's transgression is proportionate to the dignity or worthiness of the person whom one offends, and in this particular case the one offended against is infinitely worthy. Although Edwards did not originate this argument,[126] it comports well with his principle of proportionate regard as discussed in chapter 4, and he uses the argument to arrive at the far from obvious conclusion that finite creatures, by sinning, come to deserve infinite or eternal suffering.

Edwards gives definitive expression to his theory of "fitness" in Miscellany 1263, where he categorizes God's operations according to the degree in which they are "natural" or else "arbitrary."[127] An early miscellany summarizes the basic idea of the later, longer entry:

> We have shown in philosophy, that all natural operations are done immediately by God, only in harmony and proportion. But there is this difference: these being the highest kind of operations of all, are done in the most general proportion ... the proportion is with the whole series of acts and designs from eternity to eternity, as miracles are, as the creation of the world, the birth and resurrection of Christ are.[128]

God does all things in "proportion"—a word that Edwards uses, much like Butler's "analogy," to describe the likeness that two or more events have with one another. "Proportion" becomes an all-inclusive principle for understanding God's works. Yet Edwards establishes a hierarchy of "proportion," ranging from events that are done by God apart from any regular rule ("arbitrary operations") to events that are done by God in accordance with fixed laws ("natural operations").

In the opening to Miscellany 1263, Edwards notes that many persons in his day "disbelieve" in "God's immediate and arbitrary operation," and his notebook entry is devoted to finding a place in the the universe for such unique and mysterious events as the resurrection of Christ, biblical miracles, and the regeneration of the human soul. He does so, however, not by segregating miracles from all other events but by establishing a kind of sliding scale from the most supernatural events (and least natural) to the most natural (and least supernatural). Jesus' resurrection from the dead exhibits "proportion" no less than the ordinary falling of a stone. Yet to understand the "proportion," one must set this extraordinary event alongside all other extraordinary events in the history of redemption from the creation of the universe to the end of the world. As Edwards says, "The proportion is with the whole series of acts and designs from eternity to eternity."

The full implications of Miscellany 1263 will be explored in the conclusion to this chapter and to the book. Yet two important consequences follow immediately from the argument. First, there is no sharp dichotomy between the natural and the supernatural, but these two exist in fine gradations or steps from the utterly law-governed and explicable to the completely singular and inexplicable. Second, an understanding of the events of redemptive history is only possible by examining the place (or "proportion") that each event occupies within the whole. It follows that apologetics has to be pursued holistically rather than atomistically, that Christianity should be defended not by isolating individual elements and seeking to establish them one by one but rather by recounting the entire biblical narrative in such a way that its human relevance and explanatory power become fully evident.

Edwards's "Implicit Apology"

With the phrase "implicit apology" I refer to Edwards's subtle strategy, throughout his corpus, to appropriate and reinterpret various styles of thought or genres of writing so as to make them conform to his fundamental Christian convictions. He "baptized" every eighteenth-century idea and intellectual tradition he could lay hands on. Norman Fiering writes that "his purpose, contrary to that of the philosophe, was to turn the best thought of his time to the advantage of God."[129] He turned the tables on the Enlightenment, or "plundered the Egyptians"—to use the language of early Christian writers. The profane reasonings of the salons and coffee houses were converted *ad maiorem Dei gloriam*. The implicit apology appears in such varied writings as *Divine Light*, *The Mind*, *Two Dissertations*, and *History of Redemption*. In the implicit rather than explicit apology, Edwards engaged not the specific apologetic issues of his time but rather whole traditions of thought that he wished to reinterpret. To see the implicit apology one must read between the lines.

An intriguing expression of the implicit apology occurs in a short philosophical paper Edwards wrote entitled *A Rational Account of the Main Doctrines of the Christian Religion Attempted*. Though it is merely a set of short, cryptic notes and occupies but a single folio sheet, it outlines an extensive and ambitious undertaking.[130] The watermark on the paper indicates a date of 1729–30, yet the handwriting and ink of the final jottings derive from the later 1730s or the 1740s. Wallace Anderson concludes that this single sheet gives evidence that the notion of a *Rational Account* preoccupied Edwards for some fifteen years.[131] In his projected preface to the work, Edwards was "to shew how all arts and sciences, the more they are perfected, the more they issue in divinity, and coincide with it, and appear to be as parts of it." What he envisaged was nothing less than a comprehensive system of the sciences with theology as queen of them all. Probably no religious thinker of the modern age—with the possible exception of Hegel—seriously attempted such a thing. One is tempted to think of this *Rational Account* as "medieval,"[132] except that Edwards's system would assuredly have embodied the empirical and post-Lockean principles that one finds throughout his oeuvre. While Edwards did not live to author such a *Rational Account*, his published works in various ways reflect an effort to bring the arts and sciences into relation with God.

To delineate the implicit apology in Edwards, I need only summarize the results of the preceding chapters. As demonstrated in chapter 1, Edwards's teaching on spiritual perception was apologetically motivated. He presented the spiritual sense of the saints as a kind of *evidence* for God, immediately present to the mind and more certain and reliable than any rational argumentation in favor of God's existence. The Enlightenment in general laid great emphasis on direct experience of the world. Immanuel Kant defined "enlightenment" as "man's release from his self-incurred tutelage" and stressed that each individual must "dare to know."[133] Edwards in effect turned empiricism to the advantage of God. Faith was a form of seeing for oneself, not a belief at secondhand or a reliance on another's authority. God became the object of direct and unmediated encounter, with the result that the person who viewed the divine "excellency" had as good a reason to be convinced of God's reality and beauty as anyone might have reason to believe in the existence of the physical objects around him or her.

Edwards's metaphysical thought also exhibits the implicit apology. His dominating question in *The Mind*, as Wilson Kimnach explains, was the following: "How could one convince the most sophisticated audience that he had identified a functioning spiritual system as surely as Newton had identified the true physical system?"[134] *The Mind* used metaphysics as an instrument to establish the supremacy of God and spiritual reality. As shown in chapter 2, Edwards's philosophical speculations are so profuse and so diverse that it is difficult to see any unity to them. Yet the disparate lines of reasoning converge in a conception of God as foremost in being, knowing, beauty, and causality. "Now God is the prime and original being, the first and the last, and the pattern of all, and has the sum of all perfection."[135] The "corollaries" contained within *The Mind* generally spell out the theological significance of the metaphysical reasoning. Edwards did not regard his philosophical task as completed until he passed beyond the creature to the

Creator. His metaphysics shows a strong unifying tendency, since every entity stands in direct and constant relation to God, and every instance of truth, beauty, or goodness in creatures participates in the supreme truth, beauty, and goodness of God. In sum, philosophy was a handmaiden to theology.

Another intellectual discipline that Edwards sought to appropriate and reinterpret was British moral philosophy, a study that was departing from its theological underpinnings during the early 1700s. The task of *End of Creation* was the ethicizing of the divine, while that of *True Virtue* was the divinizing of ethics. As chapter 4 showed vis-à-vis the principle of proportionate regard, God has ultimate regard for Godself in creating the world while creatures are bound to show supreme regard for God in all their actions. Because the *Two Dissertations* apply a single and encompassing ethical principle to God and human agents, the net effect of the argument is to integrate and unify the entire domain of ethics, while giving central place to God. The general tendency of Enlightenment thought was to subordinate religion to ethics. Christianity was a useful prop for public morals, providing supernatural sanctions from God (i.e., heaven and hell) as incentives to good behavior. In the *Two Dissertations*, Edwards subverted and inverted Enlightenment thought, subordinating ethics to religion. *True Virtue* implied that all truly ethical actions are guided by "worthiness," hence tacitly if not overtly refer to "Being in general" or God. *End of Creation* argued that the world is a single teleological system of superordinate and subordinate ends, directed toward the glory of God. All the same, the *Two Dissertations* embodied and exemplified key Enlightenment principles, as shown previously in the discussion of Edwards's ethicizing and anthropomorphizing of God.

It would be stretching the truth to claim that *Personal Narrative* falls into the genre of Christian apology, even an implicit apology. Yet this work exhibits the same tendency as many others "to shew how all arts and sciences . . . issue in divinity." Even as Puritan autobiographies go, this one is exceptionally preoccupied with God and the soul. There is little context for action and no genuine plotline. An analysis of the vocabulary, as shown earlier, indicates that the terms "appear" and "seem," with their cognates, occur some sixty times in this brief text. The leitmotif of the *Personal Narrative* is how things "appear" to Edwards, above all how God "appears." Once again, Edwards adapts a specific genre, namely, the spiritual autobiography, to serve his larger aims. In the text of the *Personal Narrative*, Edwards himself as a flesh-and-blood individual is virtually dissolved into God. Autobiography is not a means of disclosing the self but becomes a mode of divine manifestation. The natural world makes its appearance in the *Personal Narrative* yet has its sole significance in reflecting and transmitting an awareness of God. "There seemed to be, as it were, a calm, sweet cast, or appearance of divine glory in every thing." "Sun," "moon," "stars," "clouds," "sky," "grass," "flowers," "trees," "water," and "all nature" conveyed a sense of

the divine glory.[136] Neither the woodlands of Edwards's youth in East Windsor
nor his own mental geography have importance in the *Personal Narrative* except
as providing a context for God to "appear."

The general thesis of *History of Redemption*, as Perry Miller noted, is the unity
of history.[137] It suggests a way of discerning the plan and pattern of God's "work
of redemption" in history. Edwards writes: "God's providence may not unfitly
be compared to a large and long river, having innumerable branches beginning
in different regions . . . at length discharging themselves at one mouth into the
same ocean." Yet our limited and human perspective makes it difficult for us to
perceive this: "The different streams of this river are ready to look like mere
jumble and confusion to us because of the limitedness of our sight." In the end,
however, "not one of all the streams fail of coming hither at last."[138] Essentially
History of Redemption is a book about discernment, not a mere compilation of
facts. One understands history only if one properly uses the hermeneutical key
provided in holy scripture. John F. Wilson calls attention to the elaborate if not
artificial structure of the work, which owes more to Edwards's dominant theological interest than to the historical data themselves.[139] The work is organized so
that the reader can trace the stepwise *progress* of God's redemptive plan. Everything presses toward the conclusion. Edwards conceives history eschatologically,
that is, backward from the end and not forward from the beginning. History is
like a novel in which the final chapter explains all that precedes, and its inmost
secret is God's complete and final triumph over all adversaries. Properly interpreted, the course of world affairs becomes a means of "seeing" God, and implicitly an apology for the reality and activity of God.

Conclusions

Eighteenth-century apologetics shows three different ways of locating and identifying God in the post-Enlightenment intellectual world: as the worker of miracles and supernatural events (Paley), as the moral Governor who exercises
providential rule in analogy with the scheme of natural experience (Butler), and
as the all-pervasive Infinite that manifests itself in each finite entity and in each
moment of finite experience (Schleiermacher). As the discussion made clear, each
of the apologetic positions has serious liabilities, and it is not clear that any of
the positions can overcome its characteristic deficiencies. In comparison with
these other thinkers, Edwards developed an apology that was broader in scope
and hence harder to refute. While his apology has specific affinities with those
of Paley, Butler, and Schleiermacher, it also moves in a new and unprecedented
direction in his implicit apology.

Edwards's explicit apology most closely resembles that of Paley and comprises
an argument from miracles and an argument for the authority of Scripture. Edwards agrees with Paley to the extent that particular, attested events in history

demonstrate the truth of Christianity, for example, the apostolic witness to Jesus' resurrection from the dead. Edwards presents a parallel to Butler's method of systematically pondering the relationship between the truths of everyday experience and the truths communicated in biblical revelation. Butler used the term "analogy," while Edwards more often spoke of "proportion"—an ancient Latinate synonym for the former.[140] Edwards's appeals to "proportion" suggested that God's ways were not wholly inscrutable but could be understood as extensions of principles observable in ordinary life. He also devoted considerable attention to the traditional proofs for God (ontological, cosmological, teleological, and moral), which were a not a characteristic concern of Butler or Paley. This stress on the proofs for God can be seen, following Norman Fiering, as an indication of the "rationalist foundations" of Edwards's philosophy and a sign that Continental thinkers such as Nicolas Malebranche and English Platonists such as John Norris and Henry More were as strong an influence on Edwards as was John Locke.[141]

However, there are decisive differences between Edwards and the mainline eighteenth-century British apologists. First, Edwards was far more concerned about the subjective dimension of Christianity than were Paley or Butler. His teaching on the spiritual sense placed him closer to Schleiermacher and other theological Romantics than to these more prosaic and earthbound defenders of the faith. Through his writings, Edwards sought to engender not only a rational conviction that Christianity is true but a sense of the unspeakable beauty of God's holiness. He stated unequivocally that the perception of the divine "excellency" is the highest and most reliable of all evidences for God. Edwards certainly was not content with merely probable or conjectural knowledge of God such as Bishop Butler afforded in the *Analogy*. A sound apology for the faith, no less than genuine religion itself, required a direct experience of God. Douglas Elwood is essentially correct in saying that for Edwards, "without a living experience of God there is no conclusive evidence of his reality."[142]

Second, Edwards differed from Paley and Butler in the conspicious absence of any moralistic or prudential argument for Christianity. In contrast to the great bulk of eighteenth-century writers, ranging the spectrum from freethinker to church thinker, Edwards never argued for Christianity on the basis of its socially useful function in maintaining morality. His lack of moralism may be attributed to the Puritan notion that it was perfectly possible to be a "good person" and still be damned. To promote religion for the sake of morality was to encourage the mistaken belief that external appearances alone could serve as an adequate index of salvation. Furthermore, Edwards's rejection of moralism reflects his exalted conception of religion as a love for God for God's own sake, apart from self-interest. As chapter 3 demonstrated, Edwards's contemplation was an activity that had no end beyond itself and thus required no justification. Simply to enjoy God was to fulfill one's ultimate destiny. F. D. Maurice sarcastically summarized the "home-baked theology" of the Enlightenment era: "It is safer to believe in a God, lest, if there should happen to be one, he might send us to hell for denying his existence."[143] From Edwards's point of view, such a selfishly motivated and halfhearted version of religion is scarcely worthy of God.

Edwards stands at the divide between differing tendencies in modern religious thought. The common criticisms of Paley and Schleiermacher are antipodal. Paley's religion, as Coleridge objected, was far too external and objectified; Schleiermacher's religion, as Barth maintained, was too subjective and internalized. Paley implied that God is absent from the world when not performing miracles, while Schleiermacher abolished any conception of miracles as distinct from other events. Paley and Butler, it is objected, used religion as a mere external prop for morality; Schleiermacher, however, divorced religion from morality altogether. Edwards embodies a mediating position that in effect corrects Paley by Schleiermacher and Schleiermacher by Paley. "Miracle" for Edwards was both a special kind of event in the physical universe and a unique sensibility and perception of God's "excellency." The subjective and objective aspects of religion did not compete in Edwards as they seemed to do in such otherwise diverse thinkers as Paley and Schleiermacher. Edwards did not abandon the task of rational apologetics or separate religion from knowledge, yet he also did not slip into a formalistic, dry-as-dust argument for Christianity that neglected personal experience. In terms of Coleridge's contrast between apologists who "look out" and those who "look into their own souls," Edwards falls into both categories. For all these reasons, Edwards occupies a unique middle ground between liberalizing and conservative tendencies in modern Christian thought.[144]

Conclusion

The Religious Outlook in Edwards

Historians have generally concurred that the early eighteenth century was a trying time for religion in Western societies. Paul Tillich, summarizing the century and a half from the waning of Puritanism to the early 1800s, wrote: "First among the educated classes, then increasingly in the mass of industrial workers, religion lost its 'immediacy'; it ceased to offer an unquestioned sense of direction and relevance to human living."[1] Edwards himself bemoaned the tendency in his day to set God at a distance from the world and from human affairs: " 'Tis a strange disposition that men have to thrust God out of the world, or to put Him as far out of sight as they can, and to have in no respect immediately and sensibly to do with Him. Therefore so many schemes have been drawn to exclude, or extenuate, or remove at a great distance, any influence of the Divine Being."[2] Some scholars have seen this period as a dramatic crisis for religion, not a slow defection from the faith but a pointed rejection of it. Paul Hazard said that the burning question in Europe at the beginning of the eighteenth century was, "Shall Europe be Christian, or shall it not?" He adds that this was "a case the like of which had never yet been heard of, for it was God, God Himself, who was the prisoner at the Bar." Carl Becker put it bluntly: "In those years God was on trial."[3]

Among the intelligentsia of eighteenth-century Europe and America, a common response to the challenges of their time was to preserve religion by mitigating it. The backdrop to Edwards's apology for Christianity was a complex cultural shift in New England, described as "Anglicization" by Harry S. Stout in *The New England Soul* and as the "moderate Enlightenment" in Henry F. May's *The Enlightenment in America*.[4] Stout's study documents a trend toward liberalism and toleration in early-eighteenth-century New England, muting the shriller notes of the old-time Calvinism. The career of Charles Chauncy, who opposed Edwards during the Great Awakening and later in life wrote a tract defending universal salvation, is emblematic of the gradual transition in New England that eventually led from Puritanism to Unitarianism.[5] Henry May describes the hallmarks of this era in America as balance and the avoidance of extremes. While the French philosophes were flamboyantly anticlerical, the "dominant English ideas about man and the universe tended to be compromises."[6] For adherents of the moderate Enlightenment, a little religion was a good thing.

Yet Edwards abhorred moderation in religion. In an early entry in the *Miscellanies*, he went so far as to say that a saint would be "no less useful even in this world" if his devotion were "to keep him all his lifetime in an ecstasy." The earlier examination of Edwards's spirituality showed just how painstakingly he sought after ecstasy. A cool acquiescence in the abstract validity of religion was to him as good as no religion at all, and he saw the fundamental failure of his age in its sheer insensibility to God, that "the being of God and another world don't seem real to them."[7] Edwards became, in Henry May's estimation, the moderate Enlightenment's "most powerful enemy."[8] He was the self-appointed apostle to the spiritually indifferent.

Edwards's teaching on spiritual perception expressed a subtle interpretation of and response to the religious malaise. People were not so much denying Christianity as drifting from it. They defected from religious practice because of the deadness and dullness of the churches rather than from a clear-cut logical argument against the creed or a well-defined alternative to Christian faith. The typical eighteenth-century apologist tirelessly argued for the "reasonableness of Christianity," under the supposition that establishing this single point was sufficient. As Mark Pattison quipped, "Christianity appeared made for nothing else but to be 'proved'; what use to make of it when it was proved was not much thought about."[9] Edwards, in contrast, looked beyond mere reasonableness to consider the fate of religion in his day as a total cognitive-affective-practical response to God. Reasonableness alone would not move the heart and engage the self, convey a sense God's actuality, or motivate anyone to new action. Reasonableness did not change sinners into saints. Edwards sought therefore to make God real by making God perceptible, to make God perceptible by making God visible, and to make God visible by making God beautiful. The "excellency" of God was something that could not be seen at all without being appreciated. He did not intend to leave any room for religious neutrality.

Edwards's message was almost as challenging for believers as for unbelievers, since it summoned all persons to conform to a saintly ideal of living constantly and consciously in the presence of God. In a sense, he made everyone an outsider and no one an insider.[10] When judged by Edwards's lofty standards of disinterested delight in God, all fell short. Perhaps this problem was a root cause of the dissension in the Northampton congregation: they simply grew tired of feeling spiritually deficient.[11] He expected much, almost certainly too much, of himself and others. He made no concession to the weakness of the flesh, no allowance for those who were uncertain, undecided, or halfhearted. All such persons when brought within his totalizing vision became sinners against the light. To fail to see God's "excellency" could only be an act of willful and culpable blindness. It is not difficult to comprehend the combined admiration and exasperation toward Edwards that one finds among later Americans. Mark Twain, on reading *Freedom of the Will*, called him a "drunken lunatic," a "resplendent intellect gone mad."[12] What repelled and offended many readers was Edwards's relentlessness. He asked more of humans than was humane.

No one came up to Edwards's standards, including Edwards himself. The *Diary* and *Personal Narrative* show him burdened by his own unrelenting insistence on living each moment with a perfect awareness of and dedication to God. The entire *Personal Narrative* stands under a self-censure: "I have reason to be infinitely humbled, when I consider how much I have failed of answering my obligation."[13] Where he himself failed, how could he expect others to succeed? In Edwards's religious outlook, no one ever attained the goal, and everyone was called to perpetual questing after God. Not even heaven offered a place of quiescence and repose! The final tableau in *End of Creation*, depicting the saints in heaven as everlastingly drawing nearer to God yet everlastingly falling short,[14] was simply Edwards's vision of the Christian life writ large, the church's progressive pilgrimage toward God extrapolated into eternity.

Ronald Knox, in his classic study *Enthusiasm: A Chapter in the History of Religion*, defined an "enthusiast" as an "ultrasupernaturalist" who "expects more evident results from the grace of God than we others." Knox continues:

> He sees what effects religion can have, does sometimes have, in transforming a man's whole life and outlook; these exceptional cases (so we are content to think them) are for him the average standard of religious achievement. He will have no "almost-Christians," no weaker brethren who plod and stumble, who (if the truth must be told) would like to have a foot in either world, whose ambition is to qualify, not to excel.[15]

These words ring true of Edwards. Even if he rejected the characteristic shibboleths of the "enthusiast"—voices and visions from God, the rebirth of prophecy, anti-intellectualism, a sense of superiority to others, separatism, predictions of Christ's return, and so on—Edwards still manifested the "enthusiastic" requirement that the entirety of human life be, as Knox says, "visibly penetrated with supernatural influences." Nothing less was sufficient for him. He was an "enthusiast" in the intensity of his religious vision, if not in the specifics of its experiential, practical, and institutional expressions.

The previous chapters on spiritual perception and spirituality (chapters 1 and 3) have demonstrated the *intensiveness* of Edwards's religious outlook, while the chapters on metaphysics, ethics, history, and apologetics (chapters 2, 4, 5, and 6) have demonstrated its *extensiveness*. His perspective combined subjective depth and cosmic sweep. In one of his rare moments of emotive utterance, Immanuel Kant exclaimed: "Two things fill the mind with ever new and increasing admiration and awe, the oftener and the more steadily we reflect on them, the starry heavens above and the moral law within."[16] Although Edwards did not use identical terminology, he too felt admiration and awe at the inner manifestation of God to the human awareness and the external revelation of God's presence and power in the physical universe. As Perry Miller wrote, "Beneath the dogmas of the old theology he discovered a different cosmos . . . a dynamic world, filled with the presence of God, quickened with divine life, pervaded with joy and ecstasy."[17] One is struck at how Edwards's notion of the immediate apprehension of God and his sense of the world's unity in God exist alongside one another without any apparent tension or conflict. His religious thought is a reconciliation and synthesis of diverse elements or, as Daniel Shea writes, "the expression of a profound experience of the interrelatedness of things."[18]

Edwards's position was roughly equidistant between the usual versions of naturalism and supernaturalism. It might be termed a graduated supernaturalism whose dominant characteristic was the blurring of any sharp line between the natural and the supernatural.[19] As I showed earlier in regard to Miscellany 1263, all phenomena in the universe were direct and immediate expressions of God's agency.[20] God did everything. The falling of a leaf from a tree and the resurrection of Jesus from the dead belonged to the very same order of reality. Thus, on one level, everything was unified and everything was quite supernatural. Yet, on another level, Edwards drew distinctions in the *degree* to which specific events could be classed as "arbitrary" or else "natural." He thought in terms of a scale that ranged from the utterly law-governed and regular to the utterly singular and unpredictable. James Hoopes comments: "In Edwards's metaphysics, the only distinction between nature and supernature is operative regularity or irregularity, since all phenomena are . . . created immediately by God."[21] Faced with a choice between the monotonous naturalism of the deists and the dichotomous supernaturalism of the orthodox, Edwards rejected both and developed his own idiosyncratic alternative. Just as with Edwards's distinctive notion of spiritual perception, so with his graduated supernaturalism he forged a brilliant, mediating position between the eighteenth-century intellectual options. Although it is only a matter of conjecture, the programmatic quality of Miscellany 1263 and its references to the plan of redemptive history may indicate that this text provided the basic conceptual framework or scaffolding for Edwards to build his massive *History of the Work of Redemption*.

In reference to Edwards's worldview, Douglas Elwood wrote: "Religion is not a way of looking at certain things, but a certain way of looking at all things."[22] This statement is true in what it affirms yet false in what it denies. As the preceding chapters have shown, the religious outlook in Edwards includes both "a way of looking at certain things" and "a certain way of looking at all things." His perspective incorporates particular and universal aspects. Religion, on the one hand, implies a way of looking at certain things, since the saints (and they alone) see the "excellency" of God. Miracles are a particular cluster of events. Conversion is a specific experience. God's holiness is a definite attribute. Religion, on the other hand, implies a certain way of looking at all things, since the entire worldview of the regenerate person is transformed by the vision of God. As Edwards wrote in the *Personal Narrative* following his conversion experience, "the appearance of every thing was altered."[23] The religious way of looking involves a change in subjective sensibility. One sees differently.

Speaking in generalities, the distinction between religion as a way of looking at certain things and religion as a certain way of looking at all things is one of the hotly contested issues in modern religious thought. The question is whether a religious outlook on the world requires a distinct, delimited sphere of God or the sacred or the supernatural, or instead requires only a special form of human apprehension without any such distinct external sphere. William Paley and Friedrich Schleiermacher serve as convenient points of reference. It was as inconceivable to Paley that religion could exist without miracles as a special class of events in the physical universe as it was inconceivable to Schleiermacher that religion should require such miracles.

Yet both Paley's and Schleiermacher's perspectives have something in common, in that each in a slightly different way opens the door to a nonreligious outlook on the world. If, as in Paley, religion is viewed solely as a way of looking at certain things, then religion can easily become privatized. When religion is only a way of looking at *certain* things, then the world becomes partitioned between the sacred and the secular. The implicit though often unacknowledged logic of the position is that where God is not working miracles God is absent. The privatization of religion and the secularization of culture stride hand in hand. This line of thinking brings us back once again to the "God of the gaps," to which Dietrich Bonhoeffer and others have so strenuously objected. Yet if, as in Schleiermacher, religion is only a certain way of looking at all things, then religion may lose its distinctiveness and dissolve without a trace into the sea of culture. The implicit though often unacknowledged logic of this position is that the religious outlook is simply one among others. Nothing conclusive can be said in favor of a religious outlook vis-à-vis a secular worldview. For if there is no *specific* element in human experience that requires one to invoke God, then what definitive case can be made for a religious (i.e., theistic) outlook in general?

Religion for Edwards was neither, strictly speaking, a way of looking at certain things nor a certain way of looking at all things. It was instead—to bring these two conceptions into appropriate alignment—a certain way of looking at all things, based on a way of looking at certain things. The logical and chronological priority lies with the way of looking at certain things. Regeneration is the epistemological foundation of Edwards's entire religious outlook. As I argued at the end of chapter 1, the *Personal Narrative* suggests that the transformation in Edwards's vision of the world took place only because of a prior transformation in his vision of God. As he passed from incredulity to grudging belief, and finally to a "delightful conviction" regarding God's beauty and "excellency," his entire perspective on the world changed as well. He saw the beauty of God not only in the pages of the Bible but throughout the natural world and mirrored also in the souls of the saints. The secular perspective, for Edwards, was literally unthinkable. Allen Guelzo dubs him "the most consistently unsecular thinker in American history."[24]

The late Hans Frei of Yale University described the development of early modernity as a "great reversal," whereby the biblical narrative was gradually displaced from its centrality. No longer was the Bible regarded as the "story-encompassing story" within which the communities of Western culture located themselves. Instead of the Genesis-to-Revelation narrative, secular humanity located itself within another narrative centered on humanity's conquest of the natural world, its growing self-mastery, and advancing freedom. Hegel wrote that "the history of the world is nothing but the development of the idea of freedom."[25] The great reversal occurred when the world of the biblical narrative was accepted as valid only to the extent that it fit into a secular narrative of human advancement.[26] If Frei's analysis of early modernity is correct, then Edwards's lifework might be seen as a massive attempt to reverse the great reversal and reestablish a theocentric perspective within a culture increasingly alienated from God.[27] Rather than striking a deal with secularity by limiting God's activity to special, supernatural occurrences (Paley), or abandoning the attempt to prove God's presence and activity in the world by rational argument (Schleiermacher), Edwards set for himself the prodigious task of rethinking the entire intellectual culture of his day and turning it to the advantage of God.

Notes

1. *Works* 9:520.

2. M. X. Lesser, *Jonathan Edwards: A Reference Guide* (Boston: G.K. Hall, 1981), and *Jonathan Edwards: An Annotated Bibliography, 1979–1993* (Westport, Conn.: Greenwood Press, 1994).

Introduction

1. Perry Miller, *Jonathan Edwards*, American Men of Letters Series (New York: William Sloane, 1949).

2. Each of these volumes includes a substantial "Editor's Introduction" that provides background for understanding the texts; for an evaluation of the most recent decade in the *Works*, see my forthcoming article "The Protean Puritan: *The Works of Jonathan Edwards*, volumes 8 to 16," *Religious Studies Review* 24 (1998).

3. M. X. Lesser, *Jonathan Edwards: A Reference Guide* (Boston: G.K. Hall, 1981), xli. This work, together with Lesser's successor volume, *Jonathan Edwards: An Annotated Bibliography, 1979–1993* (Westport, Conn.: Greenwood Press, 1994), provides a comprehensive annotated listing of secondary literature on Edwards and is indispensable for serious research.

4. Miller, *Jonathan Edwards*, xii. For Miller, Edwards presents "an intelligence which as much as Emerson's, Melville's or Mark Twain's, is both an index of American society and a comment upon it" (xiii).

5. On the history of the interpretation of Edwards there are three excellent works: Daniel B. Shea, "Jonathan Edwards: The First Two Hundred Years," *Journal of American Studies* 14 (1980): 181–97; Donald Louis Weber, "The Image of Jonathan Edwards in American Culture," Ph.D. diss., Columbia University, 1978; and, most recently, Joseph Conforti, *Jonathan Edwards, Religious Tradition, and American Culture* (Chapel Hill: University of North Carolina Press, 1995). Conforti's study provides an in-depth examination of the nineteenth century; meanwhile, Stephen Crocco of Princeton Theological Seminary is completing a book on twentieth-century interpretations of Edwards.

6. The recent biography by Iain H. Murray, *Jonathan Edwards: A New Biography* (Edinburgh: Banner of Truth Trust, 1987), falls into line with earlier Calvinist appreciations of Edwards. It begins with a series of encomiums to Edwards by various authors (xv–xvii)

and argues that he was "a teacher of the Christian Faith" rather than a "great philosopher" (xix–xxxi).

7. During the late nineteenth and early twentieth centuries, Edwards evoked a rich literature of denigration. Among the most prominent and influential attacks on Edwards were Joseph Crooker, "Jonathan Edwards: A Psychological Study," *New England Magazine*, n.s. 2 (1890): 159–72; Oliver Wendell Holmes, "Jonathan Edwards," in *Pages from an Old Volume of Life: A Collection of Essays: The Writings of Oliver Wendell Holmes*, vol. 8 (Cambridge, Mass.: Riverside Press, 1891), 361–401; Leslie Stephen, "Jonathan Edwards," in *Hours in a Library*, 4 vols. (London: Smith, Elder, 1907), 2:42–102; Vernon Louis Parrington, "The Anachronism of Jonathan Edwards," in *Main Currents in American Thought*, vol. 1, *1620–1800*, 3 vols. (New York: Harcourt, Brace, 1927), 1:148–63; Henry Bamford Parkes, *Jonathan Edwards: The Fiery Puritan* (New York: Minton, Balch, 1930); Charles Angoff, *A Literary History of the American People*, vol. 1, *From 1607 to the Beginning of the Revolutionary Period* (New York: Tudor, 1935), 289–310. Crooker diagnosed Edwards as having a form of "delusional insanity" (163). Holmes attacked Edwards's God as "a piece of iron machinery which would have held back the father's arms stretching out to embrace his son, and shed the blood of the prodigal, instead of that of the fatted calf" (395). His morbid theology was due, at least in part, to ill health. Stephen described Edwards as "a speculative recluse, with little faculty of literary expression, and given to utter opinions shocking to the popular mind" (43). He regrets that so great a mind was imprisoned within the narrow confines of Calvinist doctrine. For Parrington, "Edwards devoted his logic to an assiduous stoking of the fires of hell" (159). Parkes speaks of Edwards's "blight upon posterity." A number of these criticisms are echoed, more or less distinctly, in Ola Winslow, Perry Miller, and many later writers.

8. Conrad Cherry, *The Theology of Jonathan Edwards: A Reappraisal* (Bloomington: Indiana University Press, 1990 [1966]).

9. Daniel B. Shea, Jr., "Jonathan Edwards: Historian of Consciousness," in *Major Writers of Early American Literature*, ed. Everett Emerson (Madison: University of Wisconsin Press, 1972), 180.

10. See the comprehensive interpretation of Edwards's corpus of sermons in Wilson H. Kimnach, "General Introduction to the Sermons: Jonathan Edwards' Art of Prophesying," in *Works* 10:1–258.

11. The *Miscellanies* support this conclusion, since they give indication of Edwards's preoccupations throughout his career and contain little sign of long-term preparations for writing *Freedom of the Will*. Judging by the *Miscellanies*, there is much more evidence that *End of Creation*, for instance, was the culmination of a lengthy process of reflection. As discussed in chapter 4, there are some forty-five entries in the *Miscellanies* devoted to a discussion of God's "end" in creating, and these served as Edwards's preparation for writing *End of Creation*. On the other hand, *Freedom of the Will* sparked theological discussion in America for several generations, as brilliantly chronicled by Allen C. Guelzo in *Edwards on the Will: A Century of American Theological Debate* (Middletown, Conn.: Wesleyan University Press, 1989).

12. The letter, dated 19 October 1757, is reprinted in Sereno Dwight, "Memoirs of Jonathan Edwards," in *Works* (Hickman), 1:clxxiv–clxxv. He writes:

> I have had on my mind and heart . . . a great work, which I call a *History of the Work of Redemption*, a body of divinity in an entire new method, being

thrown into the form of a history; considering the affair of christian theology, as the whole of it, in each part, stands in reference to the great work of redemption by Jesus Christ ... particularly considering all parts of the grand scheme, in their historical order.

Basing his conclusion on the brief page of jottings entitled *A Rational Account of the Main Doctrines of the Christian Religion Attempted*, Perry Miller judged that Edwards's uncompleted magnum opus was to be not so much a "history of redemption" as an apologetic vindication of the Christian faith. It was to draw on the *Miscellanies* and digest the argument of the *Two Dissertations* (Miller, *Edwards*, 49, 127, 285). My analysis in this book shows, however, that the "history of redemption" and the "rational account" were not mutually exclusive projects; Edwards's projected summa may well have incorporated both redemptive-historical and apologetic aspects.

13. Quoted in Clyde A. Holbrook, *The Ethics of Jonathan Edwards: Morality and Aesthetics* (Ann Arbor: University of Michigan Press, 1973), ix.

14. James Hoopes, "Jonathan Edwards's Religious Psychology," *Journal of American History* 69 (1983): 850.

15. See the still valuable study by Thomas H. Johnson, "Jonathan Edwards's Background of Reading," *Publications of the Colonial Society of Massachusetts* 28 (1931): 193–222.

16. *Works* 6:396–97. The character of Edwards's *A Rational Account* is discussed in chapter 6.

17. I am in partial agreement with the conclusion of Peter Gay that Edwards "exploited modern ideas and modern rhetoric to confirm convictions that he had held all his life, and accepted on other grounds." *A Loss of Mastery: Puritan Historians in Colonial America* (Berkeley: University of California Press, 1966), 114. Gay discloses his own intellectual allegiances when he contrasts Puritan historians with the European thinkers who were "rushing forward into secularism" (25). Why should the acceptance of "secularism" be a step "forward," unless religion is necessarily retrograde? Gay writes that Edwards's *History of Redemption* was "reactionary" and "fundamentalist," his reasoning was "pathetic," and he "philosophized in a cage that his fathers had built" (104, 113). Although Gay approached Edwards unsympathetically and polemically, he accurately perceived what some others overlooked, namely, that Edwards often used modern or enlightened notions to serve essentially theological purposes. He writes: "Locke's psychology gave him useful material for understanding the quality of religious emotion, but little else" (113). What Edwards regarded as paramount—"understanding the quality of religious emotion"—is clearly of little significance to Gay.

18. Responding to Perry Miller's interpretation of Edwards as modern, Vincent Tomas argued that Edwards was a "medieval philosopher" inasmuch as "his philosophy placed itself at the service of Scripture and was willing to take orders from it." "The Modernity of Jonathan Edwards," *New England Quarterly* 25 (1952): 60–84, quoting 70–71. John E. Smith puzzled over Edwards's odd combination of the very traditional and the very modern, in "Jonathan Edwards as Philosophical Theologian," *Review of Metaphysics* 30 (1976): 306–24. In somewhat less overt fashion, the debate still goes on. Sang Lee argues that Edwards's writings express a "dispositional ontology" with striking parallels to trends within twentieth-century theology. *The Philosophical Theology of Jonathan Edwards* (Princeton: Princeton University Press, 1988), 3–7. In *The Philosophy of Jonathan Edwards: A Study in Divine Semiotics* (Bloomington: Indiana University Press, 1994), Stephen H. Daniel in

effect turns Edwards into a postmodern thinker with affinities to Michel Foucault and Julia Kristeva. See my review of Daniel's book in *Journal of Religion* 76 (1996): 121–22. For a wide-ranging postmodernist reading of Edwards, see the difficult book by R. C. De-Prospo, *Theism in the Discourse of Jonathan Edwards* (Newark: University of Delaware Press, 1985), reviewed by Daniel B. Shea in "Deconstruction Comes to Early 'America': The Case of Edwards," *Early American Literature* 21 (1986–87): 268–74.

1. Spiritual Perception in Jonathan Edwards

1. Perry Miller, *Harvard Theological Review* 41 (1948): 123–45. This article published Edwards's Miscellany 782 for the first time, together with Miller's commentary on it.

2. Among the most important discussions of the "new sense," in addition to the article already referenced, are the following: Perry Miller, "The Rhetoric of Sensation," in *Errand into the Wilderness* (Cambridge: Belknap Press of Harvard University, 1964), 167–83;
Perry Miller, *Jonathan Edwards,* American Men of Letters Series (New York: William Sloane, 1949), passim; John E. Smith, "Editor's Introduction" to *Religious Affections,* in *Works* 2:1–83; Conrad Cherry, *The Theology of Jonathan Edwards: A Reappraisal* (Bloomington: Indiana University Press, 1990 [1966]), especially 12–43; Edward H. Davidson, "From Locke to Edwards," *Journal of the History of Ideas* 24 (1963): 355–72; Terence Erdt, *Jonathan Edwards, Art, and the Sense of the Heart* (Amherst: University of Massachusetts Press, 1980); Paul Helm, "John Locke and Jonathan Edwards: A Reconsideration," *Journal of the History of Philosophy* 7 (1969): 51–61; James Hoopes, "Jonathan Edwards's Religious Psychology," *Journal of American History* 69 (1983): 849–65, and *Consciousness in New England: From Puritanism and Ideas to Psychoanalysis and Semiotic,* New Series in American Intellectual and Cultural History (Baltimore: Johns Hopkins University Press, 1989), 64–87; David Laurence, "Jonathan Edwards, John Locke, and the Canon of Experience," *Early American Literature* 15 (1980): 107–23; David Lyttle, "The Supernatural Light," in *Studies in Religion in Early American Literature* (Lanham: University Press of America, 1983), 1–20; Miklos Vetö, "La connaissance spirituelle selon Jonathan Edwards," *Revue de theologie et de philosophie* 111 (1979): 233–45, in English translation by Michael J. McClymond, as "Spiritual Knowledge According to Jonathan Edwards," *Calvin Theological Journal* 31 (1996): 161–81; and William J. Wainwright, "Jonathan Edwards and the Sense of the Heart," *Faith and Philosophy* 7 (1990): 43–62, and *Reason and the Heart: A Prolegomenon to a Critique of Passional Reason* (Ithaca, N.Y.: Cornell University Press, 1995), 7–54.

3. In what follows, "spiritual sense" will be used as synonymous with "new sense," yet both these terms will be distinguished from "sense of the heart." Almost alone among Edwards's interpreters, James Hoopes notes that Edwards uses "sense of the heart" for *any* state of awareness in which the will and affections, as well as the reason, are actively engaged by some object ("Religious Psychology," 857–8). In contrast to "sense of the heart" is "speculative [or notional] understanding," in which the reason is involved but not the affections. Thus the *object* of the "sense of the heart" may or may not be God or spiritual things. "Spiritual sense" or "new sense" implies two things, that the will and affections as well as the reason are engaged, and that the object of the mind and affections is God or spiritual things. It follows that every "spiritual sense" (or "new sense") is a "sense of the heart," but not every "sense of the heart" is a "spiritual sense." For Edwards, the unre-

generate and the regenerate alike possess the "sense of the heart," but only the regenerate have the "spiritual sense."

4. *Works* 2:205.

5. See Perry Miller, "From Edwards to Emerson," in *Errand*, 184–203.

6. Miller, *Jonathan Edwards*, 52,62.

7. Miller, *Jonathan Edwards*, 139.

8. Perry Miller, "Rhetoric of Sensation," 169–70; citing Locke, *Essay*, book 3, chapter 2, section 7.

9. See Perry Miller, "Sense of the Heart," 127: "As life is lived from day to day, the name imperceptibly takes the place of the sensation, and ultimately becomes the only object for the idea. . . . To our horror we realize that we are lost among signs, none of which any longer have reality."

10. Miller, "Rhetoric of Sensation," 171–81.

11. Miller, "Sense of the Heart," 127–28.

12. Compare the comments of Edward H. Davidson:

> Both natural and supernatural knowledge are not inexplicable occurrences in the life of specially receptive men, of converted men, but are part of an actual, a daily process of living. . . . 'Experience' is not, therefore, divided between 'natural' and 'supernatural' events and 'natural' and 'supernatural' knowledge, for everything is part of daily cognition. Everything, as Edwards tirelessly argued, is contained within the data of sensing and knowing. ("From Locke to Edwards," 362–4)

13. In his book on Edwards, Miller was as interested in castigating the 1930s Progressives for their shallow optimism as expounding the sage of Northampton. Recent scholars have upbraided Miller for presenting the Puritans in intellectualistic terms and for overlooking the role of the Bible and of spirituality in their life and thought. For a sampling of the criticisms, see George M. Marsden, "Perry Miller's Rehabilitation of the Puritans: A Critique," *Church History* 39 (1970): 91–105. From a different direction, Norman Fiering charges that Miller exaggerated the influence of Locke's philosophy on Edwards and argues that Edwards was substantially indebted to Continental thinkers (e.g., Malebranche, Leibniz, et al.). See Fiering, "The Rationalist Foundations of Jonathan Edwards's Metaphysics," in *Jonathan Edwards and the American Experience*, ed. Nathan O. Hatch and Harry S. Stout (New York: Oxford University Press, 1988), 73–101.

14. Hoopes, "Religious Psychology," 856.

15. Cherry writes that "for good or ill, Edwards was a Calvinist theologian" and adds that "his philosophical and scientific interests were bent to a theological purpose." *Theology*, 3–4. Cherry's new introduction to the 1990 reprint of the book indicates that he has not deviated from his earlier judgment (xxiii–xxiv). John E. Smith's 1959 introduction to the *Religious Affections* (in *Works* 2:1–83), highlighted the affective aspect of religious experience in Edwards but did not break away from Miller's interpretation of the new sense as decidedly as Cherry did.

16. In *Freedom of the Will*, Edwards made it clear that "the will itself is not an agent that has a will," for "that which has the power of volition or choice is the man or the soul, and not the power of volition itself." *Works* 1:163. Thus "will" in effect refers to the whole person in the mode of volition, just as "understanding" refers to the whole person

in the mode of cognition. Moreover, Edwards did not distinguish the affections or feelings from the will, but wrote that "the affections are no other, than the vigorous and sensible exercises of the inclination and will of the soul." *Works* 2:96–7; see *Works* 1:163.

17. Cherry, *Theology*, 22, citing Ola Winslow, *Jonathan Edwards, 1703–1758: A Biography* (New York: Collier Books, 1961), 216, and Miller, *Jonathan Edwards*, 184. Alfred Owen Aldridge went so far as to suggest that Edwards represented an "anti-intellectual tradition." *Jonathan Edwards* (New York: Washington Square Press, 1964), 22, cited in Cherry, *Theology*, 22.

18. Cherry, *Theology*, 25–43. Paul Ramsey, in his 1957 "Editor's Introduction" to *Freedom of the Will* noted that Edwards speaks of God's relation to the redeemed soul sometimes in terms of Locke's "new simple idea" and sometimes "in the terms of Platonic, Johannine, and Augustinian illuminism." *Works* 1:43. Ramsey anticipated some of Miller's later critics when he added that Locke's influence on Edwards did not render the latter "some sort of religious naturalist or sensational empiricist" but served "to provide him with a different philosophical manner of stating the truth contained in . . . earlier theological points of view." (1:43 n. 5).

19. Cherry, *Theology*, 27.

20. *Works* 2:203.

21. Cherry, *Theology*, 28–30. Consider the passage in *Religious Affections*, where he uses the words "partaker," "fellowship," "communion," and "participation" and concludes that the Christian's "grace" is "as the brightness that is in a diamond which the sun shines upon, is of the same nature with the brightness of the sun, but only that it is as nothing to its in degree." *Works* 2:201–2. See *Works* 8:441–4, 531–4.

22. Cherry, *Theology*, 30.

23. Helm, "John Locke and Jonathan Edwards," 54, 57–8. By way of qualification, Helm adds that Edwards himself "seems to equivocate," since in principle a person possessing a "sixth sense" would know more facts than a person with only five senses, and yet Edwards denies that the elect in general know any more notional or speculative truths than others (60).

24. Hoopes, "Religious Psychology," 859.

25. Hoopes, "Religious Psychology," 857.

26. See Erdt, *Jonathan Edwards*, 1–42. Steven R. Yarbrough and John C. Adams, *Delightful Conviction: Jonathan Edwards and the Rhetoric of Conversion*, Great American Orators 20 (Westport, Conn.: Greenwood Press, 1993), xiii. Later Yarbrough and Adams seem to contradict their quoted statement, in rejecting Hoopes's notion of a "new, exclusive sense" in Edwards, peculiar to the saints (17–8). David Lyttle writes: "The experience of the Supernatural Light is, so to speak, a new dimension so basically different from our natural experiences that Edwards did not know how to talk about it precisely." "Supernatural Light," 3. Moreover, "all his references to the senses when he spoke about the Supernatural Light are metaphorical. But what he meant to express literally by these metaphors, to repeat, is the absolute difference between Revelation and natural experience" (6). Edwards taught a "sixth sense" (9). Compare the comment of Harold Simonson:

> Whatever else regeneration implies, a fundamental principle of it establishes a new vision radically different from that of natural understanding and sight. . . .
> Regenerate perception enabled one to see what he could not see before, namely, the spiritual meanings in scripture, history, nature, and as Edwards believed, in

all creation. ("Typology, Imagination, and Jonathan Edwards," in *Radical Discontinuities: American Romanticism and Christian Consciousness* [Rutherford, N.J.: Fairleigh Dickinson University Press, 1983], 28–9)

27. Perry Miller, "Rhetoric of Sensation," 168; Voltaire, as quoted in Gerald R. Cragg, *Reason and Authority in the Eighteenth Century* (Cambridge: Cambridge University Press, 1964), 6. Cragg sums up: "Locke, beyond any other writer, was to be the moving spirit of the eighteenth century. . . . In every branch of intellectual endeavor his influence was supreme" (5–6). Norman Kemp Smith claims that on the appearance of the *Essay*, Locke "became the dominant philosophical influence throughout Europe." *John Locke* (Manchester, England: Manchester University Press, 1933) 8, 12–3, quoted in Gerald R. Cragg, *From Puritanism to the Age of Reason: A Study of Changes in Religious Thought within the Church of England, 1660–1700* (Cambridge: Cambridge University Press, 1966), 114 n. 1. Paul Hazard writes in *European Thought in the Eighteenth Century: From Montesquieu to Lessing* (New Haven: Yale University Press, 1954) that Locke's "supremacy seemed unchallenged, and unchallengeable" and that there may be "no thinker who exerted a profounder influence on the minds of his contemporaries than did he" (41).

28. Hoopes, *Consciousness in New England*, 64–5, 73–4.

29. Locke, *Essay* 4.19.4. The edition of Locke consulted here is Robert Maynard Hutchins et al., ed., *Great Books of the Western World*, vol. 35, *Locke, Berkeley, Hume* (Chicago: Encyclopaedia Britannica, 1952). Locke's chapters "Faith and Reason" and "Enthusiasm" (*Essay* 4.18–9) were profoundly influential in the eighteenth century, and they are indispensable for understanding Edwards's fully developed position on spiritual perception.

30. John Toland, *Christianity Not Mysterious* (London, 1696), 16–7, cited by Hoopes, *Consciousness in New England*, 64–5. On the unique position of Toland in the deist controversy, see the carefully researched study by Robert E. Sullivan, *John Toland and the Deist Controversy: A Study in Adaptations*, Harvard Historical Studies 101 (Cambridge: Harvard University Press, 1982).

31. Locke, *Essay* 4.18.3.

32. Locke, *Essay* 4.18.4.

33. David Laurence, "John Locke," 121; see 108–12.

34. Locke seemed to leave open the possibility that God might give new "original revelations," for he writes: "God, I own, cannot be denied to be able to enlighten the understanding by a ray darted into the mind immediately from the fountain of light" (*Essay* 4.19.5). Yet, as David Laurence points out, he rejected as arrogant the view that such a ray of supernatural light was prerequisite to being a Christian. What made people Christians was not supernatural illumination but intellectual assent to the truths taught in the Bible. As Laurence comments, "Christianity was of divine origin; but individual Christians were not." "John Locke," 110. Given the general tone of the chapter on "Enthusiasm," Locke's reference to the "ray darted" from God may simply be sarcastic.

35. Charles Chauncy, *Seasonable Thoughts on the State of Religion in New England* (Boston: Rogers and Fowle, 1743), 324, quoted in Cherry, *Theology of Edwards*, 166; see 19, 221 n. 29.

36. Hoopes, *Consciousness in New England*, 81.

37. *Works* 2:206 and *Treatise on Grace*, in *Treatise on Grace and Other Posthumously Published Writings*, ed. Paul Helm (Cambridge, England: James Clarke, 1971), 32–7.

38. Edwards was, if anything, even more adamant than Locke in opposing the idea of new "original revelations" in the present age. In his reflections on the "glorious times of the church" that lie ahead, Edwards says that he does not expect a restoration of the gifts of prophecy and inspiration. He quips that he himself would rather have fifteen minutes of "humble joy in God" than "prophetical visions and revelations for a whole year." *Works* 4:281.

39. Some aspects in Locke's characterization of "enthusiasm" parallel Edwards's teaching on the "divine light," especially with regard to the certitude it confers: "They see the light infused into their understandings and cannot be mistaken; it is clear and visible there, like the light of bright sunshine; shows itself, and needs no other proof but its own evidence. . . . Would he not be ridiculous, who should require to have it proved to him that the light shines, and that he sees it?" *Essay* 4.19.8; see *Works* 13:177–8 (Misc. aa).

40. Hoopes, *Consciousness in New England*, 65.

41. The most important texts on the spiritual sense include the following, with the editions I will cite (see list of abbreviations): *Religious Affections* (*Works* 2); the sermon *A Divine and Supernatural Light* (*Divine Light*); the *Personal Narrative* (*Personal Narrative*); the sermons "The Pure in Heart Blessed," "Man's Natural Blindness in Religion," and "True Grace Distinguished from the Experience of Devils" (*Works* [Hickman], 2:905–13, 2:247–56, 2:41–50); *Treatise on Grace*; *Miscellanies* aa, 123, 141, 201, 212, 239, 248, 390, 397, 408, 410, 419, 460, 471, 476, 481, 489 (*Works* 13); *Miscellanies* 541, 628, 1090 (*PJE*); *Miscellanies* 537–9, 540, 567, 580, 626, 628, 629, 686, 732, 853, 1029 (Yale MSS); and *Miscellany* 782, (in Miller, "Sense of the Heart").

42. John E. Smith writes: "The divine nature is always held up as the true foundation of the believer's response." "Editor's Introduction," in *Works* 2:30.

43. *Works* 2:240.

44. Douglas Elwood, *The Philosophical Theology of Jonathan Edwards* (New York: Columbia University Press, 1960), 7; Clyde Holbrook, *The Ethics of Jonathan Edwards: Morality and Aesthetics* (Ann Arbor: University of Michigan, 1973), 3.

45. *Works* 13:177–8 (Misc. aa).

46. See *Works* 2:305–7; 13:338 (Misc. 201); 13:470 (Misc. 408); 13:522 (Misc. 476); Misc. 628 (Yale MSS); Misc. 686 (Yale MSS); *Divine Light*, 81–6.

47. *Works* (Hickman) 2:907. Compare Edwards's reflections on the biblical description of Christians as "witnesses" to God, in *Works* 2:305–7.

48. *Divine Light*, 86.

49. *Works* 2:307.

50. *Divine Light*, 72.

51. *Works* (Hickman), 2:158.

52. In Misc. 539 (Yale MSS), Edwards writes that "the matter which the principle of grace acts upon is those notions or ideas that the mind is furnished with of the things of religion. . . . If there could be a principle of grace in the heart without these notions or ideas, yet it could not act, because it could have no matter to act upon." The "notional understanding" is thus a necessary but not a sufficient condition for spiritual perception.

53. *Divine Light*, 70. See *Works* (Hickman), 2:905–6.

54. *Works* (Hickman), 2:906.

55. *Works* 13:463 (Misc. 397).

56. "That there is a Christ, and that Christ is holy and gracious, is conveyed to the

mind by the word of God: but the sense of the excellency of Christ by reason of that holiness and grace, is nevertheless immediately the work of the Holy Spirit" (*Divine Light*, 77).

57. One finds a subtle difference in Edwards's use of the terms "notion" and "idea." "Notion" always denotes a mental content of the "speculative understanding," divorced from the "sense of the heart." "Idea" is ambiguous, for it can refer to a mental content either with or without an attendant "sense of the heart."

58. See Edwards's sermon "True Grace Distinguished from the Experience of Devils," where the demons are a test case for demonstrating that a speculative knowledge of God differs from a sense of the divine beauty. *Works* (Hickman), 2:41–50. "The devil has undoubtedly a great degree of speculative knowledge in divinity; having been, as it were, educated in the best divinity school in the universe, *viz.* the heaven of heavens" (43). Yet, for the demons, "the more holiness they see in him, the more hateful he appears" (48). See the insightful analysis of this sermon in Vetö, "La connaissance spirituelle selon Jonathan Edwards."

59. Augustine's theory is similar but not identical to Edwards's. For the former, illumination is an explanation for human knowing in general and not merely for the human knowing of God and spiritual things. Augustine taught "that man can know this present temporal, corporeal world only because he first knows the eternal, incorporeal, intelligible world of ideas that exists in the mind of God." Ronald H. Nash, *The Light of the Mind: St. Augustine's Theory of Knowledge* (Lexington: University of Kentucky Press, 1969), viii. Nash's analysis makes clear, however, that Augustine has the same difficulty as Edwards in clarifying whether the human mind in illumination is an active agent or merely a passive recipient of ideas. See also Etienne Gilson, *The Christian Philosophy of Saint Augustine*, trans. L. E. M. Lynch (New York: Random House, 1960), 66–111, and Frederick Copleston, *A History of Philosophy*, vol. 2, *Medieval Philosophy, Augustine to Scotus* (Paramus, N.J.: Newman Press, 1971 [1950]), 51–67.

60. *Divine Light*, 76.

61. *Divine Light*, 88. "The prime alteration that is made in conversion . . . is the alteration of the temper and disposition and spirit of the mind," and "the nature of the soul being thus changed, it admits divine light." *Works* 13:462 (Misc. 397). Following conversion, the cumulative effect of the Spirit over time is a qualitative change in the human person and a quantitative increase in spiritual knowledge. *Works* 13:287 (Misc. 123); *Works* 13:297 (Misc. 141).

62. See note 21. A recent study by Anri Morimoto, *Jonathan Edwards and the Catholic Vision of Salvation* (University Park: Pennsylvania State University Press, 1995), interprets Edwards's teaching on salvation as "ontological transformation" or "participation" in God (see especially 4–8, 37–50).

63. *Works* 13:513 (Misc. 471); *Works* 13:462 (Misc. 397). A number of other passages make the same distinction between the regenerate and the unregenerate: *Works* 13:455, with n. 9 (Misc. 390); *Works* 13:523–4 (Misc. 481); Misc. 626, 732 (Yale MSS); *Divine Light*, 68–70; and *Treatise on Grace*, 25–39.

64. *PJE*, 186 (Misc. 1263). The whole of Miscellany 1263 is devoted to expounding God's "arbitrary operation" as the foundational principle of the created universe. *PJE*, 184–93. See the discussion of this miscellany in the conclusion to this book.

65. On the "arbitrariness" of grace, see *Works* 13:189–91 (Misc. tt); 13:327 (Misc. 178); 13:523–4 (Misc. 481); Misc. 537, 580, 629, 1029 (Yale MSS); and *Divine Light*, 83–5. On the other hand, Edwards inveighed against the idea that divine illumination occurs apart from

the stated "means of grace." Otherwise there would be no point in Bible reading, Sunday worship, and participation in the sacraments (Misc. 538, Yale MSS; see Misc. 539).

66. Roland Delattre, in his major study *Beauty and Sensibility in the Thought of Jonathan Edwards: An Essay in Aesthetics and Theological Ethics* (New Haven: Yale University Press, 1968) writes: "Taken together, beauty and sensibility may be said to be the objective and subjective components of the moral or spiritual life. They must be taken and considered together, for they are essentially and internally related" (3).

67. *Divine Light*, 72–3.

68. *Personal Narrative*, 29.

69. Edwards's stress on the subjective response to "excellency" or "beauty" corresponds to a general trend in eighteenth-century aesthetics. "The nature of the aesthetic cannot be known by mere concepts," writes Ernst Cassirer, and "the immediate impression, with which all formulation of aesthetic concepts must start and to which it must constantly refer, cannot be replaced by any deductions." *The Philosophy of the Enlightenment*, trans. Fritz C. A. Koelln and James P. Pettegrove (Boston: Beacon Press, 1955), 303. The aesthetic of immediate impressions, as Cassirer explains, is explicated with reference to "taste," a capacity that some persons have and others lack. "Taste" cannot be replaced with a set of rules, and cannot, strictly speaking, be learned or be taught (304). In *Religious Affections*, Edwards drew on this eighteenth-century tradition to describe the nature of religious sensibility. See especially his quotation from the entry on "Taste" in Ephraim Chamber's *Cyclopaedia* (London, 1728) in *Works* 2:282–3.

70. *Divine Light*, 73.

71. Cherry points out that the metaphor of "tasting" God occurs in John Calvin, in various Puritan authors, and in the Cambridge Platonists. See John Calvin, *Institutes of the Christian Religion*, ed. John T. McNeill, 2 vols. (Philadelphia: Westminster Press, 1960), 581 (bk. 3, ch. 2, sec. 33); Geoffrey F. Nuttall, *The Holy Spirit in Puritan Faith and Experience* (Oxford: Basil Blackwell, 1947), 38–9; and John Smith, *Select Discourses* (London: Rivingtons and Cochran, 1821), 19. Cited in Cherry, *Theology of Edwards*, 21, 221 n. 40.

72. *Divine Light*, 86.

73. The literature on Schleiermacher, like that on Edwards, is simply enormous. Among the works that have influenced my discussion here are the following: Richard Crouter, "Introduction," to Friedrich Schleiermacher, *On Religion: Speeches to Its Cultured Despisers*, trans. Richard Crouter (Cambridge: Cambridge University Press, 1988), 1–73; B. A. Gerrish, *A Prince of the Church: Schleiermacher and the Beginnings of Modern Theology* (Philadelphia: Fortress Press, 1984) and "Friedrich Schleiermacher," in *Nineteenth-Century Religious Thought in the West*, ed. Ninian Smart et al., 3 vols. (Cambridge: Cambridge University Press, 1985) 1:123–56; Van Harvey, "A Word in Defense of Schleiermacher's Theological Method," *Journal of Religion* 42 (1962): 151–70, and "On the New Edition of Schleiermacher's *Addresses on Religion*," *Journal of the American Academy of Religion* 39 (1971): 488–512; Wayne Proudfoot, *Religious Experience* (Berkeley: University of California, 1985); and Wayne Proudfoot et al., "Symposium on Schleiermacher's 'On Religion: Speeches to Its Cultured Despisers,'" *Harvard Divinity Bulletin* 24 (1995): 10–3. The two primary works by Schleiermacher consulted here are: *On Religion: Speeches to Its Cultured Despisers*, trans. John Oman (New York: Harper and Row, 1958 [1893]), and *The Christian Faith*, ed. H. R. Macintosh and J. S. Stewart (Edinburgh: T. and T. Clark, 1986).

74. Proudfoot, "Symposium," 10.

75. Schleiermacher, *Speeches*, 36, 102.

76. One is reminded of Schleiermacher's fellow Romantics Samuel Taylor Coleridge and Ralph Waldo Emerson, who split the human intellectual faculties into the so-called Reason (which was lofty and spiritual) and Understanding (which was dull, unimaginative, and earthbound). In his "Divinity School Address," Emerson comments that "there is no doctrine of the Reason which will bear to be taught by the Understanding." *Essays and Lectures*, ed. Joel Porte (New York: Library of America, 1983), 80. Emerson and Coleridge did not overtly separate religion from knowledge as Schleiermacher did, but the distinction between Reason and Understanding was a step in the same direction.

77. Schleiermacher, *Speeches*, 48.

78. Schleiermacher, *Speeches*, 49–50, 282. Scholars still debate to what extent Schleiermacher changed his mind in the later editions of the *Speeches* (1806, 1821, 1831) and in his text in systematic theology, *The Christian Faith*. On the basis of the radical statements in the 1799 edition, I am inclined to agree with Richard Crouter and Van Harvey that the younger Schleiermacher was a religious naturalist whose position did not require the existence of a personal God or perhaps any God at all (see Crouter, "Introduction," 64–6, and Proudfoot, "Symposium," 10–1).

79. Schleiermacher, *The Christian Faith*, 12–26 (secs. 4–5).

80. Immanuel Kant, *Critique of Pure Reason*, trans. Norman Kemp Smith (New York: St. Martin's Press, 1965 [1929]), 29 (Bxxx).

81. Locke, *Essay* 4.18.3.

82. Nicholas Wolterstorff, in his intricately argued piece "Locke's Philosophy of Religion," concludes that for Locke "faith is not a mode of knowledge." In *The Cambridge Companion to Locke*, ed. Vere Chappell (New York: Cambridge University Press, 1994), 190. Knowledge and the assent of faith were wholly different phenomena (176). In his letter to Bishop Stillingfleet, Locke had written that "to talk of . . . the knowledge of believing" was "a way of speaking not easy to me to understand." *The Works of John Locke*, 10 vols., 1964 [1823] 4:146, quoting 189–90. As Wolterstorff explains, Locke held that we are immediately to believe something only if we directly *perceive* it to be so, and yet the only facts the mind directly perceives are those concerning the mind's existence and its modifications. "God is never directly present to the mind; that assumption is fundamental to Locke's epistemology of religion. . . . The sacramental view, that at least some of us human beings at some points in our lives experience God, was not an assumption Locke made. If asked about it, he would firmly have rejected it" (182, 186). See also Wolterstorff's *John Locke and the Ethics of Belief*, Cambridge Studies in Religion and Culture 2 (New York: Cambridge University Press, 1996).

83. Richard E. Brantley has argued that both Edwards and Wesley "theologize empiricism" and seek to show that "the great principle of empiricism, that one must see for oneself and be in the presence of the thing one knows, applies . . . to evangelical faith." Brantley traces their commonalities and differences through a careful scrutiny of Wesley's 1773 abridgement of Edwards's 1746 treatise *Religious Affections*. See Brantley, "The Common Ground of Wesley and Edwards," *Harvard Theological Review* 83 (1990): 271–83, and his *Coordinates of Anglo-American Romanticism: Wesley, Edwards, Carlyle, and Emerson* (Gainesville: University Press of Florida, 1993), 7–42.

84. Delattre speaks of "Edwards' conception of beauty" as "primarily objective, structural, and relational rather than subjective, emotional, and relativist" (*Beauty and Sensibility*, 4; see 15–26).

85. *Works* 13:177–8 (Misc. aa). For an interesting discussion of the possibility of per-

ceiving God without knowing that it is God that one perceives, see William P. Alston, *Perceiving God: The Epistemology of Religious Experience* (Ithaca, N.Y.: Cornell University Press, 1991), 11–2. John Baillie held the view, somewhat like Schleiermacher's, that at some level everyone "knows" God: "We cannot reach a time when we did not 'know God' by going back to the beginnings either of our individual or of our racial consciousness." *Our Knowledge of God* (New York: Scribner's, 1959), 47; see 4, 54, 62.

86. Cherry, *Theology*, 230 n. 54.

87. Wilson H. Kimnach, "Jonathan Edwards's Pursuit of Reality," in *Jonathan Edwards and the American Experience*, ed. Nathan O. Hatch and Harry S. Stout (New York: Oxford University Press, 1988), 102–17.

88. At least since the middle of the nineteenth century, Edwards and Franklin have been regarded as two quintessential representatives of the "Puritan" and "Yankee" types in American culture. Yet a recent and important collection of essays suggests that there are important commonalities, as well as contrasts, between the two figures. See Barbara B. Oberg and Harry S. Stout, eds., *Benjamin Franklin, Jonathan Edwards, and the Representation of American Culture* (New York: Oxford University Press, 1993).

89. Thomas Aquinas, for instance, discusses the vision of God under the rubric of eschatology, in his *Summa Theologica* (supplement, q. 92, a.1–3). See Kenneth E. Kirk, *The Vision of God: The Christian Doctrine of the "Summum Bonum"* (New York: Harper and Row, 1966 [1931]). When Edwards discusses the vision of God that the saints enjoy in heaven, he portrays it as the completion of that vision that the saints on earth already possess. It is also the supreme means of human blessedness, much as in Aquinas. *Works* (Hickman), 2:906–9.

90. *Personal Narrative*, 29, 31.

91. Diana Hochstedt Butler likewise stresses the priority for Edwards of regenerate experience and the idea that "God's greatest glory is visible only to those who have eyes to see." "God's Visible Glory: The Beauty of Nature in the Thought of John Calvin and Jonathan Edwards," *Westminster Theological Journal* 52 (1990): 13–26, citing 21.

92. See Edwards's discussion in *True Virtue*, where he argues that "experience plainly shows that men's approbation of this sort of beauty [i.e., secondary] does not spring from any virtuous temper, and has no connection with virtue." *Works* 8:573–4. Earlier in the treatise, however, he maintains that "secondary beauty" has "a tendency to assist those whose hearts are under the influence of a truly virtuous temper, to dispose them to the exercises of divine love, and enliven in them a sense of spiritual beauty" (565).

93. Robert W. Jenson, *America's Theologian: A Recommendation of Jonathan Edwards* (New York: Oxford University Press, 1988), 22.

2. The Theocentric Metaphysics of The Mind

1. Dugald Stewart, *A General View of the Progress of Metaphysical, Ethical, and Political Philosophy, Since the Revival of Letters in Europe: First Dissertation* (Boston: Wells and Lilly, 1823), 2:256–7, quoted in M. X. Lesser, *Jonathan Edwards: A Reference Guide* (Boston: G. K. Hall, 1981), 29. See the successor volume of Lesser's invaluable bibliography: *Jonathan Edwards: An Annotated Bibliography, 1979–1993* (Westport, Conn.: Greenwood Press, 1994).

2. Wallace E. Anderson, "Note on 'The Mind,'" in *Works* 6:313.

3. Sereno Dwight asserted that Edwards began writing *The Mind* in 1717, when he was only some thirteen or fourteen years old. As Thomas Schafer suggested to me in personal

conversation, Dwight's early dating of *The Mind* helped to foster a "cult of genius" that long surrounded Edwards. Unfortunately, the manuscript for *The Mind* vanished soon after Dwight transcribed it into his *Life of President Edwards*, and therefore the manuscript itself cannot be examined in assigning a date. However, based on evidence derived from Schafer's dating of Edwards's other manuscripts, Wallace E. Anderson suggests that Edwards commenced *The Mind* in 1723, when he was roughly twenty, and that certain entries were probably not written until after 1747. See Anderson's discussion, "Note on 'The Mind,' " 325–9.

4. Perry Miller, "General Editor's Note," in *Works* 1:viii.

5. Stephen Daniel writes: "For in spite of their affinities to themes developed in the modernist mentality, Edwards's texts assume practices that are simply unimaginable in terms of modernity." *The Philosophy of Jonathan Edwards: A Study in Divine Semiotics*, Indiana Series in the Philosophy of Religion (Bloomington: Indiana University Press, 1994), 4; see 1–10. For Daniel, Edwards does not fall within "modernity" but rather within a "Renaissance episteme" along with such contemporary writers as Michel Foucault and Julia Kristeva. Daniel's interpretation of Edwards's writings as a web of "discursive exchanges" works much better for his typological writings than for other texts in his corpus. See my review of Daniel's book in *Journal of Religion* 76 (1996): 121–2.

6. Frederick J. E. Woodbridge, "The Philosophy of Edwards," in *Exercises Commemorating the Two-Hundredth Anniversary of the Birth of Jonathan Edwards*, ed. John Winthrop Platner, (Andover, Mass.: Andover Press, 1904), 71–2, 58.

7. James Carse, *Jonathan Edwards and the Visibility of God* (New York: Scribners, 1967), 34–5.

8. Anders Nygren explains the notion of the "fundamental motif" as "the basic idea or the driving power of the religion concerned, or what it is that gives it its character as a whole and communicates to all its parts their special content and colour." *Agape and Eros*, rev. ed., trans. Philip S. Watson (Philadelphia: Westminster, 1953), 35.

9. Douglas Elwood, *The Philosophical Theology of Jonathan Edwards* (New York: Columbia University Press, 1960); Norman Fiering, *Jonathan Edwards's Moral Thought and Its British Context* (Chapel Hill: University of North Carolina Press, 1981); Sang Lee, *The Philosophical Theology of Jonathan Edwards* (Princeton: Princeton University Press, 1988); Daniel, *The Philosophy of Jonathan Edwards*. Delattre seems to have claimed Edwards's notion of beauty as a "fundamental motif," saying that "the aesthetic aspect of Jonathan Edwards' thought and vision . . . provides a larger purchase on the essential and distinctive features of his thought than does any other aspect." *Beauty and Sensibility in the Thought of Jonathan Edwards: An Essay in Aesthetics and Theological Ethics* (New Haven: Yale University Press), vii.

10. Cherry, *The Theology of Jonathan Edwards: A Reappraisal*, 7.

11. See the brief piece on Edwards's *Two Dissertations* by Mark A. Noll, "God at the Center: Jonathan Edwards on True Virtue," *Christian Century* 110 (1993): 854–8, which stresses Edwards's "boldness in affirming a God-centered vision of the cosmos" (854).

12. The most thorough analysis of Edwards's metaphysics to date is that by Wallace E. Anderson, "Editor's Introduction," *Works* 6:1–143.

13. Robert W. Jenson, *America's Theologian: A Recommendation of Jonathan Edwards* (New York: Oxford University Press, 1988), 22. Others have noted the same feature of Edwards's thought. Paul Ramsey says: "He is nothing if not ontological and theological or bib-

lical at the same time." "Editor's Introduction," *Works* 8:22. James Orr comments: "Philosophy to him was at no time an end in itself, but was valued only as it led back to, or had relations with, God and religion." Conversely, "Religion, as it moves back on ultimate questions, always becomes to him again a kind of philosophy; is lifted up into a region of more or less lofty speculation." "The Influence of Edwards," in Platner, *Exercises*, 114.

14. *The Mind* is unquestionably the locus classicus for a study of Edwards's metaphysics, yet such a study cannot confine itself to that work, inasmuch as he returned again and again to metaphysics in such later writings as the *Two Dissertations* and the *Miscellanies*. *The Mind* has been republished, with extensive notes and commentary by Wallace E. Anderson, in *Works* 6:313–93.

15. Elwood, *Philosophical Theology*, 11.

16. V. L. Parrington, *Main Currents of American Thought* (New York: Harcourt, Brace, 1927), 1:252, quoted in Henry F. May, "Jonathan Edwards and America," in *Jonathan Edwards and the American Experience*, ed. Nathan O. Hatch and Harry S. Stout (New York: Oxford University Press, 1988), 30.

17. Egbert Smyth, "The Theology of Edwards," in Platner, *Exercises*, 79.

18. Thomas Schafer, "Jonathan Edwards," in *Encyclopedia Britannica*, 15th ed. (Chicago: Encyclopedia Britannica, 1986), 4:381–2 (Micropedia).

19. *Works* (Hickman), 2:3.

20. *Works* 8:405–536.

21. *Works* 6:363.

22. *Works* 6:345. See Isaiah 45:5, 14, 18, 21, 22.

23. Analogously for Karl Barth, "the supreme problem of theology is not the existence of God, as natural theology supposes, but the independent existence of creaturely reality." G. W. Bromiley and T. F. Torrance, "Editor's Preface," in Karl Barth, *Church Dogmatics* volume 3, part 1 (Edinburgh: T. and T. Clark, 1958), vii.

24. H. Richard Niebuhr, "Value Theory and Theology," 174, quoted in Paul Ramsey, "The Transformation of Ethics," in *Faith and Ethics: The Theology of H. Richard Niebuhr*, ed. Paul Ramsey (New York: Harper, 1957), 143.

25. For Barth's treatment of the Creator's "affirmation" of the creature, see *Church Dogmatics*, vol. 3, part 1, 344–5.

26. Augustine writes, "Wherever we taste the truth, God is there." *Confessions*, trans. R. S. Pine-Coffin (Harmondsworth, England: Penguin Books, 1961) book 4, chapter 12.

27. *Works* 8:441.

28. Edwards, *Works* 8:550–1.

29. One textual feature of *The Mind* that seems hitherto to have passed unnoticed is the presence of the "corollaries" in which Edwards at the end of the entries draws out further conclusions from his preceding reasoning. In all, *The Mind* contains *eighteen* such references (*Works* 6:338, 341, 342, 343, 345, 351, 352, 355, 361, 362, 381, 382, 385). Commonly, though not invariably, these "corollaries" encapsulate the theological significance of the foregoing discussions. A notable instance is the essay *Of Atoms*, which proceeds much like any eighteenth-century scientific treatise, lettered diagrams and all, and then suddenly in its "corollaries" explodes into such theological declarations as that "it is God himself . . . that keeps the parts of atoms or two bodies touching" and that "the substance of bodies at last becomes nothing but the Deity acting." *Works* 6:214–6. Thus the "corollaries" point toward the underlying theological agenda of the metaphysical writings.

30. The most extensive study of Edwards's ontology to date is Thomas Anton Schafer,

"The Concept of Being in the Thought of Jonathan Edwards" (Ph.D. diss. Duke University, 1951).

31. John Locke, *An Essay Concerning Human Understanding*, book 1, chapter 1 section 7.

32. See Norman Fiering, "The Rationalist Foundations of Jonathan Edwards's Metaphysics," in Hatch and Stout, *Jonathan Edwards and the American Experience*, 73–101, where Edwards is compared to such Continental pundits as Malebranche and Leibniz.

33. The most important passages identifying God as "Being" or "Being in general" are as follows: *Works* 6:345, 363; *Works* 8:461, 621; and *PJE*, 74 (Misc. 27a), 87 (Misc. 880). Compare Malebranche's description of God as "Being without any limitation, Being infinite, and in general" (*Recherche de le verite*, book 3, chapter 2, section 8), as analyzed in Craig Walton, "Malebranche's Ontology," *Journal of the History of Philosophy* 7 (1969): 143–161, and A. Bremond, "Le théocentrisme de Malebranche," *Archives de philosophie* 6 (1928): 281–303.

34. Nineteenth- and early-twentieth-century writers often judged Edwards to be pantheistic. Recently this claim has been repeated by Rem B. Edwards, *A Return to Moral and Religious Philosophy in Early America* (Washington, D.C.: University Press of America, 1982), 65.

35. George Rupp, "The 'Idealism' of Jonathan Edwards," *Harvard Theological Review* 62 (1969): 214.

36. Miklos Vetö, *Le pensée de Jonathan Edwards* (Paris: Les Editions du Cerf, 1987), 49.

37. *Works* 8:424.

38. See *Works* 8:546; *Works* (Hickman), 2:125; and *PJE*, 127 (Misc. tt).

39. *Works* 8:546 n. 6.

40. A certain ambiguity arises at this point in Edwards's ontology, inasmuch as the supremacy of God can be served either by placing God at the summit of the chain of being or by making God into an ontological ground, not located on the chain but undergirding it at every point. Edwards seems to vacillate on this point, sometimes affirming that God differs from creatures only by virtue of his infinite degree of being (*PJE*, 183; Misc. 150), at other times insisting that God differs from creatures because God is an "all-comprehending being" (*PJE*, 262). Douglas Elwood denies any chain-of-being idea in Edwards, but this position is contradicted by the texts themselves and seems to reflect Elwood's Tillichian notion of "Being-itself . . . as the *creative power-to-be* that is present in every particular being." *Philosophical Theology*, 28.

41. See Bennett Ramsey, "The Ineluctable Impulse: 'Consent' in the Thought of Edwards, James, and Royce," *Union Seminary Quarterly Review* 37 (1983): 302–22.

42. *Works* 6:336.

43. Jonathan Edwards, "An Essay on the Trinity," in *Treatise on Grace and Other Posthumously Published Writings*, ed. Paul Helm (Cambridge, England: James Clarke, 1971), 99–131.

44. This crucial assertion of Edwards I designate "the principle of proportionate regard," which might be stated in Edwards's own words as follows: "For 'tis fit that the regard of the Creator should be proportioned to the worthiness of objects, as well as the regard of creatures." *Works* 8:424. The pervasiveness of this principle in his thinking is evidenced by its frequent repetition: *Works* 6:356, 362, 382; *Works* 8:421–4, 426, 460, 548–9, 553, 571; *PJE*, 129. For a further discussion of this principle, see the analysis of *End of Creation* in chapter 4.

45. Definitions of "idealism" vary, but a couple would equally apply to Edwards: (1)

the theory that makes mind or minds the ultimate principle of reality and (2) the viewpoint that only that which is perceptible to minds has metaphysical status as real.

46. In addition to Anderson, "Editor's Introduction," *Works* 6, see his "Immaterialism in Jonathan Edwards' Early Philosophical Notes," *Journal of the History of Ideas* 25 (1964): 181–200. Other recent studies include: George Rupp, "The 'Idealism' of Jonathan Edwards," 209–26; Charles J. McCracken, *Malebranche and British Philosophy* (Oxford: Clarendon Press, 1983), 329–40; and Claude A. Smith, "Jonathan Edwards and 'The Way of Ideas,' " *Harvard Theological Review* 59 (1966): 153–73. The earlier studies of Edwards's idealism, mostly around the turn of the century, were preoccupied with discovering its sources. See the following: H. N. Gardiner, "The Early Idealism of Jonathan Edwards," *Philosophical Review* 9 (1900): 573–96; J. H. McCracken, "The Sources of Jonathan Edwards' Idealism," *Philosophical Review* 11 (1902): 537–55; and Clarence Gohdes, "Aspects of Idealism in Early New England," *Philosophical Review* 39 (1930): 537–55. No real consensus has ever been reached on the question of Edwards's sources, except the negative conclusion that Edwards almost certainly *did not* read George Berkeley before coming to his own distinctive idealist position. Very recently Richard A. S. Hall has revived the "long dormant" theory of Berkeley's influence on Edwards, and yet he does not assert that Edwards's idealism is derived from Berkeley's. Instead he points to remarkable continuities between Edwards's *Nature of True Virtue* and Berkeley's *Alciphron* that may reflect Edwards's dependence on Berkeley's critique of the moral sense theorists. See Hall's "Did Berkeley Influence Edwards? Their Common Critique of the Moral Sense Theory," in *Jonathan Edwards's Writings: Text, Context, Interpretation*, ed. Stephen J. Stein (Bloomington: Indiana University Press, 1996), 100–21.

47. *PJE*, 193 (Misc. f). Berkeley, too, showed a keen sense of the threat posed by materialist philosophy: "Particularly, *matter*, or *the absolute existence of corporeal objects*, hath been shown to be that wherein the most avowed and pernicious enemies of all knowledge, whether human or divine, have ever placed their chief strength and confidence." *A Treatise Concerning the First Principles of Human Knowledge* in *The Works of George Berkeley, Bishop of Cloyne*, 9 vols., ed. A. A. Luce and T. E. Jessop (London: Thomas Nelson, 1948–57), 1: 133. Though the old theory of a direct dependence of Edwards's idealism on Berkeley's is now universally rejected, there are indeed remarkable parallels in their independent versions of idealism.

48. *Works* 6:216. Jenson comments: "Edwards' critique of mechanism is an encompassing piece of demythologizing: there are no little self-sufficient agencies besides God, natural entities are not godlets, and therefore the world harmony is not self-contained." *America's Theologian*, 25.

49. *Works* 6:344, 380, 398.

50. Thus Spinoza writes: "Besides God no substance can be granted or conceived." *Ethics*, in *The Chief Works of Benedict de Spinoza*, 2 vols., trans. R. H. M. Elwes (New York: Dover, 1951), 1:15.

51. *Works* 6:398. Edwards's little phrase "as it were" often occurs in contexts where he draws nearest to some form of monistic teaching, as indicated in Rufus Suter, "A Note on Platonism in the Philosophy of Jonathan Edwards," *Harvard Theological Review* 52 (1959): 283–4.

52. *Works* 6:344.

53. Edwards does not adequately explain how it is that the ideas in God's mind are related to their analogues in human minds, though his language suggests a direct causal

relation. One might term his viewpoint an "epistemic occasionalism," in that it attributes to God's agency those acts of human perceiving that might ordinarily be attributed to creaturely causes.

54. Aquinas, *Summa Theologiae*, first part, question 14, article 8.

55. Edwards enunciates his essential agreement with Lockean empiricism as follows: "All acts of the mind are from sensation; all ideas begin from thence, and there can never be any idea, thought or act of the mind unless the mind first received some ideas from sensation." *Works* 6:390. Sense-experience thus has a self-evidential character: "Things that we know by immediate sensation, we know intuitively, and they are properly self-evident truths: as, grass is green, the sun shines, honey is sweet." *Works* 6:346; see 369.

56. *PJE*, 85 (Misc. 749).

57. Anderson, "Editor's Introduction," *Works* 6:78–9.

58. *Works* 8:432.

59. *Works* 6:204.

60. The outstanding work on Edwards's aesthetics is Delattre, *Beauty and Sensibility*, a concise summary of which is available as "Beauty and Theology: A Reappraisal of Jonathan Edwards," *Soundings* 51 (1968): 60–79. Also worthy of note are: A. O. Aldrich, "Edwards and Hutcheson," *Harvard Theological Review* 44 (1951): 35–53, and Terence Erdt, *Jonathan Edwards, Art, and the Sense of the Heart* (Amherst: University of Massachusetts Press, 1980).

61. See *Works* 8:561–74.

62. Fiering, *Jonathan Edwards's Moral Thought*, 82.

63. *Works* 2:298. Such comments might create the impression that beauty is an even more basic metaphysical category for Edwards than being. Yet even Delattre admits that "Beauty . . . is ultimately to be resolved into being, rather than the reverse." *Beauty and Sensibility*, 25.

64. *Works* 6:216.

65. *Works* 3:402. Edwards expresses a doctrine of continuous creation in his notebooks as well: *PJE*, 76 (Misc. 125), 130 (Misc. 346), and *Works* 13:210 (Misc. 18).

66. Thus James Carse claims that he "abruptly ceased these avid philosophical inquiries." *Jonathan Edwards and the Visibility of God*, 34–5. Yet his *Two Dissertations* and *Miscellanies* certainly do not bear out the claim that Edwards ever outgrew his philosophizing. He was a born philosopher, if such a thing exists.

67. A variety of contemporary theological perspectives on metaphysics is exhibited in *Rethinking Metaphysics* (Oxford: Basil Blackwell, 1995), a collection of essays edited by L. Gregory Jones and Stephen E. Fowl.

68. Karl Barth, *Church Dogmatics*, vol. 1, part 1, *The Doctrine of the Word of God*, trans. G. T. Thomson (Edinburgh: T. and T. Clark, 1936–77), x.

69. See the commentary in Hans Urs von Balthasar, *The Theology of Karl Barth*, trans. John Drury (Garden City, New York: Doubleday, 1972), 136–8. There are other common antimetaphysical arguments, for example, that metaphysics reduces God to impersonality, that it fails to capture the radical freedom and spontaneity of interpersonal relationships, and that it abolishes the concreteness and specificity of essential theological affirmations through illicit generalizing. It is enough here to note that *one* of the most important objections to theological metaphysics is inapplicable to Edwards.

70. I refer to Pascal's famous dichotomy between philosophical and religious conceptions of God, as implied in "The Memorial," describing his life-changing experience in 1654: "Monday, 23 November. . . . From about half past ten in the evening until half past

midnight. Fire. 'God of Abraham, God of Isaac, God of Jacob,' not of philosophers and scholars." Blaise Pascal, *Pensées*, trans. A. J. Krailsheimer (Harmondsworth, England: Penguin Books, 1966), 309. In Edwards one finds religious experience and religious sensibility that is no less profound than Pascal's, yet without a rejection of rational and metaphysical approaches to God.

3. The Spirituality of the Personal Narrative and Diary

1. Martin E. Marty, "American Religious History in the Eighties: A Decade of Achievement," *Church History* 62 (1993): 335–77, quotation from 376.

2. The Paulist Press series of primary texts, *The Classics of Western Spirituality*, has some eighty volumes to date, with more anticipated. Crossroads Publishers' projected twenty-five-volume series, *World Spirituality*, comprises secondary studies of spirituality in the various cultural spheres of the world.

3. For the *Personal Narrative*, I will be citing the text as given in *Selected Writings of Jonathan Edwards*, ed. Harold P. Simonson (New York: Frederick Ungar, 1970), 27–44. For the *Diary* I follow the text given in Sereno E. Dwight, "Memoirs of Jonathan Edwards," in *Works* (Hickman), xx–xxii, xxiv–xxxi, and xxxiii–xxxvi. The first pages (xx–xxii) contain the *Resolutions* of Edwards, the latter the *Diary* properly speaking. Unfortunately the extant *Diary* has almost no entries after 1725.

4. Published for the Institute of Early American History and Culture, Williamsburg, Virginia (Chapel Hill: University of North Carolina Press, 1982).

5. *Works* 7.

6. Unfortunately, Daniel Walker Howe's *Making the American Self: Jonathan Edwards to Abraham Lincoln* (Cambridge: Harvard University Press, 1997) appeared too recently to be consulted for this chapter.

7. *Personal Narrative*, 39–40.

8. On the place of theocentrism in Edwards's writings, see chapter 2.

9. In addition to Hambrick-Stowe's *Practice*, I am dependent on various sources in my exposition of Puritan spirituality: Joseph Dedieu, "Calvin et Calvinisme," in *Dictionnaire de Spiritualité*, ed. M. Viller et al. (Paris: Beauchesne, 1937–), 2:23–50; Richard C. Lovelace, "The Anatomy of Puritan Piety: English Puritan Devotional Literature," in *Christian Spirituality*, vol. 3, *Post-Reformation and Modern*, ed. Louis Dupré and Don E. Saliers (New York: Crossroad, 1989), 294–323; N. H. Keeble, "Puritan Spirituality," in *The Westminster Dictionary of Christian Spirituality*, ed. Gordon Wakefield (Philadelphia: Westminster, 1982), 323–6; Charles E. Hambrick-Stowe, "Puritan Spirituality in America," in Dupré and Saliers, *Christian Spirituality*, 338–53; Charles Lloyd Cohen, *God's Caress: The Psychology of Puritan Religious Experience* (New York: Oxford University Press, 1986); and Jerald C. Brauer, "Types of Puritan Piety," *Church History* 56 (1987): 39–58.

10. Lucien Joseph Richard, *The Spirituality of John Calvin* (Atlanta, Georgia: John Knox Press, 1974), 1.

11. Luke 10:38–42.

12. Hambrick-Stowe, *Practice*, 285.

13. The technical distinction drawn by many authors between "meditation" and "contemplation"—the former involving discursive thought, the latter having transcended it—will not figure into this discussion. On the meaning of these terms, see J. Neville Ward, "Contemplation," in Wakefield, *Westminster Dictionary of Christian Spirituality*, 95.

14. Lovelace, "Anatomy," 302–3; Gordon Wakefield, *Puritan Devotion: Its Place in the Development of Christian Piety* (London: Epworth, 1957), 160.

15. In *Religious Affections* and elsewhere in his writings, Edwards perpetuated the Puritan tradition of seeking to distinguish genuine from spurious religion. Ava Chamberlain, in her penetrating article "Self-Deception as Theological Problem in Jonathan Edwards's 'Treatise Concerning Religious Affections,'" *Church History* 63 (1994): 541–56, notes that as Edwards matured he became more aware of the complexity of human nature and of the many ways that sinners and saints resemble one another. Edwards's "hypocrites" not only deceived others but themselves as well, and so "a sincere hypocrite was as possible as a sincere convert" (543).

16. Edmund Morgan, *Visible Saints: The History of a Puritan Idea* (Ithaca, N.Y.: Cornell University Press, 1963), 66, and passim, 66–72.

17. To give some idea of the intricacy of the Puritan morphologies, one might mention William Perkins, who identified no less than ten stages in the process of conversion (Morgan, *Visible Saints*, 68–9). Four of these were preparatory (hearing the Word, coming to know one's sins, "legal fear," etc.), and six were gracious (faith, combat of the soul, assurance, "evangelical sorrow," etc.).

18. Hambrick-Stowe, *Practice*, viii.

19. Hambrick-Stowe, *Practice*, 79.

20. The vast majority of entries in the *Diary* occur in the years from 1722 to 1725, with only a few lines devoted to later years. The exact time at which Edwards composed the *Personal Narrative* is not known, but it must have been sometime after January 1739—the last date mentioned in the text—and was probably soon thereafter.

21. The quotation is from the excellent article entitled "The Art and Instruction of Jonathan Edwards's *Personal Narrative*," in *Puritan New England: Essays on Religion, Society, and Culture*, ed. Alden T. Vaughan and Francis J. Bremer (New York: St. Martin's Press, 1977), 299–311, quoting 300–1.

22. *Personal Narrative*, 30.

23. Dwight, "Memoirs," xxiv.

24. The key paragraph on conversion is in Edwards, *Personal Narrative*, 29–30. One reason for calling this moment a conversion is Edwards's later, oblique reference to it as such (43). The penitential experiences of the *Personal Narrative* are recounted toward the end; the first of them is dated in 1737 (40–3).

25. *Personal Narrative*, 33.

26. Dwight, "Memoirs," xxi, xxvii.

27. *Personal Narrative*, 30.

28. There is a first reference to the father in connection with an "awakening" in "my father's congregation" (*Personal Narrative*, 27) and a second in relation to a conversation that Jonathan had with him (31). Even though Edwards was "much affected" by the conversation, he does not describe it at all but rather speaks of the aftermath, when he was alone again: "When the discourse was ended, I walked abroad alone in a solitary place."

29. At the risk of anachronism, one might describe Edwards in the *Personal Narrative* as a phenomenologist of sorts. Gerardus van der Leeuw wrote that "phenomenology is the systematic discussion of what appears." *Religion in Essence and Manifestation*, 2 vols., trans. J. E. Turner (New York: Harper and Row, 1963), 2:683. Another wellknown feature of phenomenology is the technique of *epoche* or "bracketing," whereby the observer sets aside prejudices and self-interest so that the object of study can "appear" just as it is.

C. J. Bleeker says that "the phenomenological method . . . aims at excluding all kinds of preconceptions . . . and at sharpening the eye for what is genuinely religious." *The Sacred Bridge: Researches into the Nature and Structure of Religion* (Leiden: E. J. Brill, 1963), viii. See Douglas Allen, "Phenomenology of Religion," in *Encyclopedia of Religion*, ed. Mircea Eliade et al. (New York: Macmillan, 1987), 11:272–85. Analogously, Edwards's practice of contemplation in the *Personal Narrative* involves a delight in God for God's own sake, a bracketing of self-interest, and an attempt simply to describe how God "appears."

30. One finds the characteristic stress on solitude in the fifteenth-century spiritual classic, Thomas à Kempis, *The Imitation of Christ*: "The greatest Saints used to avoid the company of men whenever they were able, and chose rather to serve God in solitude. . . . No man can safely speak unless he who would gladly remain silent. . . . In silence and quietness the devout soul makes progress and learns the hidden mysteries of the Scriptures." Trans. Leo Shirley-Price (London: Penguin Books, 1952), 50–1; book 1, ch. 20.

31. Ola Winslow, *Jonathan Edwards, 1703–1758: A Biography* (New York: Farrar, Straus and Giroux, 1940), 45.

32. *Personal Narrative*, 30, 32, 36; see 31, 40.

33. Dwight, "Memoirs," xl. The entire paragraph in praise of Sarah conveys the sense of a quite individualistic and otherworldly spirituality:

> They say . . . that she hardly cares for any thing, except to meditate on him— that she expects after a while to be received up where he is, to be raised up out of the world and caught up into heaven . . . to be ravished with his love and delight for ever. Therefore, if you present all the world before her, with the richest of its treasures, she disregards it and cares not for it (xxxix).

Based on a scrutiny of Sarah's firsthand account of her religious experiences in 1742 (see *Works* 4:331–41, with C. C. Goen's commentary in the "Editor's Introduction," 68– 70), Julie Ellison speaks of "the facility with which Sarah Edwards was able to absent herself from the interpersonal realm and to withdraw into religious meditation" and notes that Jonathan's presentation of his wife's piety expresses his own "isolationist impulse." "The Sociology of 'Holy Indifference': Sarah Edwards' Narrative," *American Literature* 56 (1984): 479–95, quoting 483, 494.

34. Dwight, "Memoirs," xxxv.

35. *Personal Narrative*, 37.

36. Dwight, "Memoirs," xxvi.

37. In a very early entry into the *Miscellanies*, Edwards writes: "Religious thoughts are of such an high, internal and spiritual nature as very much abstracts the soul from the body, and so the operations of the body are deadened . . . This abstraction of the soul, in its height, leaves the body even dead; and then the soul is in a trance." *Works* 13:176 (Misc. x). One recalls Plato's statement that philosophical thinking, like death, tends to separate the soul from the body. *Phaedo*, 64–65, in *The Dialogues of Plato: Translated into English With Analyses and Introductions*, trans. B. Jowett, 4th ed., 4 vols. (Oxford: Clarendon Press, 1953), 1: 414–15.

38. On the whole, Edwards's experience as a bodily human being was not sanguine, and his health was rather frail. In the *Diary* he more than once refers to his headaches (Dwight, "Memoirs," xxiv, xxxv). In the last months of his life, he wrote to the trustees of the College of New Jersey (later to become Princeton University), detailing his many health ailments as possible disqualifications from becoming the new president of the institution:

"I have a constitution, in many respects, peculiarly unhappy, attended with flaccid solids, vapid, sizy, and scarce fluids, and a low tide of spirits." Dwight, "Memoirs," clxxiv. It is hard from this quaint language to tell exactly what Edwards experienced, but one senses that it was not pleasant! Perhaps a person of stronger physical constitution would have survived the poorly administered smallpox vaccination that killed Edwards.

39. Dwight, "Memoirs," xxv. On "mortification," see xxiv, xxvi, xxix. My judgment that "mortification" for Edwards relates almost exclusively to eating and drinking is based on the context of the whole *Diary*.

40. Edwards's "resolutions" on eating and drinking are given in Dwight, "Memoirs," xxi. There are many passages in the *Diary* related to eating (xxv, xxvi, xxviii, xxxiv, xxxv).

41. Winslow, *Jonathan Edwards*, 67.

42. *Personal Narrative*, 35; Dwight, "Memoirs," xxix.

43. Dwight, "Memoirs," xxix. Edwards's censoriousness was a trait shared by other members of his immediate family. Jerusha, his younger sister by six years, was said to abhor "froth and levity in conversation" and kept aloof from merrymaking at social events. On Saturday evenings she stayed up later than the rest of the family in preparation for the Sabbath, and on Sunday mornings she walked alone to the house of God in silent meditation. Considering it her duty to reprove others, she censured her own sweetheart to "preserve him against the infection of vice" and so blighted a budding romance. In this way she won the admiration of the family, and "even before her death she seems to have been all but canonized in the Edwards household." Winslow, *Jonathan Edwards*, 47–8. Winslow depicts Timothy Edwards—much like his son in later years—as exacting in daily affairs and as recalcitrant in controversy (21–2, 39–40).

44. Edwards expressed a desire for "religious conversation" in the *Diary* only after he discovered that he learned more of "natural philosophy" in talking with others than in solitary study. Dwight, "Memoirs," xxxiv. He does not come across as someone who needed other people!

45. Dwight, "Memoirs," xxxvi.

46. Edwards writes, "Observe to remember the meditations which I had . . . under the oak tree," and then adds, "I *read* over and reviewed those reflections and remarks." Dwight, "Memoirs," xxvii; emphasis mine.

47. *Personal Narrative*, 30. On the sensuality of Edwards's notion of love, see Paula M. Cooey, "*Eros* and Intimacy in Edwards," *Journal of Religion* 69 (1989): 484–99.

48. Jerald Brauer, "Conversion: From Puritanism to Revivalism," *Journal of Religion* 58 (1978): 240. With reference to the Puritan themes of pilgrimage and holy warfare, he comments: "Emphasis was placed on the subject, the major character, the one who underwent the pilgrimage and fought the good fight. This tended to shift the center of attention from the givenness of God's work in history to man's personal religious experience." Other scholars of Puritanism have come to the same conclusion. Sacvan Bercovitch writes: "We cannot help but feel that the Puritans' urge for self-denial stems from the very subjectivism of their outlook, that their humility is coextensive with personal assertion." *The Puritan Origins of the American Self* (New Haven: Yale University Press, 1975), 18. Everett Emerson is harsh in his judgment of the Puritan diarists Thomas Shepard, Michael Wigglesworth, and Cotton Mather: "None of these three diarists makes an attractive impression. As they poured their energies into introspection, these active creative people become egotists before our eyes: their only concern is themselves." *Puritanism in America, 1620–1750* (Boston: Twayne, 1977), 134.

49. Cohen, *God's Caress*, 20.

50. M. Van Beek, *An Enquiry into Puritan Vocabulary* (Groningen: Wolters-Noordhof, 1969), 117–20. Van Beek's list makes for interesting reading: "self-affection," "self-revenging," "self-intended," "self-sophistry," "self-guiltiness," "self-flattery," and so forth.

51. Winslow, *Jonathan Edwards*, 129.

52. See Paul S. Nagy, "The Beloved Community of Jonathan Edwards," *Transactions of the Charles S. Pierce Society* 7 (1971): 93–104.

53. Dwight, "Memoirs," clxxviii.

54. See Gerald R. McDermott, *One Holy and Happy Society: The Public Theology of Jonathan Edwards* (University Park: Pennsylvania State University Press, 1992). McDermott's assertion of a "public theology" is not, I believe, inconsistent with my stress on Edwards's solitary spirituality and contemplative practice. In his article "Jonathan Edwards and the Culture Wars: A New Resource for Public Theology and Philosophy," *Pro Ecclesia* 4 (1995): 268–80, McDermott underscores Edwards's conception of the Christian's duty to participate in civil community but then qualifies this emphasis by adding that Edwards's faith was "profoundly private" (273) and that Edwards was convinced that politics is "relatively unimportant in the ultimate scheme of things" and "incapable of bringing happiness or salvation" (275).

55. Quoted in Dwight, "Memoirs," xxxix. The section from Hopkins's memoir quoted here gives a glimpse into Edwards's absorption with his solitary studies.

56. The word "affection" in *Personal Narrative* occurs frequently in the earliest paragraphs, where Edwards is describing his life *prior* to his conversion. Consequently, "affection" may be part of a spurious religious experience. Yet when Edwards slips into his optical vocabulary (e.g., "view," "apprehension," and "appear") he invariably uses such language to describe genuine religious experience.

57. *Personal Narrative*, 39–40.

58. See the discussion of the development from Edwards to Hopkins in Stephen Garrard Post, *Christian Love and Self-Denial: An Historical and Normative Study of Jonathan Edwards, Samuel Hopkins, and American Theological Ethics* (Lanham, Md.: University Press of America, 1987), and Post's later book *A Theory of Agape: On the Meaning of Christian Love* (Lewisburg, Pa.: Bucknell University Press, 1990).

59. See *PJE*, 202–5 (Misc. 530). Here Edwards argues that "self-love" and "love to God" are not in competition with one another, since "one enters into the nature of the other." He concludes that "'tis impossible for any person to be willing to be perfectly and finally miserable for God's sake." Edwards later took up the theme of "self-love" in one chapter of *True Virtue* (*Works* 8:575–88) and in *Charity and Its Fruits* (*Works* 8:252–71). See the commentary by Paul Ramsey in "Editor's Introduction," in *Works* 8:12–27.

60. On Brainerd's spirituality and Edwards's interpretation of it, see: Norman Pettit, "Editor's Introduction," in *Works* 7:1–85; Joseph Conforti, "Jonathan Edwards's Most Popular Work: 'The Life of David Brainerd' and Nineteenth-Century Evangelical Culture," *Church History* 54 (1985): 188–201; and David L. Weddle, "The Melancholy Saint: Jonathan Edwards's Interpretation of David Brainerd as a Model of Evangelical Spirituality," *Harvard Theological Review* 81 (1988): 297–318. Herbert W. Richardson suggested, in conversation, that Edwards's conception of the Christian life during his last years became more overtly self-sacrificial because of the trying experiences of his dismissal in Northampton.

61. Misc. 724, Yale MSS.

62. *Works* 8:534–6.

63. *Works* 2:376–83. Compare the words of Gregory of Nyssa: "This truly is the vision of God: never to be satisfied in the desire to see him. But one must always, by looking at what he can see, rekindle his desire to see more. Thus no limit would interrupt growth in the ascent to God, since no limit to the God can be found nor is the increasing desire for good brought to an end because it is satisfied." *The Life of Moses*, quoted in Wakefield, *Westminster Dictionary of Christian Spirituality*, 388.

64. Both Edwards's practice and his theory embody what Andrew Louth has called the distinctive trait of Greek religion, "the realization that the divine is the beautiful." "Greek Spirituality," in Wakefield, *Westminster Dictionary of Christian Spirituality*, 180.

4. Ethics and Divinity in End of Creation

1. While certain scholars distinguish the terms "ethical" and "moral," there is no agreed-on difference in meaning among writers in English; hence I will use these words as synonyms here.

2. John Locke, *The Reasonableness of Christianity*, ed. I. T. Ramsey (Stanford: Stanford University Press, 1958), 49.

3. Quoted in Mark Pattison, "Tendencies of Religious Thought in England, 1688–1750," in *Essays and Reviews*, 8th ed. (London: Longman, Green, 1861), 274.

4. Leslie Stephen, *History of English Thought in the Eighteenth Century*, 2 vols. (New York: G. P. Putnam, 1876), 2:1–2.

5. Nowhere has this story been told in greater detail than in the two works by Norman Fiering, *Moral Philosophy at Seventeenth-Century Harvard: A Discipline in Transition*, published for the Institute of Early American History and Culture (Chapel Hill: University of North Carolina Press, 1981), and *Jonathan Edward's Moral Thought and Its British Context* (Chapel Hill: University of North Carolina Press, 1981).

6. See Harry S. Stout, *The New England Soul: Preaching and Religious Culture in Colonial New England* (New York: Oxford University Press, 1986), 127–47, 222–228, and Henry F. May, *The Enlightenment in America* (New York: Oxford University Press, 1976), 3–101.

7. Fiering, *Jonathan Edwards's Moral Thought*, 60–1.

8. An illuminating elaboration of this point is provided in William C. Spohn, "Sovereign Beauty: Jonathan Edwards and The Nature of True Virtue," in *Theological Studies* 42 (1981): 394–421. The text of the *Two Dissertations* is in *Works* 8:403–640.

9. *Works* 8:552–3.

10. Francis Hutcheson, in *An Inquiry Concerning the Original of Our Ideas of Virtue or Moral Good* (1725), seemed to suggest that moral excellence or benevolence may exist apart from religious devotion: "Here again we might appeal to all mankind, whether there be no Benevolence but what flows from a View of Reward from the Deity? Nay, do we not see a great deal of it among those who entertain few if any Thoughts of Devotion at all?" *British Moralists, Being Selections from Writers Principally of the Eighteenth Century*, ed. L. A. Selby-Bigge, 2 vols. (New York: Dover, 1965), section 2, article 7, 1:91. Hutcheson returned to the issue in more explicit terms in his subsequent work, *An Essay on the Nature and Conduct of the Passions and Affections, With Illustrations on the Moral Sense* (1728), where he concludes that "the bare absence of the idea of a Deity, or of affections to him, can evidence no evil; otherwise it would be a crime to fall asleep, or to think of any thing else." In *Illustrations on the Moral Sense*, ed. Bernard Peach (Cambridge, Mass.: Belknap Press of Harvard University, 1971), 191.

11. Ola Winslow, *Jonathan Edwards, 1703–1758: A Biography* (New York: Farrar, Straus and Giroux, 1940), 310 a. In the same context Winslow intimates that *End of Creation* may have been intended as a propadeutic to Edwards's intended but never completed magnum opus. Perry Miller, *Jonathan Edwards,* American Men of Letters Series (New York: William Sloane, 1949), 285. Arthur Cushman McGiffert [Sr.], *Protestant Thought before Kant* (New York: Scribners, 1951), 182. Perhaps the most sweeping claim in behalf of *End of Creation* was made by the eminent Yale historian Sydney E. Ahlstrom, who called the work "the true center of Edwards's rational account of the Christian religion, around which his earliest thoughts revolved and around which all his sermons, polemics, and treatises must be grouped. It defines the lines of force according to which the other writings arrange themselves." *A Religious History of the American People* (New Haven and London: Yale University Press, 1972), 310. See also Mark A. Noll's brief appreciation of the *Two Disser-tations* in "God at the Center: Jonathan Edwards on True Virtue," *Christian Century* 110 (1993): 854–8.

12. The secondary literature on Edwards is exhaustively summarized in two works by M. X. Lesser: *Jonathan Edwards: A Reference Guide* (Boston: G. K. Hall 1981), and *Jonathan Edwards: An Annotated Bibliography, 1979–1993* (Westport, Conn.: Greenwood Press, 1994). These volumes together list nearly three thousand books, articles, dissertations, and stray references on Edwards from the eighteenth century up to 1993. Yet there seems to be only one article or book devoted exclusively to *End of Creation*, and it was published almost one hundred and fifty years ago: William C. Wisner, "The End of God in Creation," *American Biblical Repository*, 3rd series, 6 (1850): 430–56. George S. Hendry, "The Glory of God and the Future of Man," *Reformed World* 34 (1976): 147–57, deals with *End of Creation*, but purely in connection with eschatology. Paul Ramsey's "Editor's Introduc-tion" to *Works* 8 (1–121) contains some helpful comments on *End of Creation* but is pri-marily concerned with *True Virtue* and Edwards's sermon series *Charity and Its Fruits*.

13. Karl Dietrich Pfisterer, *The Prism of Scripture: Studies on History and Historicity in the Work of Jonathan Edwards*, Anglo-American Forum, no. 1 (Frankfurt: Peter Lang, 1975), 237.

14. Jonathan Edwards, *Two Dissertations: I. Concerning the End for which God Created the World; II. The Nature of True Virtue* (Boston: S. Kneeland, 1765).

15. *Works* 8:552, 557.

16. Ramsey, "Editor's Introduction," in *Works* 8:7; Ramsey, in *Works* 8:552 n. 3.

17. *Works* 8:424.

18. See *Works* 8:421, 422–3, 424, 426, 460, 548–9, 553, 571; and *Works* 6:356, 362, 381.

19. *Works* 8:540. On Edwards's ontology, see my discussion of God and being in chapter 2, where I argue that the notion of "Being in general" does not imply a pantheistic con-ception of God but rather establishes God's distinction from and superiority to the world. Precisely because of God's *all-inclusive* being, God differs from every finite entity. See also Thomas Schafer, "The Concept of Being in the Thought of Jonathan Edwards" (Ph.D. diss., Duke University, 1951).

20. Aquinas argues, in *Summa Theologica*, first part, question 20, that "in God there is love" (article 1), that "God loves all existing things" (article 2), and that "the better things are more loved by God" (article 4). Thus Aquinas anticipates Edwards's principle of proportionate regard. *The Summa Theologica of St. Thomas Aquinas*, 5 vols., trans. Fathers of the English Dominican province (Westminster, Md.: Christian Classics, 1981 [1911]), 1:114–5.

21. See *Works* 8:422–3, 548–9, 571; *Works* 6:356, 362, 382. Though Edwards's proposed

calculus is rich in potential applications for ethical theory, as noted in chapter 2, he never follows it up by analyzing the various possible relations between creatures of differing degrees of "existence" and "excellence." Instead, as I argue there, his whole intent is to reinforce his theocentrism, by setting the infinite "existence" and "excellence" of God over against the merely finite reality of creatures.

22. The notebook collection known as the *Miscellanies*, spanning four decades of Edwards's life and containing some fourteen hundred entries, was fully transcribed by Dr. Thomas Schafer in the 1950s but is only partially published at this time in volume 13 of the Yale edition. Based on my study of the published and as yet unpublished *Miscellanies* in the collection held at the Beinecke Rare Book and Manuscript Library of Yale University, I estimate that there are some forty-five entries in the *Miscellanies* devoted to the theme of God's "end in creation."

23. Samuel Hopkins, who was responsible for the publication of *Two Dissertations*, commented in his preface to the 1765 edition that the published texts were not as polished as Edwards might have wished: "'Tis probable that if his life had been spared, he would have revised them, and rendered them in some respects more complete." In *Works* 8:401. Hopkins's opinion on *End of Creation* carries special weight, since his diary indicates that he and Joseph Bellamy (Edwards's two closest disciples) listened to Edwards read aloud the text of *End of Creation* in February 1755, with the author presumably soliciting some response from them. Iain Murray, *Jonathan Edwards: A New Biography* (Edinburgh: Banner of Truth Trust, 1987), 391.

24. The analysis here will highlight the first chapter, which is primarily philosophical, and will pass over the second chapter, devoted to biblical exegesis. While the chapter division conveys the superficial impression that Edwards separates "reason" and "revelation," a closer scrutiny of *End of Creation* and the *Miscellanies* contradicts this impression. Miscellany 243 demonstrates that Edwards's conviction that God's glory is an "ultimate end" of creation, a prominent idea in the first chapter of *End of Creation*, originated in his exegesis of such biblical texts as Isaiah 42:8 and 48:11, and John 12:28. In *End of Creation*, as elsewhere, Edwards is an Augustinian sort of thinker for whom reason and revelation are interpenetrating.

25. The *Miscellanies* reveal three stages in Edwards's thinking on God's "end." In the initial phase, Edwards maintained the position—surprising in light of the final argument of *End of Creation*—that human happiness per se was God's end in creating. He reasoned that a perfect Creator does not need anything, such as happiness, from creatures. During an intermediate phase, he held that human happiness and divine glory were both "ultimate ends" in God's creating, but stood independent of one another. In his final phase, as expressed in *End of Creation*, he merged human happiness and divine glory under the rubric of God's "communication." According to my reading of the *Miscellanies*, the initial phase is reflected in Misc. 3, the intermediate phase is signalled by Misc. 243, and the final phase appears with Misc. 332.

26. *Works* 8:458–9.

27. The appeals to "reason" in *End of Creation* clearly reflect the eighteenth-century context. Edwards presupposes that his readers—whether orthodox or heterodox, Christian, deistic, or even atheistic—think of "God" in terms of classical Christian or theistic categories. Thus he does not argue *for* his assertion that God is perfectly "blessed" and "independent" of creatures, but rather argues *from* this assertion in defense of his thesis that God creates for God's own sake.

28. *Works* 8:420–1.

29. Such terms as "fit", "amiable", and so on serve as verbal signals that Edwards is speaking from an aesthetic frame of reference. This dimension of Edwards's thought has been well characterized by Roland Andre Delattre in *Beauty and Sensibility in the Thought of Jonathan Edwards: An Essay in Aesthetics and Theological Ethics* (New Haven: Yale University Press, 1968).

30. *Works* 8:429.

31. This point is related to Edwards's oft-discussed idealism. For an idealist, whatever is not present to consciousness is as good as nonexistent. Hence the glory of God, to be truly real, must reverberate in the minds of creatures. Edwards adds a distinctive twist to the idealist position, however, when he says in *End of Creation* that God's glory must not only be *known* by created minds, but also *loved* by created wills (*Works* 8:432–3).

32. *Works* 8:435; highlighted in the original.

33. Jonathan Edwards's use of tree imagery has been noted in David L. Weddle, "Jonathan Edwards on Men and Trees, and the Problem of Solidarity," *Harvard Theological Review* 67 (1974): 155–75.

34. *Works* 8:433.

35. Rufus Orlando Suter notes that Edwards uses qualifying phrases (e.g., "as it were") wherever he wishes to downplay an appearance of monistic teaching. See Suter, "A Note on Platonism in the Philosophy of Jonathan Edwards," *Harvard Theological Review* 52 (1959): 283–4.

36. *Works* 8:436.

37. *Works* 8:437.

38. *Works* 8:445–63.

39. *Works* 8:467–536. On the relation between the two chapters in *End of Creation*, see note 24.

40. *Works* 8:534–6.

41. Miller, *Jonathan Edwards*, 302.

42. *Works* 8:405–6.

43. In his *Miscellanies* Edwards writes: "Were it not for divine revelation, I am persuaded that there is no one doctrine of that which we call natural religion, which . . . would not be for ever involved in darkness, doubts, endless disputes and dreadful confusion." He points out that it is one thing to show a truth "agreeable to reason" after it has already been revealed to us, and quite another to discover a truth by "mere reason" in the first place. *Works* (Hickman), 2:462.

44. An account of the intellectualist and sentimentalist schools, in contrast to one another, and in their common opposition to the ethical egoism of Thomas Hobbes and Bernard Mandeville, is given in the following: Stephen, *History of English Thought*, 2:1–129; Henry Sidgwick, *Outlines of the History of Ethics* (London: Macmillan, 1931), especially 158–234; and Alasdair MacIntyre, *A Short History of Ethics* (New York: Macmillan, 1966), 157–77.

45. Stephen, *History of English Thought*, 2:6, quoting Samuel Clarke, *Works* (1738), 2:618.

46. It should be noted that the sentimentalist school was not altogether averse to mathematical computation in the sphere of ethics, though such computation was not its prime concern. Francis Hutcheson developed an elaborate moral calculus to determine the value of a given action. *Inquiry*, 3.8–15. And while Hutcheson is not normally regarded as a utilitarian per se, he introduced a phrase that was to prove seminal in the development

of later British moral thought: "That Action is best, which procures the greatest Happiness for the Greatest Numbers." *Inquiry* 3.8, in Selby-Bigge, *British Moralists*, 1:107. So even in his principle of proportionate regard, Edwards may be drawing as much from Hutcheson as from Clarke and other ethical intellectualists.

47. "Introduction," in Selby-Bigge, *British Moralists*, 1:lxx.

48. Hutcheson, *Inquiry* 2.10, 5.2, in Selby-Bigge, *British Moralists*, 1:97,130.

49. *Works* 8:411.

50. Hutcheson, *Inquiry* 7.5, 7.11, in Selby-Bigge, *British Moralists*, 1:158,175.

51. To speak most accurately, Edwards would have denied that God's creation of the world was a "benevolent" action, since "love or benevolence strictly taken presupposes an existing object." *Works* 8:439. This distinction leads Edwards to shift the focus in *End of Creation* from "benevolence" to "emanation." Yet the outflowing goodness of God exhibited in creation or "emanation" is at least analogous to "benevolence," if not identical with it.

52. Shaftesbury, *An Inquiry Concerning Virtue or Merit* (1699), treatise 1, part 2, section 2; treatise 2, part 1, section 1; in Selby-Bigge, *British Moralists*, 1:8–9,26. Hutcheson, *Inquiry* 3.6, in Selby-Bigge, *British Moralists*, 1:104.

53. Shaftesbury taught that good actions were engendered by good breeding: "A man of thorough good breeding, whatever else he be, is incapable of doing a rude or brutal action. He never deliberates in this case, or considers of the matter by prudential rules of self-interest and advantage. He acts from his nature, in a manner necessarily, and without reflection." *Characteristics of Men, Manners, Opinions, Times, Etc.*, 2 vols., ed. John M. Robertson (Gloucester, Mass.: Peter Smith, 1963), 1:86.

54. *Works* 8:453,457–8.

55. *The Ethics of Aristotle*, trans. J. A. K. Thomson, (Harmondsworth, England: Penguin Books, 1953), 121–2.

56. John Norris, "A Divine Hymn on the Creation," 1706, quoted in Arthur O. Lovejoy, *The Great Chain of Being: A Study of the History of an Idea*, William James Lectures, Harvard University, 1933 (Cambridge: Harvard University Press, 1936), 159.

57. Edwards's notion of the "emanative disposition" within God implies that God *needed* to create a world. Because creation derives from a "disposition" that Edwards calls "an original property of his nature" (*Works* 8:436), it seems that God had no choice but to create a world. Regarding *End of Creation*, Douglas Elwood comments that "*a* universe is necessary because it is the very nature of God to seek to communicate himself." *The Philosophical Theology of Jonathan Edwards* (New York: Columbia University Press, 1960), 15. Other scholars corroborate this conclusion: John E. Smith, "Jonathan Edwards as Philosophical Theologian," *Review of Metaphysics* 30 (1976): 316–7; Schafer, "Concept of Being," 295–6; and Patricia Wilson-Kastner, "God's Infinity and His Relationship to Creation in the Theologies of Gregory of Nyssa and Jonathan Edwards," *Foundations* 21 (1978): 311. With respect to God's freedom, it is worth noting that the deterministic position on human volition set forth in Edwards's *Freedom of the Will* assumes a *compatibility* between the responsible exercise of the will and the determination of the will by "motives." According to Edwards, God's goodness, although "necessary," is nonetheless volitional and is praiseworthy. *Works* 1:277–80, 375–96. Hence it may be possible to say, in Edwardsean terms, that creation was "necessary" yet took place through a responsible and praiseworthy act of God. Edwards, at one point in *End of Creation*, turns the objection to his position back on his imagined opponents and challenges them to find an alternative account of God's

motivation in creation that is superior to his own. *Works* 8:448–9. Implicitly, he acknowledges that no human explanation for divine creation will ever be free of logical difficulties.

58. See the discussion "True Virtue and Its Early Critics", in Clyde Holbrook, *The Ethics of Jonathan Edwards* (Ann Arbor: University of Michigan Press, 1973), 113–33. Edwards's defender, Samuel Hopkins, responding to a broadside by Rev. William Hart, entitled *Remarks on President Edwards's Dissertation Concerning the Nature of True Virtue* (1771), insisted that "he who loves being in general loves God and his fellow creatures and, therefore, obeys the two great commandments." Hopkins, *Works*, 3 vols. (Boston: Doctrinal Tract and Book Society, 1852), 3:69, cited in Holbrook, *Ethics*, 119.

59. Alexander V. G. Allen, *Jonathan Edwards*, American Religious Leaders (Boston: Houghton, Mifflin, 1889), 388.

60. John F. Wilson, in his analysis of *History of Redemption*, noted Edwards's tendency toward universalism: "Beside these grim notes he sounded the theme that redemption would reconcile the whole creation to God as the means of his glorification. In this he displayed an incipient universalism that appears more as a tone of exultation and rejoicing than as a clear claim, at least in his published works." "Editor's Introduction," in *Works* 9:89. Wilson's comments on *History of Redemption* are especially pertinent to *End of Creation*, since Edwards left behind a jotting indicating his intention to incorporate the argument of *End of Creation* in the extensive work he intended to write on redemptive history. "Editor's Introduction," 69.

61. Hutcheson, *Inquiry* 7.13, in Selby-Bigge, *British Moralists*, 1:176–7.

62. Edwards's stern teaching regarding hell is well known and well documented in the sources: "And there are none there but whom God hates with a perfect and everlasting hatred. He exercises no love, no mercy to any one object there; there he pours out his wrath without mixture." *Works* 8:390. For several generations prior to Edwards, European intellectuals had been emancipating themselves from traditional notions of hell, as expertly chronicled by D. P. Walker, *The Decline of Hell: Seventeenth-Century Discussions of Eternal Torment* (London: Routledge and Kegan Paul, 1964). Yet Edwards attempted to turn the tables by arguing that it was unreasonable *not* to believe in hell. See Bruce W. Davidson, "Reasonable Damnation: How Jonathan Edwards Argued for the Rationality of Hell," *Journal of the Evangelical Theological Society* 38 (1995): 47–56.

63. *Works* 8:443.

64. See Thomas A. Schafer, "Jonathan Edwards' Conception of the Church," *Church History* 24 (1955): 51–66.

65. A passing comment in *End of Creation*, one of two references to hell in the treatise, makes just this point: "God's judgments on the wicked world, and also their eternal damnation in the world to come, are spoken of as being for the happiness of God's people." *Works* 8:509. See also the sermon "The End of the Wicked Contemplated by the Righteous," *Works* (Hickman), 2:207–12.

66. Kenneth R. Morris, in "The Puritan Roots of American Universalism," *Scottish Journal of Theology* 44 (1991): 457–87, tries to link the revivalism of the 1740s with the universalism that became more common in America around 1800. Yet there is no clear connection between the "universal availability of salvation" (457) and the assertion of actual salvation for all. In any case, broad cultural factors rather than theological argument alone must be considered. In Edwards's case, one might speak of an implicit tendency toward universalism constrained or counteracted by a strong sense of the particularity of grace.

67. See the following comparative studies of Wesley and Edwards: Charles Rogers, "John Wesley and Jonathan Edwards," *Duke Divinity School Review* 31 (1966): 20–38; Robert Doyle Smith, "John Wesley and Jonathan Edwards on Religious Experience: A Comparative Analysis," *Wesleyan Theological Journal* 25 (1990): 130–46; and Richard E. Brantley, "The Common Ground of Wesley and Edwards," *Harvard Theological Review* 83 (1990): 271–303.

68. John Wesley, "A Plain Account of Genuine Christianity," in *John Wesley*, ed. Albert C. Outler (New York: Oxford University Press, 1964), 183–96, quoting 184–5.

5. *Drama and Discernment in* History of Redemption

1. Quoted in J. M. Cohen and M. J. Cohen, *The Penguin Dictionary of Quotations* (Harmondsworth, England: Penguin Books, 1960), 167,407.

2. R. G. Collingwood, in his brilliant work on the philosophy of history, wrote that "Gibbon finds the motive force of history in human irrationality itself." *The Idea of History* (Oxford: Clarendon Press, 1946), 79.

3. On the cyclical theory of the Greeks, see Karl Löwith, *Meaning in History* (Chicago: University of Chicago Press, 1949), 4–9. Oswald Spengler, *The Decline of the West*, trans. Charles Francis Atkinson (New York: Alfred A. Knopf, 1926–8), from the German edition *Der Untergang des Abendlandes; Umrisse einer Morphologie der Weltgeschichte* (München: Beck, 1919–22). See the discussion of Spengler in Collingwood, *The Idea of History*, 181–3.

4. The older work by J. B. Bury, *The Idea of Progress: An Inquiry into Its Origin and Growth* (London: Macmillan, 1924), viewed the notion of progress as largely a creation of post-Renaissance and secular thought, in contrast to the allegedly pessimistic and world-negating tendencies in Augustine and in medieval thought. The more recent work by Robert A. Nisbet, *History of the Idea of Progress* (New York: Basic Books, 1980), sees Augustine's *City of God* as the foundation of all Western philosophies of history, and as providing the basis for later Western assertions of the ultimate unity and intelligibility of world history. For Nisbet, progress was a secularized version of the theological notion of divine providence. Nonetheless, this theory of the secularization of providence into progress has been criticized because of confusions inherent in the very notion of secularization. See Hans Blumenberg, *The Legitimacy of the Modern Age*, trans. Robert M. Wallace (Cambridge: MIT Press, 1983), 27–51. Morris Ginsberg argues much like Bury that there is a basic disparity between divine providence and humanistic notions of progress. "Progress in the Modern Era," in *Dictionary of the History of Ideas*, gen. ed. Philip P. Wiener, 5 vols. (New York: Scribners, 1973), 3:633–50, especially 636. This debate over the relationship between providence and progress is germane to the interpretation of Edwards's *History of Redemption*, because if progress in general *is not* providence secularized, then Goen's and Heimert's position—that Edwards's providentialism helped spawn later American notions of progress, utopianism, or manifest destiny—is weakened.

5. The text of *A History of the Work of Redemption*, edited by John F. Wilson, is given in *Works* 9:113–528.

6. C. A. Patrides, *The Grand Design of God: The Literary Form of the Christian View of History* (London: Routledge and Kegan Paul, Toronto: University of Toronto Press, 1972), 29. Patrides took the main title for his erudite study from Jonathan Edwards's letter to the Princeton trustees (xiii, 119). Many of the universal chronicles of the medieval period used Augustine's theory of "Six Ages" of the world, corresponding to the six days of creation and the six periods in the life of an individual human being (18).

7. Jacques-Bénigne Bossuet, *Discourse on Universal History*, Classic European Historians Series, trans. Elborg Forster, edited with introduction by Orest Ranum (Chicago: University of Chicago Press, 1976). In the preface, Leonard Krieger interprets the *Discourse* as a fusion of Christian history and humanist rhetoric, hence as an intermediate stage between the providentialism of Augustine and the secularism of modern historians (x–xi).

8. Perry Miller, *Jonathan Edwards*, American Men of Letters Series (New York: William Sloane, 1949), 310–2.

9. John F. Wilson, "Editor's Introduction," in *Works* 9:97.

10. Peter Gay, *A Loss of Mastery: Puritan Historians in Colonial America* (Berkeley: University of California Press, 1966), 88–117, quoting 94, 97, 104, 91.

11. Wilson, "Editor's Introduction," in *Works* 9:2, 37, 73. In his analysis of the organization of Edwards's work, Wilson calls attention to the use of a "branching structure" and explains: "The use of a branching structure . . . is an index of the degree to which uthe Discourse was governed theologically. . . . This is the sense in which the Discourse, in spite of the title under which it was published, is profoundly unhistoriographical in any modern sense" (73). Compare Wilson's statement that Edwards saw human affairs as "the production of a play that God had authored" (73) with Gay's observation that "God settled everything at the beginning." *Loss of Mastery*, 95. Both authors seem to agree that Edwards's theological interests overrode a sense of genuine contingency in human affairs.

12. Compare the judgment of Gerhard Hoffman that "die formale Periodierung der Heilsgeschichte ist durchaus herrkömmlich," and "Edwards' philosophierendes Denken durchaus 'ungeschichtlicher' Struktur ist." "Seinsharmonie und Heilsgeschichte bei Jonathan Edwards" (Th.D. diss., Göttingen University, 1957), 148, 165.

13. H. Richard Niebuhr, *The Kingdom of God in America* (Middletown, Conn.: Wesleyan University Press, 1988 [1937]), 142–3.

14. C. C. Goen, "Jonathan Edwards: A New Departure in Eschatology," in *Critical Essays on Jonathan Edwards*, ed. William J. Scheick (Boston: G. K. Hall, 1980), 151–65, reprinted from *Church History* 28 (1959) 25–40, quoting 152. More recently, Goen in his "Editor's Introduction" in *Works* 4:1–95 reiterates the position taken in his groundbreaking article. Edwards contributed to the notion of America as a "redeemer nation" and "anticipated the messianic impulses of crusading churchmen and politicans for the next two centuries" (71–2). Ernest Lee Tuveson's brilliant study, *Redeemer Nation: The Idea of America's Millennial Role* (Chicago: University of Chicago Press, 1980 [1968]), interprets the historical development of the notion that America plays a unique role in world affairs. The "redeemer nation" idea was stated succinctly by Albert J. Beveridge around the turn of this century: "And of all our race He has marked the American people as His chosen nation to finally lead in the redemption of the world" (vii).

15. Describing the optimistic tendency of Edwards's vision of history, Alan Heimert wrote: "No longer did the tendency of history seem toward judgment, or the thoughts of the pious bent on despair. . . . Indeed the Edwardean Deity seemed designed as a guarantor of the millennium . . . in the last analysis cataclysm was inconsistent with a vision of history as the progressive enlargement of the realm of the spirit." *Religion and the American Mind: From the Great Awakening to the Revolution* (Cambridge: Harvard University Press, 1966), 62–3, 65. Heimert called attention to Edwards's elaborate argument in *An Humble Attempt* (see *Works* 5:378–94) showing that the "slaying of the witnesses" in chapter 11 of the Book of Revelation had already transpired in the period prior to the Protestant Reformation, so

that the darkest times of the church were already past. *Religion and the American Mind*, 65.

16. See Stephen Stein, "Editor's Introduction," in *Works* 5:1–93, especially 54–74. Stein sees a connection between Moses Lowman (1680–1752) and Edwards's optimism: "Lowman confirmed Edwards in his conviction that the lowest days of the church were past and the times were becoming increasingly favorable for the saints" (59).

17. Wilson, "Editor's Introduction," in *Works* 9:56.

18. Miller, *Jonathan Edwards*, 313.

19. Miller, *Jonathan Edwards*, 315.

20. Hoffman, "Seinsharmonie und Heilsgeschichte bei Jonathan Edwards," 161–2,167. Hoffman is one of the few authors to underscore the role of the Holy Spirit in *History of Redemption*, though Edwards regularly mentions this point. *Works* 9:143, 189, 233, 266, 300, 314, 364–5, 377, 436, 438, 441, 459–62.

21. William J. Scheick, "The Grand Design: Jonathan Edwards' *History of the Work of Redemption*," in Scheick, *Critical Essays on Jonathan Edwards* (reprinted from *Eighteenth-Century Studies* 8 [1975]: 300–14), 177–88, quoting 178.

22. Scheick, "Grand Design," 182–3, citing quotation in *Images and Shadows of Divine Things*, ed. Perry Miller (New Haven: Yale University Press, 1948), 53. The same text is now included in *Works* 11:61.

23. The literature on Edwards's typology is especially rich. The key primary texts have been published or republished in *Works* 11: *Images of Divine Things* (51–142), *Types* (146–53), and *Types of the Messiah* (191–324). Among the notable secondary studies are the following: Wallace E. Anderson, "Editor's Introduction to 'Images of Divine Things' and 'Types,' " in *Works* 11:3–33; Mason I. Lowance, Jr., and David H. Watters, "Editor's Introduction to 'Types of the Messiah,' " in *Works* 11:157–182; Mason I. Lowance, Jr., " 'Images or Shadows of Divine Things' in the Thought of Jonathan Edwards," in *Typology in Early American Literature*, ed. Sacvan Bercovitch (Amherst: University of Massachusetts, 1972), 209–44, and *The Language of Canaan: Metaphor and Symbol in New England from the Puritans to the Transcendentalists* (Cambridge: Harvard University Press, 1980); Conrad Cherry, *Nature and Religious Imagination: From Edwards to Bushnell* (Philadelphia: Fortress Press, 1980), and "Symbols of Spiritual Truth: Jonathan Edwards as Biblical Interpreter," *Interpretation* 39 (1985): 263–71; and Clyde A. Holbrook, *Jonathan Edwards, the Valley, and Nature: An Interpretive Essay* (London: Associated University Presses, 1987).

24. Wilson, "Editor's Introduction," in *Works* 9:43.

25. In Edwards's biblical exposition, as Kenneth P. Minkema notes, "his unifying concept was Jesus Christ as the reference point of all promises." "The Other Unfinished 'Great Work': Jonathan Edwards, Messianic Prophecy, and 'The Harmony of the Old and New Testament,' " in *Jonathan Edwards's Writings: Text, Context, Interpretation*, ed. Stephen J. Stein (Bloomington: Indiana University Press, 1996), 62.

26. John F. Wilson writes: "His antitype, in nature as well as in apocalyptic literature, was Christ. This meant that his understanding of nature was finally determined by a Christocentric construction of the world." "Editor's Introduction," in *Works* 9:47–8.

27. *Works* 11:152.

28. See *Works* 9:129, 136, 138, 144, 151–2, 163–4, 175, 177–8, 181–4, 192–3, 196, 198, 204, 213, 218, 220, 224–5, 227, 236, 253, 263, 281, 286–7, 289, 318, 331, 351, 484.

29. Heimert, *Religion and the American Mind*, 153.

30. *Works* 9:116.

31. *Works* 9:516; see 9:512–3.

32. *Works* 9:121.

33. *Works* 9:144.

34. *Works* 9:292.

35. *Works* 9:517–8, 525.

36. *Works* 9:520.

37. Edwards uses "church" indiscriminately to refer to Israelites prior to the coming of Jesus and to Christians subsequently. Thus one encounters such odd-sounding phrases as "the Jewish church," "the church under the Old Testament," and "the Mosaic church of Israel." *Works* 9:252, 230, 376–7. The terminology reflects Edwards's belief in the fundamental unity of God's people through space and time: "The church of God from the beginning has been one society." *Works* 9:443.

38. *Works*, 9:113. Gerhard Hoffman stresses the "comforting" character of *History of Redemption*: "Die Betrachtung der 'history of redemption' hat Predigtcharakter; sie soll der Kirche Trost geben in Leiden und Verfolgung." "Seinsharmonie und Heilsgeschichte bei Edwards," 166.

39. *Works* 9:444.

40. See the following passages in *History of Redemption*: *Works* 9:120–1, 123, 130–1, 148, 155, 175–6, 48–9, 298, 315, 327, 345, 347–8, 356, 375, 380–2, 390–1, 393, 396–8, 403–11, 415–18, 424–32, 434, 463, 488–89, 499–500, 509, 519, 523, 525.

41. On ancient apocalypticism in biblical and and extrabiblical texts, see Paul D. Hanson et al., "Apocalypses and Apocalypticism," *Anchor Bible Dictionary*, ed. David Noel Freedman (New York: Doubleday, 1992), 1:279–92. On the later development of apocalypticism, see the works of Bernard McGinn, including: *Visions of the End: Apocalyptic Traditions in the Middle Ages* (New York: Columbia University Press, 1979); "Introduction," in *Apocalyptic Spirituality: Treatises and Letters of Lactantius, Adso of Montier-en-Der, Joachim of Fiore, the Franciscan Spirituals, Savonarola* (New York: Paulist Press, 1979), 1–16; and *Apocalypticism in the Western Tradition* (Aldershot, England: Variorum, 1994).

42. *Works* 9:444, 454.

43. Based in part on his identification of Rome with "the great city" in Revelation 17: 18—a passage he called "the plainest of any one passage in the whole book"—Edwards was convinced that the Roman papacy was the Antichrist. Stephen Stein, "Editor's Introduction," in *Works* 5:12. On the identification of the Roman Catholic church with "Antichrist," see the recent and definitive book by Bernard McGinn, *Antichrist: Two Thousand Years of the Human Fascination with Evil* (San Francisco: Harper, 1994), especially 143–230.

44. *Works* 9:380.

45. *Works* 9:409–11.

46. *Works* 9:450–1.

47. *Works* 9:411.

48. The number 1260 was derived from references in the Book of Daniel and Book of Revelation to a period of three and a half years, or forty-two months, traditionally interpreted so that each day represented an entire year. See Stein, "Editor's Introduction," in *Works* 5:13–5.

49. Edwards, *Works* 9:456–7. Stephen Stein points out that Edwards at one point calculated that Antichrist would fall by 1866. Yet he was generally hesitant to make public his conjectures regarding the fulfillment of the biblical prophecies: "Speculation in private,

but discretion in public came to be characteristic of him." Stein, "Editor's Introduction," in *Works* 5:13, 19.

50. Stephen Stein, "A Notebook on the Apocalypse by Jonathan Edwards," in Scheick, *Critical Essays on Jonathan Edwards* (reprinted from *The William and Mary Quarterly* 29 [1972]: 623–34), 174. Stein adds: "Edwards stands in a long line of bigoted polemicists who drew upon the Revelation for inspiration. He drank deeply from the tradition and added his own imaginative contributions as well as a new sense of urgency." As early as the beginning of the *Miscellanies*, Edwards spoke of the Church of Rome as the most dangerous of Christ's enemies and like "a viper or some loathsome, poisonous crawling monster." *Works* 13:186 (Misc. hh).

51. *Works* 9:419.

52. *Works* 9:254, 282, 430–3, 469. The Jewish people had a somewhat paradoxical place in Edwards's conception of God's plan for history. While most of the Jews were cut off from Christ during the present era, the biblical prophecies pointed toward a future "conversion" of the people, which was to signal the arrival of the "glorious times" of the church. Stein, "Editor's Introduction," in *Works* 5:19.

53. Perry Miller spoke of history as following a "zigzag course" in which "a declension . . . should be interpreted as a preparation for the next and greater exertion." *Jonathan Edwards*, 315. Along similar lines Alan Heimert writes that "Edwards adopted and announced a 'cyclical' theory of history—one not of mere repetition, but of recurrence and periodically renewed and increased momentum." *Religion and the American Mind*, 67.

54. *Works* 9:448. See *Works* 9:186.

55. *Works* 9:367. The quoted statement contains a biblical allusion: "But the path of the just is as the shining light, that shineth more and more unto the perfect day." Proverbs 4:18, Authorized Version.

56. *Works* 9:248. See *Works* 9:279, 523.

57. *Works* 9:394.

58. In one of his *Miscellanies*, Edwards himself used the image of rebuilding from ruins: "When he has any thing very glorious to accomplish he accomplishes it and builds it up out of the ruins of something that was excellent but is destroyed." Misc. 907 (Yale MSS). Somewhat similar is the notion of the "wilderness" that Edwards set forth in *Thoughts on the Revival* in support of his suggestion that the millennium might begin in America:

> When God is about to turn the earth into a paradise, he don't begin his work where there is some good growth already, but in a wilderness, where nothing grows, and nothing is to be seen but dry sand and barren rocks; that the light may shine out of darkness, and the world be replenished from emptiness, and the earth watered by springs from a droughty desert. (*Works* 4:356)

God does so in order "that the power of God might be the more conspicuous; that the work might appear to be entirely God's."

59. Thomas Schafer writes: "The course of the Church in history, he believed, has been on the whole an upward one. In fact, the worst is past, Antichrist is soon to fall." "Jonathan Edwards' Conception of the Church," *Church History* 24 (1955): 56.

60. *PJE*, 135 (Misc. 547).

61. *Works* 9:189.

62. *Works* 9:351–2.

63. Perry Miller commented: "He preached chiliasm in its starkest form. According to

this ancient doctrine, there will come 'a very dark time,' which will be followed by a thousand years of the reign of Christ on earth." *Jonathan Edwards*, 316. This statement makes Edwards sound like an undoubted premillennialist. Goen and Heimert sought to correct this misapprehension and designated him a postmillennialist.

64. The *Personal Narrative* attests to Edwards's lifelong effort to interpret current events in the light of biblical prophecies:

> If I heard the least hint of any thing that happened, in any part of the world, that appeared, in some respect or other, to have a favorable aspect on the interests of Christ's kingdom, my soul eagerly catched at it; and it would much animate and refresh me. I used to be eager to read public news letters, mainly for that end; to see if I could not find some news favorable to the interest of religion in the world. (*Personal Narrative*, 35)

65. *Works* 9:457–8.

66. *Works* 4:353.

67. Stein, "Editor's Introduction," in *Works* 5:26.

68. Letter to William McCulloch, 5 March 1743/4, in *Works* 4:560.

69. *Works* 9:122, 519.

70. *Works* 9:399. For further elaboration of this point, see the discussion of reason and revelation in chapter 6.

71. *Works* 9:291.

72. In his essay on "Historicism," C. S. Lewis applies the term to "the belief that men can, by the use of their natural powers, discover an inner meaning to the historical process." He amplifies his point: "When Novalis called history 'an evangel' he was a Historicist. When Hegel saw in history the progressive self-manifestation of absolute spirit he was a Historicist. When a village woman says that her wicked father-in-law's paralytic stroke is a 'a judgment on him' she is a Historicist." Those who find meaning in history by means of an alleged divine revelation are not "historicists." Lewis for his part judges that "historicism is an illusion." "Historicism," in *God, History, and Historians: An Anthology of Modern Christian Views of History*, ed. C. T. McIntire (New York: Oxford University Press, 1977), 225–38, quoting 225–6. While Lewis uses the term "historicist" idiosyncratically, and one might substitute the phrase "historical rationalism," Lewis's position tallies with that of Edwards: human beings cannot understand the historical process apart from special divine guidance.

73. *Works* 9:520. He also expounds the river of providence in the notebook *Images of Divine Things* (*Works* 11:77–80).

74. *Works* 6:335.

75. *Works* 8:540.

76. John Hick, *Evil and the God of Love*, rev. ed. (San Francisco: Harper and Row, 1978 [1966]), 82. According to Augustine, the existence of wicked creatures renders the world like "an exquisite poem set off with antitheses," and "as, then, these oppositions of contraries lend beauty to the language, so the beauty of the course of this world is achieved by the opposition of contraries, arranged, as it were, by an eloquence not of words, but of things." *The City of God*, book 11, chapter 18, in *A Select Library of Nicene and Post-Nicene Fathers*, ed. Philip Schaff, 2nd series, 14 vols. (Grand Rapids, Mich.: Eerdmans, 1974–76), 2:214–5.

77. Misc. 555, 777, 1061 (Yale MSS). See Misc. 778, 804, 917, 1059, 1089, 1095, 1119, 1121, 1281.

78. See the detailed and well-documented discussion by Paul Ramsey in appendix 3, "Heaven is a Progressive State," in *Works* 8:706–38.

79. My conclusions concur with those of Gerald R. McDermott in *One Holy and Happy Society: The Public Theology of Jonathan Edwards* (University Park: Pennsylvania State University Press, 1992). McDermott notes that Edwards's position is anything but jingoistic or triumphalistic: "I was also suprised to discover that Edwards was not the provincial chauvinist he has been made out to be . . . America for Edwards usually deserved condemnation, not celebration. The further he progressed in his career, the more distance he put between his country and the Kingdom of God" (viii).

80. Kenneth Minkema notes that the Bible was Edwards's "lifelong love" and that he wrote a massive work, *The Harmony of the Old and New Testaments*, extant in an unpublished draft of more than five hundred manuscript pages. "The Other Unfinished 'Great Work,' " 52.

81. *Works* 9:523, 279.

82. Bernard McGinn notes the frequent use of ocean imagery by Christian writers to describe the return of souls to God. Thus the early Christian writer Evagrius writes: "When minds flow back into him like torrents into the sea, he changes them all completely into his nature, color and taste. They will no longer be many but one in his unending and inseparable unity." *Epistola ad Melaniam*, epistle 6, in "Ocean and Desert as Symbols of Mystical Absorption in the Christian Tradition," *Journal of Religion* 74 (1994): 155–81, quoting 159.

6. Edwards as a Christian Apologist

1. Paul Hazard, in his classic study *European Thought in the Eighteenth Century: From Montesquieu to Lessing* (New Haven: Yale University Press, 1954), describes the tediousness of the defenders of religion:

> They were fine stout fellows, these champions of religion, but they were not geniuses, and geniuses were what was needed. Often enough, and with the best intentions in the world, they were tedious and long-winded; their lengthy prefaces, their pedantic dissertations, their massive periods, were not suited to the popular taste . . . and their audience paid no heed. (93)

In notable contrast to this statement, Hazard later speaks of the diversity and vitality of deism (393). His comments are fair enough if one compares the second-rate apologists of the day to Hume and Voltaire, but not if one sets them alongside Butler, Edwards, and Schleiermacher. The deists, too, wrote their share of long-winded books! Compare Peter Gay's interpretation of Edwards as "medieval" in *A Loss of Mastery: Puritan Historians in Colonial America* (Berkeley: University of California, 1966).

2. The history of Christian apologetics has not received much scholarly attention. Among the best general treatments is Avery Dulles, *A History of Apologetics* (New York: Corpus, 1971). Also worthy of note are J. K. S. Reid, *Christian Apologetics* (Grand Rapids, Mich.: Eerdmans, 1969), which is a historical survey, and Alan Richardson, *Christian Apologetics* (London: SCM, 1947), which is organized topically but with attention to historical development.

3. See *Miscellaneous Observations*, in *Works* (Hickman), 2:460–510. In the preface to this collection, written in Edinburgh in 1793, John Erskine notes that this work "may prove

an antidote to the deistical notions spreading in some parts of America." *Works* (Hickman), 2:458. A further set of selected *Miscellanies* on theological subjects, entitled *Remarks on Important Theological Controversies* (1796), is included in *Works* (Hickman), 2:511–641.

4. See the discussion by Thomas Schafer in appendix A, "Previous Publication of the 'Miscellanies,'" in *Works* 13:545–51. Regarding the *Miscellaneous Observations* and *Remarks*, Schafer concludes: "Only essays that directly addressed the controversies of the day were selected, with the result that JE was presented only as an orthodox rationalist, with scarcely a hint of other aspects of his thought that are to be found in the 'Miscellanies'." *Works* 13:546 n. 5. Schafer finds Townsend's transcriptions of the earlier *Miscellanies* to be "often very faulty." *Works* 13:550.

5. All Edwards scholars owe an unrepayable debt to Dr. Thomas Schafer for his patient labors with the manuscripts over the last forty-odd years. His introduction to the *Miscellanies* (see *Works* 13:1–160) is essential reading for anyone who seeks to understand Edwards's intellectual development. Because of our many conversations on Edwards and his generosity in allowing me access to his transcriptions while I was in Chicago, I owe a great deal to Dr. Schafer. If it is appropriate to dedicate a chapter, I dedicate this chapter to him.

6. All citations of the *Miscellanies* in this chapter will refer to the Yale edition (*Works* 13) for Misc. a–z, aa–zz, and 1–500. For later entries not yet published in the Yale edition (Misc. 501–1340), I will generally refer to Schafer's transcriptions (Yale MSS) at the Beinecke Library of Yale University and occasionally to *PJE* and the *Miscellaneous Observations* in *Works* (Hickman), 2:460–510.

7. B. A. Gerrish, *A Prince of the Church: Schleiermacher and the Beginnings of Modern Theology* (Philadelphia: Fortress, 1984), 54–5.

8. Lord Herbert of Cherbury, author of the early deistic work *De Veritate* (1624), held to a doctrine of *notitiae communes* or "innate ideas" which were so axiomatic that they needed no proof and were universally accessible to all human beings. See James C. Livingston, *Modern Christian Thought: From the Enlightenment to Vatican II* (New York: Macmillan, 1971), 14, and Reid, *Christian Apologetics*, 145.

9. On the physics of Aristotle versus that of Galileo and Newton, see Gerald Holton and Stephen G. Brush, *Introduction to Concepts and Theories in Physical Science* (Princeton: Princeton University Press, 1985), 9, 66, 89, 116. Newton believed—contrary to his later followers—that God had two specific, cosmic functions at the present time: to prevent the fixed stars from collapsing into the middle of space, and to keep the mechanism of the world in good repair. Gerald R. Cragg, *From Puritanism to the Age of Reason: A Study of Changes in Religious Thought within the Church of England, 1660–1700* (Cambridge: Cambridge University Press, 1966), 105–6.

10. Steven Ozment speaks of the Protestant Reformation as "an unprecedented revolution in religion" that "progressively ended or severely limited a host of traditional beliefs, practices, and institutions that touched directly the daily life of large numbers of people." *The Age of Reform: An Intellectual and Religious History of Late Medieval and Reformation Europe* (New Haven: Yale University Press, 1980), 435. My argument is that the Protestants' loss of certain concrete religious practices and institutions of Catholicism made it harder for them to identify a place and a role for God in everyday life.

11. On the rise of biblical criticism and its impact on the appeal to the Bible as an authoritative religious text in the period prior to 1800, see the following: Henning Graf Reventlow, *The Authority of the Bible and the Rise of the Modern World*, trans. by John

Bowden (London: SCM, 1984); Klaus Scholder, *The Birth of Modern Criticism: Origins and Problems of Biblical Criticism in the Seventeenth Century* (London: SCM, 1990); Jack B. Rogers and Donald K. McKim, *The Authority and Interpretation of the Bible: An Historical Approach* (San Francisco: Harper and Row, 1979); Hans Frei, *The Eclipse of Biblical Narrative: A Study in Eighteenth and Nineteenth Century Hermeneutics* (New Haven: Yale University Press, 1974); and *The Cambridge History of the Bible*, vol. 3, ed. S. L. Greenslade (Cambridge: Cambridge University Press, 1963).

12. Locke, *An Essay Concerning Human Understanding*, book 4, chapter 19.

13. Quoted in *The Penguin Dictionary of Quotations*, ed. J. M. Cohen and M. J. Cohen (Harmondsworth, England: Penguin Books, 1960), 85.

14. Ernst Cassirer, *The Philosophy of the Enlightenment*, trans. Fritz C. A. Koelln and James P. Pettegrove (Boston: Beacon Press, 1955), 174.

15. Paul Hazard writes: "There was not one deism, but several, all different, all mutually opposed, and even at daggers drawn with one another. Pope's deism is not Voltaire's,and Voltaire's was worlds away from Lessing's." *European Thought in the EighteenthCentury: From Montesquieu to Lessing* (New Haven: Yale University Press, 1954), 393. Seealso the chapter on "The Definition of Deism," in Roland N. Stromberg, *Religious Liberalism in Eighteenth-Century England* (Oxford: Oxford University Press, 1954), 52–69.Appeals to "reason" in this era concealed a great deal of disparity, as John Redwoodnotes: "Reason for the early eighteenth century was . . . a word thought by many to represent a consensus approach to understanding, but in effect reflecting a number of prejudices and preconceptions on the part of each individual." *Reason, Ridicule and Religion: The Age of Enlightenment in England, 1660–1750* (Cambridge: Harvard University Press, 1976), 215.

16. G. C. Joyce, quoted in Reid, *Christian Apologetics*, 147. See A. C. McGiffert, *Protestant Thought before Kant* (New York: Scribners, 1951 [1911]), 228–9. On the rise and the course of deism in England, see the old but still invaluable work by Leslie Stephen, *History of English Thought in the Eighteenth Century*, 2 vols. (New York: G. P. Putnam, 1876), 1:1–308. Stephen himself professes indebtedness to an earlier and classic treatment of the topic: Mark Pattison, "Tendencies of Religious Thought in England, 1688–1750," in *Essays and Reviews*, 8th ed. (London: Longman, Green, 1861), 254–329. See also the straightforward account by John Orr, *English Deism: Its Roots and Its Fruits* (Grand Rapids, Mich.: Eerdmans, 1934), and the more interpretive treatments by Frank Manuel, *The Eighteenth Century Confronts the Gods* (Cambridge: Harvard University Press, 1959), and Robert E. Sullivan, *John Toland and the Deist Controversy: A Study in Adaptations*, Harvard Historical Studies 101 (Cambridge: Harvard University Press, 1982).

17. "The Nicaeno-Constantinopolitan Creed," in *The Creeds of Christendom*, ed. Philip Schaff, 3 vols. (New York: Harper and Row, 1931), 2:58–9.

18. On the definition of "apology" and "apologetics," see Richardson, *Christian Apologetics*, 19, and Reid, *Christian Apologetics*, 9–10.

19. Paul Tillich, *Systematic Theology*, 3 vols. (Chicago: University of Chicago Press, 1951–63), 1:31.

20. Mark Pattison quipped that "the title of Locke's treatise, *The Reasonableness of Christianity*, may be said to have been the solitary thesis of Christian theology in England for the great part of a century." "Tendencies," 258.

21. The edition of the *Evidences* cited here is volume 2 of *The Works of William Paley*, 5 vols. (Boston: Joshua Belcher, 1810). Paley's *Natural Theology*, which is not as relevant

to the discussion here, presents an apology for Christianity based almost entirely on the teleological argument. The most important secondary work is that by D. L. LeMahieu, *The Mind of William Paley: A Philosopher and His Age* (Lincoln: University of Nebraska Press, 1976). See also M. L. Clarke, *Paley: Evidences for the Man* (Toronto: University of Toronto Press, 1974).

22. LeMahieu, *Mind of Paley*, 94. Leslie Stephen captures both Paley's strengths and limitations when he writes: "To originality he makes no pretences; and yet he gives so able a summary of the apologetic argument, that his book has almost the force of novelty." *History*, 1:414. The *Evidences* was so highly regarded at Cambridge University, Paley's alma mater, that it remained on the required reading list for all undergraduate students until well into the twentieth century. LeMahieu, *Mind of Paley*, 104.

23. Paley, *Evidences*, 9–16. See also *Evidences*, 200–8, where Paley refutes Hume's claim that the alleged pagan miracles cancel out any claims based on alleged Christian miracles. In both passages Hume is explicitly named.

24. LeMahieu, *Mind of Paley*, 98.

25. Paley, *Evidences*, 11.

26. LeMahieu, *Mind of Paley*, 98.

27. The twentieth-century British apologist C. S. Lewis presented an argument against Hume that is reminiscent of Paley's. See Lewis, *Miracles* (New York: Macmillan, 1947), 100–7.

28. Paley, *Evidences*, 176, 10–11, 18, 19, 22, 179.

29. Paley, *Evidences*, 85, 96–8, 104, 178.

30. Paley, *Evidences*, 356. On the image of Muhammed and Islam in Western nations, see the brilliant historical survey by Norman Daniel, *Islam and the West: The Making of an Image* (Edinburgh: University of Edinburgh Press, 1960). Paley was following a well-worn path in his interpretation of Islam.

31. Paley, *Evidences*, 408. Paley held that the church's enemies greatly exaggerated the evils committed by the church, for "the slave trade destroys more in a year, than the Inquisition does in a hundred."

32. Paley, *Evidences*, 400. In this section of the *Evidences*, Paley cites the name of Joseph Butler (398) and expresses some characteristically Butlerian opinions. Thus he writes that "the true similitude between nature and revelation consists in this; that they each bear strong marks of their original; that they each also bear appearances of irregularity and defect" (396–7). He also acknowledges that his "conclusions are formed with very different degrees of probability, and possess very different degrees of importance" (411). These comments, however, do not convey the general tone of the *Evidences*, which is sanguine and confident rather than skeptical and cautious.

33. Paley, *Evidences*, 221. Later he comments sweepingly, "The most important service that can be rendered to human life . . . is to convey to the world authorized assurances of the reality of a future existence" (222).

34. Paley, *Evidences*, 176.

35. Paley, *Evidences*, 312.

36. Among the critics was Dietrich Bonhoeffer, who writes "how wrong it is to use God as a stop-gap for the incompleteness of our knowledge" and notes that "God is no stop-gap; he must be recognized at the centre of life, not when we are at the end of our resources." *Letters and Papers from Prison*, edited by Eberhard Bethge, rev. ed. (New York: Macmillan, 1967), 164.

37. The edition cited here is [Bishop] Joseph Butler, *The Analogy of Religion, Natural and Revealed* (London: J. M. Dent, 1906). See the recent and substantial collection of essays edited by Christopher Cunliffe, *Joseph Butler's Moral and Religious Thought: Tercentenary Essays* (Oxford: Clarendon Press, 1992), especially David Brown, "Butler and Deism," 7–28, and Basil Mitchell, "Butler as a Christian Apologist," 97–116.

38. Brown, "Butler and Deism," 7. Brown mentions the contrary opinion of Ernest C. Mossner, in *Bishop Butler and the Age of Reason: A Study in the History of Thought* (New York: Columbia University Press, 1936), that deism was already on the wane when Butler sought to refute it.

39. Butler, *Analogy*, xxviii.

40. Butler, *Analogy*, xxviii, 1. The Oxford philosopher Basil Mitchell appeals to this notion of a "cumulative case argument" for religion in his *The Justification of Religious Belief* (New York: Macmillan, 1973). See also the discussion of Mitchell's approach in *The Rationality of Religious Belief: Essays in Honour of Basil Mitchell*, ed. William J. Abraham and Steven W. Holtzer (New York: Oxford University Press, 1987).

41. Butler, *Analogy*, xxiv–xxv.

42. Even a low degree of presumption, writes Butler, "in matters of practice, will lay us under an absolute and formal obligation, in point of prudence and of interest, to act upon that presumption or low probability." *Analogy*, xxv–xxvi. Later he writes: "The apprehension that religion may be true does as really lay men under obligations as a full conviction that it is true." *Analogy*, 188.

43. Taking a jab at the Continental philosophers, Butler writes: "Forming our notions of the constitution and government of the world upon reasoning, without foundation for the principles which we assume . . . is building the world upon hypothesis, like Des Cartes." *Analogy*, xxvii; see 134–5.

44. Butler, *Analogy*, 102, 107, 110, xxvii–xxviii.

45. Butler, *Analogy*, 26–9, 54; see 167.

46. Butler, *Analogy*, 113.

47. Butler, *Analogy*, 139–40, 163, 182.

48. Here Butler exemplifies what Basil Willey has aptly termed "cosmic Toryism," an eighteenth-century tendency to affirm, in the words of Alexander Pope, that "whatever is, is right." See Willey, *The Eighteenth-Century Background: Studies on the Idea of Nature in the Thought of the Period* (New York: Columbia University Press, 1950), 43–56.

49. Leslie Stephen, *History*, 1:303. Butler can be seen as a kind of "spoiler." Thus J. K. S. Reid spoke of "the bland Bishop Butler," who "ensured that in the conflict no one would win or have a prize." *Christian Apologetics*, 139.

50. Mitchell, "Butler as a Christian Apologist," 101–2, 106.

51. Butler's discussion of miracles and fulfilled prophecy is limited to the section entitled "Of the Particular Evidences for Christianity" in *Analogy*, 199–233.

52. Stephen, *History*, 1:293, 306–7. Stephen likens Butler and Pascal: both were brilliant thinkers of aristocratic bent, and deeply conscious of "the sad discords of the universe." See also the essay by Albino Babolin, "*Deus absconditus*: Some Notes on the Bearing of the Hiddenness of God upon Butler's and Pascal's Criticism of Deism," in Cunliffe, *Joseph Butler's Moral and Religious Thought*, 29–35.

53. Sydney E. Ahlstrom writes: "No single judgment of the Romantics was so universal or vehement as their dissatisfaction with the Age of Reason." "The Romantic Religious Revolution and the Dilemmas of Religious History," *Church History* 46 (1977): 155. Com-

pare the statement of Percy Bysshe Shelley, in the preface to his celebrated poem "Prometheus Unbound": "For my part, I had rather be damned with Plato and Lord Bacon, than get to heaven with Paley and Malthus." *Shelley's Prometheus Unbound: A Variorum Edition*, ed. Lawrence John Zillman (Seattle: University of Washington Press, 1959), 126, quoted in LeMahieu, *Mind of Paley*, 55. It is not clear why Bacon, in distinction from the other Englishmen, is exempted from the indictment directed against Paley and Malthus! Yet the animus toward Paley is obvious enough.

54. Samuel Taylor Coleridge, *The Collected Writings of Samuel Taylor Coleridge*, vol. 9, *"Aids to Reflection"*, ed. John Beer, Bollingen Series 75 (Princeton: Princeton University Press, 1993), xliv, lxviii, lxxxviii, 405–8. In his letter to George Fricker of 4 October 1806, Coleridge writes that if none of the biblical miracles had occurred, "yet still all the doctrines will remain untouched by this circumstance, and binding on thee" (xliv). Yet he did not altogether deny the role of miracles: "I by no means deny their importance, much less hold them useless, or superfluous. Even as Christ did, so I would teach; that is, build the miracle on the faith, not the faith on the miracle." On Coleridge as a religious thinker, see Beer's introduction, cited above, and the review by Stephen Happel of nine books on Coleridge: "Words Made Beautiful by Grace: On Coleridge the Theologian," *Religious Studies Review* 6 (1980): 201–10.

55. The edition cited here is Friedrich Schleiermacher, *On Religion: Speeches to Its Cultured Despisers*, translated by John Oman, with an introduction by Rudolf Otto (New York: Harper and Row, 1958 [1893]). Oman's translation is of the 1831 (and final) German edition, which was preceded by editions in 1799, 1806, and 1821. There is an English translation of the first edition by Richard E. Crouter, *On Religion: Speeches to Its Cultured Despisers* (Cambridge: Cambridge University Press, 1988). Crouter's "Introduction" (1–73) provides a brilliant sketch of the historical background to the *Speeches* and the major interpretive issues raised by the text.

56. Crouter, "Introduction," in Schleiermacher, *On Religion*, 9, 12–13.

57. The works that have influenced my discussion here include Richard Crouter, "Introduction," in Schleiermacher, *On Religion*, 1–73; B. A. Gerrish, *A Prince of the Church: Schleiermacher and the Beginnings of Modern Theology* (Philadelphia: Fortress, 1984), and "Friedrich Schleiermacher," in *Nineteenth-Century Religious Thought in the West*, ed. Ninian Smart et al., 3 vols. (Cambridge: Cambridge University Press, 1985), 1:123–56; Van Harvey, "A Word in Defense of Schleiermacher's Theological Method," *Journal of Religion* 42 (1962): 151–70, and "On the New Edition of Schleiermacher's *Addresses on Religion*," *Journal of the American Academy of Religion* 39 (1971): 488–512; Wayne Proudfoot, *Religious Experience* (Berkeley: University of California Press, 1985); and Wayne Proudfoot, et al., "Symposium on Schleiermacher's 'On Religion: Speeches to Its Cultured Despisers,' " *Harvard Divinity Bulletin* 24 (1995): 10–13.

58. Schleiermacher, *Speeches*, 36.

59. Schleiermacher, *Speeches*, 48.

60. Schleiermacher, *Speeches*, 50.

61. Schleiermacher, quoted in W. Dilthey, "Denkmale der inneren Entwicklung Schleiermachers," in *Leben Schleiermachers* (1870), 139; cited as epigraph to Gerhard Spiegler, *The Eternal Covenant: Schleiermacher's Experiment in Cultural Theology* (New York: Harper and Row, 1967).

62. I leave undecided the exact status and relation of "God," "the Universe," and "the Infinite" in the younger Schleiermacher. Some scholars, such as Van Harvey (see references

in note 57), have judged that the universe was more important to him than God was. Schleiermacher broadmindedly suggested that "religion" was consistent with a personal God, an impersonal God, and even with no God at all. *Speeches*, 50, 282. Crouter notes that in the 1799 edition, the German term *Universum* occurs 166 times, as compared with only fifty-six and thirty-six occurrences of "God" and "divinity." In later editions, many of the references to "the Universe" are replaced with different and more theological vocabulary. Thus Crouter concludes that the young Schleiermacher was a "religious naturalist" who later modified his "naturalism" in the direction of "theism" ("Introduction," in Schleiermacher, *On Religion*, 64–6).

63. William Blake, "Auguries of Innocence," 1, quoted in *The Oxford Dictionary of Quotations*, 3rd ed. (Oxford: Oxford University Press, 1979), 85. One could equally well cite the lines from "Aurora Leigh" by Elizabeth Barrett Browning: "Earth's crammed with heaven, / And every common bush afire with God; / But only he who sees, takes off his shoes, / The rest sit round it and pluck blackberries." *Oxford Dictionary of Quotations*, 97.

64. Schleiermacher's *Speeches* has obvious affinities to Ralph Waldo Emerson's *Nature*. The latter conceives the infinite or "the higher laws" as manifested through the realm of nature: "When in fortunate hours we ponder this miracle . . . the universe becomes transparent, and the light of higher laws than its own, shines through it." *Nature*, in Ralph Waldo Emerson, *Essays and Lectures*, ed. Joel Porte (New York: Library of America, 1983), 24–5. The insight that Emerson sought involved a harmony of the individual with the whole: "Nothing is quite beautiful alone: nothing but is beautiful in the whole." *Nature*, 18; see 29–30. On Emerson as a religious thinker in relation to the broader transcendentalist movement, see the incisive study by Catherine L. Albanese, *Corresponding Motion: Transcendental Religion and the New America* (Philadelphia: Temple University Press, 1977).

65. Schleiermacher, *Speeches*, 88. Schleiermacher goes on to say to his imagined reader: "In your sense the inexplicable and strange alone is miracle, in mine it is no miracle." Compare Emerson's statements in his "Divinity School Address": "The word Miracle, as prounounced by Christian churches, gives a false impression; it is Monster. It is not one with the blowing clover and the falling rain." *Essays and Lectures*, 80. In *Nature*, Emerson writes: "The invariable mark of wisdom is to see the miraculous in the common." *Essays and Lectures*, 47.

66. Schleiermacher, *Speeches*, 48. Emerson stressed the need for firsthand religion perhaps even more strongly than Schleiermacher did. In the opening words of his first book, he wrote: "Our age is retrospective. It builds the sepulchres of the fathers. . . . The foregoing generations beheld God and nature face to face; we, through their eyes. Why should not we also enjoy an original relation to the universe? Why should not we have a poetry and philosophy of insight and not tradition, and a religion by revelation to us, and not the history of theirs?" *Nature*, in *Essays and Lectures*, 7.

67. Gerrish, *A Prince of the Church*, 67.

68. See Karl Barth, *The Theology of Schleiermacher*, ed. Dietrich Ritschl, trans. Geoffrey Bromiley (Grand Rapids, Mich.: Eerdmans, 1982), especially 249–58. Barth concludes that Schleiermacher erroneously annuls the distinction between a religious and a nonreligious worldview: "The person who has it in his nature to personify the universum is in essentials . . . no different from the one who does not" (258). Compare the slightly more favorable estimate of Schleiermacher from a later period of Barth's career, in Karl Barth, *Protestant Thought: From Rousseau to Ritschl* (New York: Harper, 1959), 306–54.

69. Douglas Elwood, *The Philosophical Theology of Jonathan Edwards* (New York: Columbia University Press, 1960), 51.

70. The only notable discussion of Edwards as an apologist is a series of articles by John Gerstner, whose approach is basically ahistorical. See Gerstner, "An Outline of the Apologetics of Jonathan Edwards," *Bibliotheca Sacra* 133 (1976): 3–10, 99–107, 195–201, 291–8. Gerstner refashions Edwards in the likeness of a seventeenth-century rationalist and inteprets him in a rigid scheme (proofs of God followed by proofs of biblical inspiration) that owes less to Edwards himself than to such Calvinist scholastics as Francis Turrentin and Charles Hodge. He largely neglects the subjective stress in Edwards and misses entirely what I am calling the implicit apology. Scott Oliphint, in "Jonathan Edwards: Reformed Apologist," *Westminster Theological Journal* 57 (1995): 165–86, follows Gerstner's ahistorical interpretation as he seeks "to incorporate his [Edwards's] work into a presuppositional or transcendental framework" (165).

71. Misc. 832 (Yale MSS).

72. Misc. 1297, in *PJE*, 214–9.

73. See the meticulous analysis and attempted vindication of Edwards's epistemological position by William J. Wainwright, *Reason and the Heart: A Prolegomenon to a Critique of Passional Reason*, Cornell Studies in the Philosophy of Religion (Ithaca, N.Y.: Cornell University Press, 1995), 7–54, especially 7–18, 41–50. Wainwright seeks to resolve the "apparent ambiguity" of Edwards's remarks on reason by showing how "grace is needed to reason properly" (7,11).

74. *Works* 13:421–3 (Misc. 350).

75. *Works* (Hickman), 2:476–7.

76. *Works* 13:421–3 (Misc. 350). Other passages repeat these points: Misc. 514, 837, 1298 (Yale MSS).

77. *Works* 13:291 (Misc. 127).

78. Misc. 1338 (Yale MSS); see Misc. 864, 1156 (Yale MSS).

79. *Works* 13:421 (Misc. 350). See *Works* (Hickman), 2:476.

80. Misc. 598 (Yale MSS). See *Works* (Hickman), 2:465.

81. In *History of Redemption*, Edwards describes Islam as a "great kingdom of mighty power and vast extent that Satan set up against the kingdom of Christ." *Works* 9:415; see *Works* (Hickman), 2:471. See Gerald R. McDermott, "The Deist Connection: Jonathan Edwards and Islam," in *Jonathan Edwards's Writings: Text, Context, Interpretation*, ed. Stephen J. Stein (Bloomington: Indiana University Press, 1996), 39–51. McDermott argues that "Edwards was continuing a long tradition of anti-Islamic sentiment that combined fear and loathing with curious fascination," and yet he was "unusually vitriolic" because "the deists . . . were using Islam as a stick to shake at their orthodox opponents" (39,43). Many of Edwards's ideas on Islam were taken directly from Johann Friedrich Stapfer's five-volume *Institutiones theologiae polemicae* (1743–47). Edwards and Stapfer, like Paley, fall into the common Western stereotypes regarding Islam. See Daniel, *Islam and the West: The Making of an Image.* Edwards's perspective on Judaism is only slightly more positive. Like other thinkers of his day, he judged that Judaism is a "carnal religion" preoccupied with this-worldly blessings in the present life, while Christianity, with its more overt teaching on eternal life, is a "spiritual religion." *Works* 13:292 (Misc. 129). For a recent study of the "carnal" in Judaism, see Daniel Boyarin, *Carnal Israel: Reading Sex in Talmudic Culture* (Berkeley: University of California Press, 1993), especially 1–10. Ironically, while Judaism as a religion was invalid for Edwards, the Jewish people themselves

were a "standing evidence" of God and so had apologetic significance in his case for Christianity.

82. Elwood, *Philosophical Theology*, 151.

83. Gerstner, "Outline," 4.

84. Edwards, "Of Being," in *Works* 6:202–7. *Works* 13:213 (Misc. 27a). See "The Mind," nos. 27–30, in *Works* 6:350–2; *Works* 13:256 (Misc. 93); *Works* 13:436 (Misc. 365); Misc. 587, 650 (Yale MSS).

85. Edwards, *Works* 13:188 (Misc. pp).

86. Edwards, *Works* 13:254–5 (Misc. 91). Compare the analogous statements in *Freedom of the Will* (*Works* 1:180–5). In another text, Edwards comments that our imperfect notions of God prevent us from understanding how it is that God exists without being caused. Misc. 650 (Yale MSS).

87. *Works* 13:288 (Misc. 125a).

88. In one of his strongest and strangest assertions, he writes that "the mere exertion of a new thought is a certain proof of God," for the old thought cannot be what "produces and upholds" the new one, since the old is "past, and what is past is not." *Works* 13:373 (Misc. 267). Thus Edwards's occasionalism extended to human thoughts and actions as well as events in the natural world. "All men's works," he writes, are "only the regular actings of God's works." *Works* 13:338 (Misc. 200).

89. Misc. 651 (Yale MSS). See *PJE*, 103–9 (Misc. 976); *PJE*, 82–6 (Misc. 749); Misc. 896–7 (Yale MSS). A copious refutation of the idea that the order of the world is due to sheer chance is given in *PJE*, 87–103 (Misc. 880).

90. *Works* 13:288 (Misc. 124).

91. *Works* 13:334 (Misc. 192); *Works* 13:337 (Misc. 199–200). See *Works* 13:373–4 (Misc. 269).

92. Edwards, *Works* 13:373 (Misc. 268). See Edwards, *Works* (Hickman), 2:470–2.

93. *Works* 13:294 (Misc. 132).

94. *Works* 13:185 (Misc. gg). See Edwards, *PJE*, 196–7 (Misc. 1006); Misc. 1292 (Yale MSS). If humans, as the "consciousness of the creation," pass away, then it is "in vain" that the world ever existed at all. *Works* 13:197 (Misc. 1); see *Works* 13:188 (Misc. pp).

95. *Works* 13:267 (Misc. 99), *Works* 13:282 (Misc. 114).

96. Misc. 1205 (Yale MSS).

97. On heaven as a state of preeminent happiness and human fulfillment, see: *Works* 13:329 (Misc. 181–2); *Works* 13:275 (Misc. 105); *Works* 13:303 (Misc. 153); *Works* 13:331 (Misc. 188); *Works* 13:336–7 (Misc. 198); *Works* 13:369–70 (Misc. 263); *Works* (Hickman), 2:638; and Misc. 1072 (Yale MSS). See also the concluding sermon in *Charity and Its Fruits*, entitled "Heaven Is a World of Love" (*Works* 8:366–97).

98. *Works* 13:202–3 (Misc. 6). Similarly, John Calvin wrote that the Scripture possesses an "uncultivated and almost rude simplicity," which nonetheless "inspires greater reverence for itself than any eloquence." *Institutes of the Christian Religion*, ed. John T. McNeill, trans. Ford Lewis Battles, 2 vols. (Philadelphia: Westminster Press, 1960), book 1, chapter 8, sections 1, 11 (1:82–3, 90–1).

99. *Works* 13:335–6 (Misc. 195–6). Likewise, the story of Joseph in the Book of Genesis must have been written by inspiration, since it shows "so perfect a knowledge of . . . the secret springs of human affections." *Works* 13:339 (Misc. 203).

100. *Works* 13:410 (Misc. 333). See Calvin, *Institutes* 1.8.1, 1:82.

101. *Works* 13:289 (Misc. 126).

102, *Works* 13:338 (Misc. 202). See *Works* 13:376 (Misc. 276).

103. Misc. 1060 (Yale MSS). See *Works* (Hickman), 2:9/5

104. *Works* 13:448 (Misc. 378).

105. *Works* 13:393–4 (Misc. 311). This argument, along with so many others of the evidential sort, is implausible in the light of current knowledge. Circumcision was widely practiced in the ancient Near East, even prior to the patriarchal era and the Israelites' sojourn in Egypt. See Nahum M. Sarna, *Understanding Genesis* (New York: Jewish Theological Seminary of America, 1966), 131–3.

106. Edwards, *Works* (Hickman), 2:493–5. In common with many other Christian theologians, Edwards held that the Jews' special place in God's plan ended with the coming of Jesus. Moreover, the destruction of the Jewish Temple was a specific indication that God intended for Christianity to supercede and to replace Judaism. *Works* 13:491–2 (Misc. 443).

107. Misc. 1150, 702 (Yale MSS).

108. *Works* 13:293 (Misc. 131).

109. *Works* 13:352–3 (Misc. 236).

110. *Works* 13:492 (Misc. 444).

111. *Works* 13:395 (Misc. 313); *Works* 13:302–3 (Misc. 152). cf. *Works* 13:402 (Misc. 321a).

112. *Works* (Hickman), 2:469–70.

113. *Works* 13:507 (Misc. 465).

114. *Works* 13:293 (Misc. 131).

115. *Works* 13:449–50 (Misc. 379).

116. Misc. 1162 (Yale MSS).

117. Calvin, *Institutes* book 2, chapter 2, section 15–16 (1:273–5).

118. In the Yale MSS, see the following entries: Misc. 955, 956, 959, 961, 970, 973, 975, 978, 992, 1012, 1013, 1014, 1016–8, 1020–4, 1028, 1073, 1180, 1181, 1200, 1236, 1244, 1255, 1269. The material for 955, 956, and 959 is taken from Theophilus Gale's *The Court of the Gentiles*, that of 1180, 1181, and 1255 from Ramsay's *The Travels of Cyrus*, that of 1236 from a book by Philip Skelton called *Deism Revealed*, and that of 1024 and 1076 from Grotius's *The Truth of the Christian Religion*.

119. Edwards writes: "Heathens had what they had of truth in divine thing[s] by tradition from the first fathers of nations or from the Jews." Misc. 959 (Yale MSS). Here Edwards leaves open the possibility that some traditions were *borrowed* from the Jews by other nations at some early stage in history (as suggested by Justin Martyr and other early Christian writers). This speculation provides another theory of how analogous religious traditions developed in different cultural spheres, supplementing the theory of the divine inspiration of the "heathen." See *PJE*, 217 (Misc. 1297).

120. Edwards, *Works* 13:288–9 (Misc. 125b).

121. Edwards, *Works* 13:364 (Misc. 253).

122. Edwards, *Works* 13:336 (Misc. 197).

123. Edwards, *Works* 13:358 (Misc. 242).

124. Edwards, *Works* 13:359 (Misc. 244).

125. Edwards, *Works* 13:372 (Misc. 266).

126. For a cogent analysis of how early modern thinkers sought to vindicate the traditional doctrine of hell but ultimately abandoned the attempt, see D. P. Walker, *The Decline of Hell: Seventeenth-Century Discussions of Eternal Torment* (London: Routledge and Kegan Paul, 1964).

127. Misc. 1263 is transcribed in *PJE*, 184–93.

128. *Works* 13:235 (Misc. 64).

129. Norman Fiering, *Jonathan Edwards's Moral Thought and Its British Context*, published for the Institute of Early American History and Culture, Williamsburg, Virginia (Chapel Hill: University of North Carolina Press, 1981), 60–1.

130. *Works* 6:396–7.

131. Wallace Anderson, in *Works* 6:394.

132. A medieval work that adumbrated Edwards's *Rational Account* was Bonaventura's *The Reduction of the Arts to Theology*. "Since every science," he wrote, "and particularly [though not only] the science contained in the Holy Scriptures, is concerned with the Trinity before all else, every science must necessarily present some trace of this same Trinity." Quoted in Jaroslav Pelikan, *The Christian Tradition: A History of the Development of Doctrine*, vol. 3, *The Growth of Medieval Theology (600–1300)* (Chicago: University of Chicago Press, 1978), 282; see 305–7. Bonaventura attempted to apply this principle to each of the acknowledged fields of study in his day, much as Edwards sought to do vis-à-vis the fields of study as they existed in his era.

133. Immanuel Kant, "What is Enlightenment?" quoted in James C. Livingston, *Modern Christian Thought: From the Enlightenment to Vatican II* (New York: Macmillan, 1971), 1.

134. Wilson Kimnach, "Editor's Introduction," in *Works* 10:189.

135. *Works* 6:363.

136. *Personal Narrative*, 31–2.

137. Perry Miller, *Jonathan Edwards*, American Men of Letters Series (New York: William Sloane, 1949), 313.

138. *Works* 9:520.

139. John F. Wilson, "Editor's Introduction," in *Works* 9:72–4.

140. The Latin word *proportio* was used in technical writing as a synonym for the Greek term *analogia* as far back as the time of Cicero. See Joachim Track, "Analogie," in *Theologische Realenzyklopädie*, ed. Gerhard Krause and Gerhard Muller, 27 vols. to date (Berlin: Walter de Gruyter, 1976–), 2:625–6. Given this correspondence in terminology, it seems that Edwards's discussion of "proportion" and Butler's discussion of "analogy" were treating the same subject, despite the differences in their conclusions.

141. See Norman Fiering, "The Rationalist Foundations of Edwards's Metaphysics," in *Jonathan Edwards and the American Experience*, ed. Nathan O. Hatch and Harry S. Stout (New York: Oxford University Press, 1988), 73–101.

142. Elwood, *Philosophical Theology*, 24. Yet Elwood presses his point too far when he adds: "The 'God' whose existence is 'proved' by rational arguments is not really God" (ibid). This statement more accurately reflects the sentiments of Kierkegaard and Barth than Edwards.

143. Quoted in Pattison, "Tendencies," 296.

144. Another way that Edwards mediated between Paley in Schleiermacher was with respect to the divine inspiration of the "heathen," as discussed earlier. In his later *Miscellanies*, Edwards opened the door to a presence and activity of the Holy Spirit among all the nations and cultures of the world. "Inspiration" was more widely diffused for Edwards than for classical Protestantism. On the other hand, Christ clearly remained central for him—the final and definitive expression of truth and the very incarnation of God.

Conclusion

1. Paul Tillich, "Existential Philosophy," *Journal of the History of Ideas* 5 (1944): 66, quoted in Roland N. Stromberg, *Religious Liberalism in Eighteenth-Century England* (London: Oxford University Press, 1954), ix.

2. Edwards, *Treatise on Grace*, in *Treatise on Grace and Other Posthumously Published Writings*, ed. Paul Helm (Cambridge, England: James Clarke, 1971), 53.

3. Paul Hazard, *European Thought in the Eighteenth Century: From Montesquieu to Lessing* (New Haven: Yale University Press, 1954), 46. Carl Becker, quoted in Roland N. Stromberg, *Religious Liberalism in Eighteenth-Century England* (London: Oxford University Press, 1954), 1.

4. See Harry S. Stout, *The New England Soul: Preaching and Religious Culture in Colonial New England* (New York: Oxford University Press, 1986), 127–47, 222–8, and Henry F. May, *The Enlightenment in America* (New York: Oxford University Press, 1976), 3–101.

5. The well-known work attacking the Great Awakening was Charles Chauncy's *Seasonable Thoughts on the State of Religion in New England* (Boston: Rogers and Fowle, 1743). The later tract by Chauncy was *Salvation for All Men, Illustrated and Vindicated as a Scripture Doctrine* (Boston: T. and J. Fleet, 1782).

6. May, *The Enlightenment*, 5.

7. *Works* 13:191 (Misc. tt). Edwards, Unpublished MS Sermon on Gen. 19:14, Beinecke Library, Yale University, quoted in Wilson H. Kimnach, "Jonathan Edwards's Pursuit of Reality," in *Jonathan Edwards and the American Experience*, ed. Nathan O. Hatch and Harry S. Stout (New York: Oxford University Press, 1988), 105.

8. May, *Enlightenment*, 49.

9. Mark Pattison, "Tendencies of Religious Thought in England, 1688–1750," in *Essays and Reviews*, 8th ed. (London: Longman, Green, 1861), 259–60.

10. My conclusion is thus different from, but not inconsistent with, that of Jon Pahl in "Jonathan Edwards and the Aristocracy of Grace," *Fides et Historia* 25 (1993): 62–72. While Pahl correctly notes that Edwards's social ideal was "monarchical and aristocratic" (65), a "rule of the saints" (70), my stress is on the imposing spiritual obligations Edwards placed on clerics and laypersons alike.

11. My intention here is not to prejudge the very complex and controverted issue of Edwards's dismissal from the pastorate in Northampton. Edwards's defenders, past and present, have seen him as the innocent lamb led to the slaughter by a mob of ungrateful parishioners. Sereno Dwight blamed the Williams clan for fomenting opposition in Edwards's congregation. "Memoirs of Jonathan Edwards," in *Works* (Hickman), 1:cxiv-cxxvii. Ola Winslow saw the conflict as resulting from Edwards's own pastoral blunders, combined with a rising tide of democracy throughout New England that clashed with the older, authoritarian style of leadership that Edwards sought to perpetuate; see her *Jonathan Edwards, 1703–1758: A Biography* (New York: Farrar, Straus and Giroux, 1940), 215–67. The recent and carefully researched study by Patricia J. Tracy, *Jonathan Edwards, Pastor: Religion and Society in Eighteenth-Century Northampton* (New York: Hill and Wang, 1980), situates Edwards and his Northampton parish in the context of shifting social and economic conditions that led to "the fragmentation of a once integrated body into a mere geographical collection of competitive individuals." In Tracy's analysis, Edwards was out of step with the changing times (192–4).

12. Mark Twain, letter to Rev. Joseph H. Twitchell, February 1902, in *Mark Twain's Letters*, ed. Albert Bigelow Paine (New York: Harper, 1917), 2:719–21, quoted in M. X. Lesser, *Jonathan Edwards: A Reference Guide* (Boston: G. K. Hall, 1981), 137.

13. *Personal Narrative*, 35.

14. *Works* 8:534–6.

15. Ronald A. Knox, *Enthusiasm: A Chapter in the History of Religion: With Special Reference to the Seventeenth and Eighteenth Centuries* (Notre Dame, Ind.: University of Notre Dame Press, 1994 [1950]), 2. The entire chapter on "The Nature of Enthusiasm" (1–8) is filled with insights.

16. Immanuel Kant, conclusion to *Critique of Practical Reason*, in *Great Books of the Western World*, vol. 42, ed. Robert Maynard Hutchins (Chicago: Encyclopaedia Britannica, 1952), 360.

17. Perry Miller, "From Edwards to Emerson," in *Errand into the Wilderness* (Cambridge: Belknap Press of Harvard University, 1956), 195.

18. Daniel B. Shea, Jr., "Jonathan Edwards, Historian of Consciousness," in *Major Writers of Early American Literature*, ed. Everett Emerson (Madison: University of Wisconsin Press, 1972), 180.

19. Douglas Elwood commented: "The term 'supernaturalist' cannot be applied to him without careful qualification." *The Philosophical Theology of Jonathan Edwards* (New York: Columbia University Press, 1960), 18. This observation is correct, in that the term "supernaturalist" generally implies a simple straightforward dichotomy of "nature" and "supernature" such as does not exist in Edwards's thought.

20. *PJE*, 184–93.

21. James Hoopes, "Jonathan Edwards's Religious Psychology," *Journal of American History* 69 (1983): 863. Hoopes refers to Norman Fiering, *Jonathan Edwards's Moral Thought and Its British Context*, published by the Institute of Early American History and Culture, Williamsburg, Virginia (Chapel Hill: University of North Carolina Press, 1981), 98–102.

22. Elwood, *Philosophical Theology*, 23.

23. *Personal Narrative*, 31.

24. Allen C. Guelzo, *Edwards on the Will: A Century of American Theological Debate* (Middletown, Conn.: Wesleyan University Press, 1989), ix.

25. G. W. F. Hegel, *The Philosophy of History* (1832), in *The Philosophy of Hegel*, ed. Carl J. Friedrich (New York: Modern Library, 1953), 157.

26. My comments are based largely on lectures given by Hans Frei at Yale University in the early 1980s. See also his major work, *The Eclipse of Biblical Narrative: A Study in Eighteenth and Nineteenth Century Hermeneutics* (New Haven: Yale University Press, 1974).

27. See Herbert Warren Richardson, "The Glory of God in the Theology of Jonathan Edwards" (Ph.D. diss., Harvard University, 1962), 7–9, and William Morris, "The Young Jonathan Edwards: A Reconstruction" (Ph.D. diss., University of Chicago, 1955), 597–8.

Bibliography

Abraham, William J., and Steven W. Holtzer. *The Rationality of Religious Belief: Essays in Honor of Basil Mitchell.* New York: Oxford University Press, 1987.

Ahlstrom, Sydney E. *A Religious History of the American People.* New Haven: Yale University Press, 1972.

———. "The Romantic Religious Revolution and the Dilemmas of Religious History." *Church History* 46 (1977): 149–170.

Albanese, Catherine L. *Corresponding Motion: Transcendental Religion and the New America.* Philadelphia: Temple University Press, 1977.

Aldrich, A. O. "Edwards and Hutcheson." *Harvard Theological Review* 44 (1951): 35–53.

Aldridge, Alfred Owen. *Jonathan Edwards.* New York: Washington Square Press, 1964.

Allen, Alexander V. G. *Jonathan Edwards.* American Religious Leaders. Boston: Houghton, Mifflin, 1889.

Allen, Douglas. "Phenomenology of Religion." In *Encyclopedia of Religion,* edited by Mircea Eliade, et al. 11:272–85. 16 vols., New York: Macmillan, 1987.

Alston, Willliam P. *Perceiving God: The Epistemology of Religious Experience.* Ithaca, N.Y.: Cornell University Press, 1991.

Anderson, Wallace E. "Editor's Introduction." In Jonathan Edwards, *Scientific and Philosophical Writings.* Volume 6 of *The Works of Jonathan Edwards,* 1–143. New Haven and London: Yale University Press, 1980.

———. "Editor's Introduction to 'Images of Divine Things' and 'Types.'" In Jonathan Edwards, *Typological Writings.* Vol. 2 of *The Works of Jonathan Edwards.* Edited by Wallace E. Anderson, Mason I. Lowance, and David H. Watters, 3–33. New Haven and London: Yale University Press, 1993.

———. "Immaterialism in Jonathan Edwards' Early Philosophical Notes." *Journal of the History of Ideas* 25 (1964): 181–200.

Angoff, Charles. *From 1607 to the Beginning of the Revolutionary Period.* Vol. 1 of *A Literary History of the American People.* New York: Tudor, 1935.

Anonymous. *The Oxford Dictionary of Quotations.* 3rd ed. New York: Oxford University Press, 1979.

Aristotle. *The Ethics of Aristotle.* Translated by J. A. K. Thomson. Harmondsworth, England: Penguin Books, 1953.

Augustine. *The City of God*. In *A Select Library of Nicene and Post-Nicene Fathers*, edited by Philip Schaff. 2nd series, 14 vols., 2:1–511. Grand Rapids, Mich.: Eerdmans, 1974–76.

———. *Confessions*. Translated by R. S. Pine-Coffin. Harmondsworth, England: Penguin Books, 1961.

Babolin, Albino. "*Deus absconditus*: Some Notes on the Bearing of the Hiddenness of God upon Butler's and Pascal's Criticism of Deism." In *Joseph Butler's Moral and Religious Thought: Tercentenary Essays*, edited by Christopher Cunliffe, 29–35. Oxford: Clarendon Press, 1992.

Baillie, John. *Our Knowledge of God*. New York: Scribner's, 1959.

Balthasar, Hans Urs von. *The Theology of Karl Barth*. Translated by John Drury. Garden City, N.Y.: Doubleday, 1972.

Barth, Karl. *Church Dogmatics*. 14 vols. Edinburgh: T. and T. Clark, 1936–77.

———. *Protestant Thought: From Rousseau to Ritschl*. New York: Harper, 1959.

———. *The Theology of Schleiermacher*. Edited by Dietrich Ritschl. Translated by Geoffrey Bromiley. Grand Rapids, Mich.: Eerdmans, 1982.

Bercovitch, Sacvan. *The Puritan Origins of the American Self*. New Haven: Yale University Press, 1975.

Berkeley, George. *The Works of George Berkeley, Bishop of Cloyne*. Edited by A. A. Luce and T. E. Jessop. 9 vols. London: Thomas Nelson, 1948–57.

Bleeker, C. J. *The Sacred Bridge: Researches into the Nature and Structure of Religion*. Leiden: E. J. Brill, 1963.

Blumenberg, Hans. *The Legitimacy of the Modern Age*. Translated by Robert M. Wallace. Cambridge: MIT Press, 1983.

Bonhoeffer, Dietrich. *Letters and Papers from Prison*. Edited by Eberhard Bethge. Rev. ed. New York: Macmillan, 1967.

Bossuet, Jacques-Bénigne. *Discourse on Universal History*. Classic European Historians Series. Translated by Elborg Forster. Edited with an introduction by Orest Ranum, with a preface by Leonard Krieger. Chicago: University of Chicago Press, 1976.

Boyarin, Daniel. *Carnal Israel: Reading Sex in Talmudic Culture*. Berkeley: University of California Press, 1993.

Brantley, Richard E. "The Common Ground of Wesley and Edwards." *Harvard Theological Review* 83 (1990): 271–303.

———. *Coordinates of Anglo-American Romanticism: Wesley, Edwards, Carlyle, and Emerson*. Gainesville: University Press of Florida, 1993.

Brauer, Jerald C. "Conversion: From Puritanism to Revivalism." *The Journal of Religion* 58 (1978): 227–43.

———. "Types of Puritan Piety." *Church History* 56 (1987): 39–58.

Bremond, A. "Le théocentrisme de Malebranche." *Archives de philosophie* 6 (1928): 281–303.

Bromiley, G. W., and T. F. Torrance. Editor's preface to Karl Barth, *Church Dogmatics*. Volume 3, part 1, vii–viii. 14 vols., Edinburgh: T. and T. Clark, 1958.

Brown, David. "Butler and Deism." In *Joseph Butler's Moral and Religious Thought: Tercentenary Essays*, edited by Christopher Cunliffe, 7–28. Oxford: Clarendon Press, 1992.

Bury, J. B. *The Idea of Progress: An Inquiry into Its Origin and Growth*. London: Macmillan, 1924.

Butler, Diana H. "God's Visible Glory: The Beauty of Nature in the Thought of John Calvin and Jonathan Edwards." *Westminster Theological Journal* 52 (1990): 13–26.

Butler, Joseph. *The Analogy of Religion, Natural and Revealed.* London: J. M. Dent, 1906.

Calvin, John. *Institutes of the Christian Religion.* Edited by John T. McNeill. 2 vols. Philadelphia: Westminster Press, 1960.

Carse, James. *Jonathan Edwards and the Visibility of God.* New York; Scribner's, 1967.

Cassirer, Ernst. *The Philosophy of the Enlightenment.* Translated by Fritz C. A. Koelln and James P. Pettegrove. Boston: Beacon Press, 1955.

Chamberlain, Ava. "Self-Deception as a Theological Problem in Jonathan Edwards's 'Treatise Concerning Religious Affections.' " *Church History* 63 (1994): 541–56.

Chauncy, Charles. *Salvation for All Men, Illustrated and Vindicated as a Scripture Doctrine.* Boston: T. and J. Fleet, 1782.

———. *Seasonable Thoughts on the State of Religion in New England.* Boston: Rogers and Fowle, 1743.

Cherry, Conrad. *Nature and Religious Imagination: From Edwards to Bushnell.* Philadelphia: Fortress Press, 1980.

———. "Symbols of Spiritual Truth: Jonathan Edwards as Biblical Interpreter." *Interpretation* 39 (1985): 263–71.

———. *The Theology of Jonathan Edwards: A Reappraisal.* Bloomington and Indianapolis: Indiana University Press, 1990 [1966].

Clarke, M. L. *Paley: Evidences for the Man.* Toronto: University of Toronto Press, 1974.

Cohen, Charles Lloyd. *God's Caress: The Psychology of Puritan Religious Experience.* New York: Oxford University Press, 1986.

Cohen, J. M., and M. J. Cohen, *The Penguin Dictionary of Quotations.* Harmondsworth, England: Penguin Books, 1960.

Coleridge, Samuel Taylor. *"Aids to Reflection."* Vol. 9 of *The Collected Writings of Samuel Taylor Coleridge.* Edited by John Beer. Bollingen Series 75. Princeton: Princeton University Press, 1993.

Collingwood, R. G. *The Idea of History.* Oxford: Clarendon Press, 1946.

Cooey, Paul M. *"Eros* and Intimacy in Edwards." *Journal of Religion* 69 (1989): 484–99.

Conforti, Joseph. "Jonathan Edwards's Most Popular Work: 'The Life of David Brainerd' and Nineteenth-Century Evangelical Culture." *Church History* 54 (1985): 188–201.

———. *Jonathan Edwards, Religious Tradition, and American Culture.* Chapel Hill: University of North Carolina Press, 1995.

Copleston, Frederick. *Medieval Philosophy, Augustine to Scotus* Vol. 2 of *A History of Philosophy.* Paramus, N.J.: Newman Press, 1971 [1950].

Cunliffe, Christopher, ed. *Joseph Butler's Moral and Religious Thought: Tercentenary Essays.* Oxford: Clarendon Press, 1992.

Cragg, Gerald. *From Puritanism to the Age of Reason: A Study of Changes in Religious Thought within the Church of England, 1660–1700.* Cambridge: Cambridge University Press, 1966.

———. *Reason and Authority in the Eighteenth Century.* Cambridge: Cambridge University Press, 1964.

Crooker, Joseph. "Jonathan Edwards: A Psychological Study." *New England Magazine,* n.s. 2 (1890): 159–72.

Crouter, Richard. "Introduction." In Friedrich Schleiermacher, *On Religion: Speeches to Its Cultured Despisers*, 1–73. Cambridge: Cambridge University Press, 1988.

Daniel, Norman. *Islam and the West: The Making of an Image*. Edinburgh: University of Edinburgh Press, 1960.

Daniel, Stephen H. *The Philosophy of Jonathan Edwards: A Study in Divine Semiotics*. Bloomington: Indiana University Press, 1994.

Davidson, Bruce W. "Reasonable Damnation: How Jonathan Edwards Argued for the Rationality of Hell." *Journal of the Evangelical Theological Society* 28 (1995): 47–56.

Davidson, Edward H. "From Locke to Edwards," *Journal of the History of Ideas* 24 (1963): 355–72.

Dedieu, Joseph. "Calvin et Calvinisme." In *Dictionnaire de spiritualité*, edited by M. Viller et al, 2:23–50. Paris: Beauchesne, 1937–.

Delattre, Roland. *Beauty and Sensibility in the Thought of Jonathan Edwards: An Essay in Aesthetics and Theological Ethics*. New Haven: Yale University Press, 1968.

———. "Beauty and Theology: A Reappraisal of Jonathan Edwards," *Soundings* 51 (1968): 60–79.

DeProspo, R. C. *Theism in the Discourse of Jonathan Edwards*. Newark: University of Delaware Press, 1985.

Dulles, Avery. *A History of Apologetics*. New York: Corpus, 1971.

Dwight, Sereno. "Memoirs of Jonathan Edwards." In *The Works of Jonathan Edwards*. Revised by Edward Hickman. 2 vols., 1:xi–ccxxxiv. Edinburgh: Banner of Truth Trust, 1984 [1834].

Edwards, Jonathan. "A Divine and Supernatural Light." In *Selected Writings of Jonathan Edwards*. Edited by Harold P. Simonson, 65–88. New York: Frederick Ungar, 1970.

———. "An Essay on the Trinity." In *Treatise on Grace and Other Posthumously Published Writings*, 99–131. Edited by Paul Helm. Cambridge, England: James Clarke, 1971.

———. "Personal Narrative." In *Selected Writings of Jonathan Edwards*, Edited by Harold P. Simonson, 27–44. New York: Frederick Ungar, 1970.

———. *The Philosophy of Jonathan Edwards from His Private Notebooks*. Edited by Harvey G. Townsend. Eugene: University of Oregon Press, 1955.

———. "Treatise on Grace." In *Treatise on Grace and Other Posthumously Published Writings*. Edited by Paul Helm, 25–75. Cambridge, England: James Clarke, 1971.

———. *Freedom of the Will*. Vol. 1 of *The Works of Jonathan Edwards*. Edited by Paul Ramsey. New Haven: Yale University Press, 1957.

———. *Religious Affections*. Vol. 2 of *The Works of Jonathan Edwards*. Edited by John E. Smith. New Haven: Yale University Press, 1959.

———. *Original Sin*. Vol. 3 of *The Works of Jonathan Edwards*. Edited by Clyde A. Holbrook. New Haven: Yale University Press, 1970.

———. *The Great Awakening*. Vol. 4 of *The Works of Jonathan Edwards*. Edited by C. C. Goen. New Haven: Yale University Press, 1972.

———. *Apocalyptic Writings*. Vol. 5 of *The Works of Jonathan Edwards*. Edited by Stephen J. Stein. New Haven: Yale University Press, 1977.

———. *Scientific and Philosophical Writings*. Vol. 6 of *The Works of Jonathan Edwards*. Edited by Wallace E. Anderson. New Haven: Yale University Press, 1980.

———. *The Life of David Brainerd.* Vol. 7 of *The Works of Jonathan Edwards.* Edited by Norman Pettit. New Haven: Yale University Press, 1985.

———. *Ethical Writings.* Vol. 8 of *The Works of Jonathan Edwards.* Edited by Paul Ramsey. New Haven: Yale University Press, 1989.

———. *A History of the Work of Redemption.* Vol. 9 of *The Works of Jonathan Edwards.* Edited by John F. Wilson. New Haven: Yale University Press, 1989.

———. *Sermons and Discourses, 1720–1723.* Vol. 10 of *The Works of Jonathan Edwards.* Edited by Wilson H. Kimnach. New Haven: Yale University Press, 1992.

———. *Typological Writings.* Vol. 11 of *The Works of Jonathan Edwards.* Edited by Wallace E. Anderson, Mason I. Lowance, and David H. Watters. New Haven: Yale University Press, 1993.

———. *Ecclesiastical Writings.* Vol. 12 of *The Works of Jonathan Edwards.* Edited by David D. Hall. New Haven: Yale University Press, 1994.

———. *The "Miscellanies" (Entry Nos. a–z, aa–zz, 1–500).* Vol. 13 of *The Works of Jonathan Edwards.* Edited by Thomas A. Schafer. New Haven: Yale University Press, 1994.

———. *The Works of Jonathan Edwards.* With a Memoir by Sereno E. Dwight. Revised by Edward Hickman. 2 vols. Edinburgh: Banner of Truth Trust, 1984 [1834].

———. Yale MSS. Typed transcripts of the "Miscellanies" collection, Beinecke Rare Book and Manuscripts Library, Yale University.

Edwards, Rem B. *A Return to Moral and Religious Philosophy in Early America.* Washington, D. C.: University Press of America, 1982.

Ellison, Julie. "The Sociology of 'Holy Indifference': Sarah Edwards' Narrative." *American Literature* 56 (1984): 479–95.

Elwood, Douglas. *The Philosophical Theology of Jonathan Edwards.* New York: Columbia University Press, 1960.

Emerson, Everett. *Puritanism in America, 1620–1750.* Boston: Twayne, 1977.

Emerson, Ralph Waldo. *Essays and Lectures.* Edited by Joel Porte. New York: Library of America, 1983.

Erdt, Terence. *Jonathan Edwards, Art, and the Sense of the Heart.* Amherst: University of Massachusetts, 1980.

Fiering, Norman. *Jonathan Edwards's Moral Thought and Its British Context.* Published for the Institute of Early American History and Culture, Williamsburg, Virginia. Chapel Hill: University of North Carolina Press, 1981.

———. *Moral Philosophy at Seventeenth-Century Harvard: A Discipline in Transition.* Published for the Institute of Early American History and Culture, Williamsburg, Virginia. Chapel Hill: University of North Carolina Press, 1981.

———. "The Rationalist Foundations of Jonathan Edwards's Metaphysics." In *Jonathan Edwards and the American Experience,* edited by Nathan O. Hatch and Harry S. Stout, 73–101. New York: Oxford University Press, 1988.

Frei, Hans. *The Eclipse of Biblical Narrative: A Study in Eighteenth and Nineteenth Century Hermeneutics.* New Haven: Yale University Press, 1974.

Gardiner, H. N. "The Early Idealism of Jonathan Edwards." *Philosophical Review* 9 (1900): 573–96.

Gay, Peter. *A Loss of Mastery: Puritan Historians in Colonial America*. Berkeley: University of California Press, 1966.

Gerrish, B. A. "Friedrich Schleiermacher." In *Nineteenth-Century Religious Thought in the West*, edited by Ninian Smart et al. 3 vols., 1:123–56. Cambridge: Cambridge University Press, 1985.

———. *A Prince of the Church: Friedrich Schleiermacher and the Beginnings of Modern Theology*. Philadelphia: Fortress Press, 1984.

Gerstner, John. "An Outline of the Apologetics of Jonathan Edwards," *Bibliotheca Sacra* 133 (1976): 3–10, 99–107, 195–201, 291–8.

Gilson, Etienne. *The Christian Philosophy of Saint Augustine*. Translated by L. E. M. Lynch. New York: Random House, 1960.

Ginsberg, Morris. "Progress in the Modern Era." In *Dictionary of the History of Ideas*. 5 vols., 3:633–50. General editor Philip P. Wiener. New York: Scribner's, 1973.

Goen, C. C. "Editor's Introduction." In Jonathan Edwards, *The Great Awakening*. Vol. 4 of *The Works of Jonathan Edwards*, 1–95. New Haven: Yale University Press, 1972.

———. "Jonathan Edwards: A New Departure in Eschatology." In *Critical Essays on Jonathan Edwards*, edited by William J. Scheick. Boston: G. K. Hall, 1980. Reprinted from *Church History* 28 (1959): 25–40.

Gohdes, Clarence. "Aspects of Idealism in Early New England." *Philosophical Review* 39 (1930) 537–55.

Greenslade, S. L., ed. *The West, From the Reformation to the Present Day*. Vol. 3 of *The Cambridge History of the Bible*. Cambridge: Cambridge University Press, 1963.

Guelzo, Allen C. *Edwards on the Will: A Century of American Theological Debate*. Middletown, Conn.: Wesleyan University Press, 1989.

Hall, David D. "Editor's Introduction." Jonathan Edwards, *Ecclesiastical Writings*. Vol. 12 of *The Works of Jonathan Edwards*, 1–90. New Haven: Yale University Press, 1994.

Hall, Richard A. S. "Did Berkeley Influence Edwards? Their Common Critique of the Moral Sense Theory." In *Jonathan Edwards's Writings: Text, Context, Interpretation*, edited by Stephen J. Stein, 100–21. Bloomington: Indiana University Press, 1996.

Hambricke-Stowe, Charles. *The Practice of Piety: Puritan Devotional Disciplines in Seventeenth-Century New England*. Published for the Institute of Early American History and Culture, Williamsburg, Virginia. Chapel Hill: University of North Carolina Press, 1982.

———. "Puritan Spirituality in America." In *Post-Reformation and Modern*. Vol. 3 of *Christian Spirituality*, edited by Louis Dupré and Don E. Saliers, 338–53. New York: Crossroad, 1989.

Hanson, Paul D., et al. "Apocalypses and Apocalypticism." In *Anchor Bible Dictionary*, edited by David Noel Freedman. 6 vols., 1:279–92 New York: Doubleday, 1992.

Happel, Stephen. "Words Made Beautiful By Grace: On Coleridge the Theologian." *Religious Studies Review* 6 (1980): 201–10.

Harvey, Van. "On the New Edition of Schleiermacher's *Addresses on Religion*." *Journal of the American Academy of Religion* 39 (1971): 488–512.

———. "A Word in Defense of Schleiermacher's Theological Method." *Journal of Religion* 42 (1962): 151–70.

Hatch, Nathan O., and Harry S. Stout, eds. *Jonathan Edwards and the American Experience*. New York: Oxford University Press, 1988.

Hazard, Paul. *European Thought in the Eighteenth Century: From Montesquieu to Lessing.* New Haven: Yale University Press, 1954.

Hegel, G. W. F. *The Philosophy of Hegel.* Edited by Carl J. Friedrich. New York: Modern Library, 1953.

Heimert, Alan. *Religion and the American Mind: From the Great Awakening to the Revolution.* Cambridge: Harvard University Press, 1966.

Helm, Paul. "John Locke and Jonathan Edwards: A Reconsideration." *Journal of the History of Philosophy* 7 (1969): 51–61.

Hendry, George S. "The Glory of God and the Future of Man." *Reformed World* 34 (1976): 147–57.

Hick, John. *Evil and the God of Love.* Rev. ed. San Francisco: Harper and Row, 1978 [1966].

Hoffman, Gerhard. "Seinsharmonie und Heilsgeschichte bei Jonathan Edwards." Th.D. diss., Göttingen University, 1957.

Holbrook, Clyde A. "Editor's Introduction." In Jonathan Edwards, *Original Sin.* Vol. 3 of *The Works of Jonathan Edwards*, 1–101. New Haven: Yale University Press, 1970.

———. *The Ethics of Jonathan Edwards: Morality and Aesthetics.* Ann Arbor: University of Michigan Press, 1973.

———. *Jonathan Edwards, the Valley, and Nature: An Interpretive Essay.* London: Associated University Presses, 1987.

Holmes, Oliver Wendell. "Jonathan Edwards." In *Pages From an Old Volume of Life: A Collection of Essays.* Vol. 8 of *The Writings of Oliver Wendell Holmes*, 361–401. Cambridge, Mass.: The Riverside Press, 1891.

Holton, Gerald, and Stephen G. Brush. *Introduction to Concepts and Theories in Physical Science.* Princeton: Princeton University Press, 1985.

Hoopes, James. *Consciousness in New England: From Puritanism and Ideas to Psychoanalysis and Semiotic.* New Series in American Intellectual and Cultural History. Baltimore: Johns Hopkins University Press, 1989.

———. "Jonathan Edwards's Religious Psychology." *Journal of American History* 69 (1983): 849–65.

Howe, Daniel Walker. *Making the American Self: Jonathan Edwards to Abraham Lincoln.* Cambridge: Harvard University Press, 1997.

Hutcheson, Francis. *Illustrations on the Moral Sense.* Edited by Bernard Peach. Cambridge: Belknap Press of Harvard University, 1971.

———. *An Inquiry Concerning the Original of Our Ideas of Virtue or Moral Good.* In *British Moralists, Being Selections from Writers Principally of the Eighteenth Century*, edited by L. A. Selby-Bigge, 1:69–177. New York: Dover, 1965.

Jenson, Robert W. *America's Theologian: A Recommendation of Jonathan Edwards.* New York: Oxford University Press, 1988.

Johnson, Thomas H. "Jonathan Edwards's Background of Reading." *Publications of the Colonial Society of Massachusetts* 28 (1931): 193–222.

Jones, L. Gregory, and Stephen E. Fowl. *Rethinking Metaphysics.* Oxford: Basil Blackwell, 1995.

Jowett, B., trans. *The Dialogues of Plato; Translated into English with Analyses and Introductions.* 4th ed. 4 vols. Oxford: Clarendon Press, 1953.

Kant, Immanuel. *Critique of Practical Reason*. In *Immanuel Kant*. Vol. 42 of *Great Books of the Western World*, 291–379. Edited by Robert Maynard Hutchins et. al., Chicago; Encyclopedia Britannica, 1952.

———. *Critique of Pure Reason*. Translated by Norman Kemp Smith. New York: St. Martin's Press, 1965 [1929].

Keeble, N. H. "Puritan Spirituality." In *The Westminster Dictionary of Christian Spirituality*, Edited by Gordon S. Wakefield, 323–6. Philadelphia: Westminster Press, 1983.

Kimnach, Wilson H. "General Introduction to the Sermons: Jonathan Edwards' Art of Prophesying." In Jonathan Edwards, *Sermons and Discourses, 1720–1723*. Vol. 10 of *The Works of Jonathan Edwards*. Edited by Wilson H. Kimnach, 1–258. New Haven: Yale University Press, 1992.

———. "Jonathan Edwards' Pursuit of Reality." In *Jonathan Edwards and the American Experience*, edited by Nathan O. Hatch and Harry S. Stout, 102–17. New York: Oxford University Press, 1988.

Kirk, Kenneth E. *The Vision of God: The Christian Doctrine of the "Summum Bonum"*. New York: Harper and Row, 1966 [1931].

Knox, Ronald A. *Enthusiasm: A Chapter in the History of Religion: With Special Reference to the Seventeenth and Eighteenth Centuries*. Notre Dame, Indiana: University of Notre Dame Press, 1994 [1950].

Laurence, David. "Jonathan Edwards, John Locke, and the Canon of Experience." *Early American Literature* 15 (1980): 107–23.

Lee, Sang. *The Philosophical Theology of Jonathan Edwards*. Princeton: Princeton University Press, 1988.

Leeuw, Gerardus van der. *Religion in Essence and Manifestation*. Translated by J. E. Turner. 2 vols. New York: Harper and Row, 1963.

LeMahieu, D. L. *The Mind of William Paley: A Philosopher and His Age*. Lincoln: University of Nebraska Press, 1976.

Lesser, M. X. *Jonathan Edwards: An Annotated Bibliography, 1979–1993*. Westport, Conn.: Greenwood Press, 1994.

———. *Jonathan Edwards: A Reference Guide*. Boston: G. K. Hall, 1981.

Lewis, C. S. "Historicism." In *God, History, and Historians: An Anthology of Modern Christian Views of History*, edited by C. T. McIntire, 225–38. New York: Oxford University Press, 1977.

———. *Miracles*. New York: Macmillan, 1947.

Livingston, James C. *Modern Christian Thought: From the Enlightenment to Vatican II*. New York: Macmillan, 1971.

Locke, John. *An Essay Concerning Human Understanding*. In *Locke, Berkeley, Hume*. Vol. 35 of *Great Books of the Western World*. Edited by Robert Maynard Hutchins, 85–395. Chicago: Encyclopaedia Britannica, 1952.

———. *The Reasonableness of Christianity*. Edited by I. T. Ramsey. Stanford: Stanford University Press, 1958.

Louth, Andrew. "Greek Spirituality." In *The Westminster Dictionary of Christian Spirituality*, edited by Gordon S. Wakefield, 180–2. Philadelphia: Westminster Press, 1983.

Lovejoy, Arthur O. *The Great Chain of Being: A Study of the History of an Idea*. William James Lectures, Harvard University, 1933. Cambridge: Harvard University Press, 1936.

Lovelace, Richard C. "The Anatomy of Puritan Piety: English Puritan Devotional Literature." In *Christian Spirituality: Volume Three: Post-Reformation and Modern*, edited by Louis Dupré and Don E. Saliers, 294–323. New York: Crossroad, 1989.

Lowance, Mason I., and David H. Watters. "Editor's Introduction to 'Types of the Messiah.'" In Jonathan Edwards, *Typological Writings*. Vol. 11 of *The Works of Jonathan Edwards*. Edited by Wallace E. Anderson, Mason I. Lowance, and David H. Watters, 157–82. New Haven: Yale University Press, 1993.

Lowance, Mason I. "Images or Shadows of Divine Things." In *Typology in Early American Literature*, edited by Sacvan Bercovitch, 209–44. Amherst: University of Massachusetts Press, 1972.

——. *The Language of Canaan: Metaphor and Symbol in New England from the Puritans to the Transcendentalists*. Cambridge: Harvard University Press, 1980.

Löwith, Karl. *Meaning in History*. Chicago: University of Chicago Press, 1949.

Lyttle, David. "The Supernatural Light." In *Studies in Religion in Early American Literature*, 1–20. Lanham, Md.: University Press of America, 1983.

MacIntyre, Alasdair. *A Short History of Ethics*. New York: Macmillan, 1966.

Manuel, Frank. *The Eighteenth Century Confronts the Gods*. Cambridge: Harvard University Press, 1959.

Marsden, George M. "Perry Miller's Rehabilitation of the Puritans: A Critique." *Church History* 39 (1970): 91–105.

Marty, Martin E. "American Religious History in the Eighties: A Decade of Achievement." *Church History* 62 (1993): 335–77.

May, Henry F. *The Enlightenment in America*. New York: Oxford University Press, 1976.

McClymond, Michael J. "God the Measure: Toward a Theocentric Understanding of Jonathan Edwards's Metaphysics." *Scottish Journal of Theology* 47 (1994): 43–59.

——. Review of *The Philosophy of Jonathan Edwards: A Study in Divine Semiotics*, by Stephen H. Daniel. *Journal of Religion* 76 (1996): 121–2.

——. "Sinners in the Hands of a Virtuous God: Ethics and Divinity in Jonathan Edwards's *End of Creation*." *Zeitschrift für neuere Theologiegeschichte / Journal for the History of Modern Theology*, 2 (1995): 1–22.

——. "Spiritual Perception in Jonathan Edwards." *Journal of Religion* 77 (1997): 195–216.

——. trans. "Spiritual Knowledge According to Jonathan Edwards," by Miklos Vetö *Calvin Theological Journal* 31 (1996): 161–81. From "La connaissance spirituelle selon Jonathan Edwards." *Revue de theologie et de philosophie*, 111 (1979): 233–45.

McCracken, Charles J. *Malebranche and British Philosophy*. Oxford: Clarendon Press, 1983.

McCracken, J. H. "The Sources of Edwards' Idealism." *Philosophical Review* 11 (1902): 537–55.

McDermott, Gerald R. "The Deist Connection: Jonathan Edwards and Islam." In *Jonathan Edwards's Writings: Text, Context, Interpretation*, edited by Stephen J. Stein, 39–51. Bloomington: Indiana University Press, 1996.

——. "Jonathan Edwards and the Culture Wars: A New Resource for Public Theology and Philosophy." *Pro Ecclesia* 4 (1995): 268–80.

——. *One Holy and Happy Society: The Public Theology of Jonathan Edwards*. University Park: Pennsylvania State University Press, 1992.

McGiffert, Arthur Cushman [Sr.]. *Protestant Thought Before Kant.* New York: Scribner's, 1951 [1911].

McGinn, Bernard. *Antichrist: Two Thousand Years of the Human Fascination With Evil.* San Francisco: Harper, 1994.

———. *Apocalypticism in the Western Tradition.* Aldershot, England: Variorum, 1994.

———. "Introduction." In *Apocalyptic Spirituality: Treatises and Letters of Lactantius, Adso of Montier-en-Der, Joachim of Fiore, the Franciscan Spirituals, Savonarola.* New York: Paulist Press, 1979.

———. "Ocean and Desert as Symbols of Mystical Absorption in the Christian Tradition." *Journal of Religion* 74 (1994) 155–81.

———. *Visions of the End: Apocalyptic Traditions in the Middle Ages.* New York: Columbia University Press, 1979.

Miller, Perry. "From Edwards to Emerson." In *Errand into the Wilderness,* 184–203. Cambridge: Belknap Press of Harvard University, 1964.

———. *Jonathan Edwards.* American Men of Letters Series. New York: William Sloane, 1949.

———. "Jonathan Edwards on the Sense of the Heart." *Harvard Theological Review* 41 (1948) 123–45.

———. "The Rhetoric of Sensation." In *Errand into the Wilderness,* 167–83. Cambridge: Belknap Press of Harvard University, 1964.

———, ed. *Images and Shadows of Divine Things.* New Haven: Yale University Press, 1948.

Minkema, Kenneth P. "The Other Unfinished 'Great Work': Jonathan Edwards, Messianic Prophecy, and 'The Harmony of the Old and New Testament.' " In *Jonathan Edwards's Writings: Text, Context, Interpretation,* edited by Stephen J. Stein, 52–65. Bloomington: Indiana University Press, 1996.

Mitchell, Basil. "Butler as a Christian Apologist." In *Joseph Butler's Moral and Religious Thought: Tercentenary Essays,* edited by Christopher Cunliffe, 97–116. Oxford: Clarendon Press, 1992.

———. *The Justification of Religious Belief.* New York: Macmillan, 1973.

Morgan, Edmund. *Visible Saints: The History of a Puritan Idea.* Ithaca, N.Y.: Cornell University Press, 1963.

Morimoto, Anri. *Jonathan Edwards and the Catholic Vision of Salvation.* University Park: Pennsylvania State University Press, 1995.

Morris, Kenneth R. "The Puritan Roots of American Universalism." *Scottish Journal of Theology* 44 (1991): 457–87.

Morris, William. "The Young Jonathan Edwards: A Reconstruction." Ph.D. diss., University of Chicago, 1955.

Mossner, Ernest C. *Bishop Butler and the Age of Reason: A Study in the History of Thought.* New York: Columbia University Press, 1936.

Murray, Iain H. *Jonathan Edwards: A New Biography.* Edinburgh: Banner of Truth Trust, 1987.

Nagy, Paul S. "The Beloved Community of Jonathan Edwards." *Transactions of the Charles S. Pierce Society* 7 (1971): 93–104.

Nash, Ronald H. *The Light of the Mind: St. Augustine's Theory of Knowledge.* Lexington: University of Kentucky Press, 1969.

Niebuhr, H. Richard. *The Kingdom of God in America.* Middletown, Conn.: Wesleyan University Press, 1988 [1937].

Nisbet, Robert A. *History of the Idea of Progress.* New York: Basic Books, 1980.

Noll, Mark A. "God at the Center: Jonathan Edwards on True Virtue." *Christian Century* 110 (1993): 854–8.

Nuttall, Geoffrey F. *The Holy Spirit in Puritan Faith and Experience.* Oxford: Basil Blackwell, 1947.

Nygren, Anders. *Agape and Eros.* Translated by Philip S. Watson. Rev. ed. Philadelphia: Westminster, 1953.

Oberg, Barbara B., and Harry S. Stout, eds. *Benjamin Franklin, Jonathan Edwards, and the Representation of American Culture.* New York: Oxford University Press, 1993.

Oliphint, Scott. "Jonathan Edwards: Reformed Apologist." *Westminster Theological Journal* 57 (1995): 165–86.

Orr, James. "The Influence of Edwards." In *Exercises Commemorating the Two-Hundredth Anniversary of the Birth of Jonathan Edwards,* edited by John Winthrop Platner, 105–26. Andover, Mass.: Andover Press, 1904.

Orr, John. *English Deism: Its Roots and Fruits.* Grand Rapids, Mich.: Eerdmans, 1934.

Ozment, Steven. *The Age of Reform: An Intellectual and Religious History of Late Medieval and Reformation Europe.* New Haven: Yale University Press, 1980.

Pahl, Jon. "Jonathan Edwards and the Aristocracy of Grace." *Fides et Historia* 25 (1993): 62–72.

Paley, William. *The Works of William Paley.* 5 vols. Boston: Joshua Belcher, 1810.

Parkes, Henry Bamford. *Jonathan Edwards: The Fiery Puritan.* New York: Minton, Balch, 1930.

Parrington, Vernon Louis. "The Anachronism of Jonathan Edwards." In *1620–1800.* Vol. 1 of *Main Currents in American Thought.* 3 vols., 148–63. New York: Harcourt, Brace, 1927.

Pascal, Blaise. *Pensées.* Translated by A. J. Krailsheimer. Harmondsworth, England: Penguin Books, 1966.

Patrides, C. A. *The Grand Design of God: The Literary Form of the Christian View of History.* London: Routledge and Kegan Paul, University of Toronto Press, 1972.

Pattison, Mark. "Tendencies of Religious Thought in England, 1688–1750." In *Essays and Reviews.* 8th ed., 254–329. London: Longman, Green, 1861.

Pelikan, Jaroslav. *The Growth of Medieval Theology (600–1300).* Vol. 3 of *The Christian Tradition: A History of the Development of Doctrine.* Chicago: University of Chicago Press, 1978.

Pettit, Norman. "Editor's Introduction." In Jonathan Edwards, *The Life of David Brainerd.* Vol. 7 of *The Works of Jonathan Edwards,* 1–85. New Haven: Yale University Press, 1985.

Pfisterer, Karl Dietrich. *The Prism of Scripture: Studies on History and Historicity in the Work of Jonathan Edwards.* Anglo-American Forum, no. 1. Frankfurt: Peter Lang, 1975.

Platner, John Winthrop, ed. *Exercises Commemorating the Two-Hundredth Anniversary of the Birth of Jonathan Edwards.* Andover, Mass.: Andover Press, 1904.

Post, Stephen Garrard. *Christian Love and Self-Denial: An Historical and Normative Study of Jonathan Edwards, Samuel Hopkins, and American Theological Ethics.* Lanham, Md.: University Press of America, 1987.

———. *A Theory of Agape: On the Meaning of Christian Love.* Lewisburg, Pa.: Bucknell University Press, 1990.

Proudfoot, Wayne. *Religious Experience.* Berkeley: University of California Press, 1985.

Proudfoot, Wayne, et. al. "Symposium on Schleiermacher's 'On Religion: Speeches to Its Cultured Despisers'." *Harvard Divinity Bulletin* 24 (1995): 10–13.

Ramsey, Bennett. "The Ineluctable Impulse: 'Consent' in the Thought of Edwards, James, and Royce." *Union Seminary Quarterly Review* 37 (1983): 302–22.

Ramsey, Paul. Appendix 3, "Heaven is a Progressive State." In Jonathan Edwards, *Ethical Writings.* Vol. 8 of *The Works of Jonathan Edwards.* Edited by Paul Ramsey, 706–38. New Haven: Yale University Press, 1989.

———. "Editor's Introduction." In Jonathan Edwards, *Ethical Writings.* Vol. 8 of *The Works of Jonathan Edwards,* 1–121. New Haven: Yale University Press, 1989.

———. "Editor's Introduction." In Jonathan Edwards, *Freedom of the Will.* Vol. 1 of *The Works of Jonathan Edwards,* 1–128. New Haven: Yale University Press, 1957.

———. "The Transformation of Ethics." In *Faith and Ethics: The Theology of H. Richard Niebuhr,* edited by Paul Ramsey, 140–72. New York: Harper and Row, 1957.

Redwood, John. *Reason, Ridicule, and Religion: The Age of Enlightenment in England, 1660–1750.* London: Thames and Hudson, 1976.

Reid, J. K. S. *Christian Apologetics.* Grand Rapids, Mich.: Eerdmans, 1969.

Reventlow, Henning Graf. *The Authority of the Bible and the Rise of the Modern World.* Translated by John Bowden. London: SCM, 1984.

Richard, Lucien Joseph. *The Spirituality of John Calvin.* Atlanta: John Knox Press, 1974.

Richardson, Alan. *Christian Apologetics.* London: SCM, 1947.

Richardson, Herbert Warren. "The Glory of God in the Theology of Jonathan Edwards," Ph.D. diss., Harvard University, 1962.

Rogers, Charles. "John Wesley and Jonathan Edwards." *Duke Divinity School Review* 31 (1966): 20–38.

Rogers, Jack, and Donald K. McKim. *The Authority and Interpretation of the Bible: An Historical Approach.* San Francisco: Harper and Row, 1979.

Rupp, George. "The 'Idealism' of Jonathan Edwards." *Harvard Theological Review* 62 (1969): 209–26.

Sarna, Nahum M. *Understanding Genesis.* New York: Jewish Theological Seminary of America, 1966.

Schafer, Thomas A. "The Concept of Being in the Thought of Jonathan Edwards." Ph.D. diss., Duke University, 1951.

———. "Editor's Introduction." In Jonathan Edwards, *The "Miscellanies" (Entry Nos. a–z, aa–zz, 1–500).* Vol. 13 of *The Works of Jonathan Edwards,* 1–160. New Haven: Yale University Press, 1994.

———. "Jonathan Edwards." In *Encyclopedia Britannica: Micropedia,* 4:381–2. 15th ed. Chicago: Encyclopedia Britannica, 1986.

———. "Jonathan Edwards' Conception of the Church." *Church History* 24 (1955): 51–66.

Schaff, Philip, ed. *The Creeds of Christendom*. 3 vols. New York: Harper and Row, 1931.

Scheick, William J. "The Grand Design: Jonathan Edwards' *History of the Work of Redemption*." In *Critical Essays on Jonathan Edwards*, edited by William J. Scheick, 177–88. Boston: G. K. Hall, 1980. Reprinted from *Eighteenth-Century Studies* 8 (1975): 300–14.

Schleiermacher, Friedrich. *The Christian Faith*. Edited by H. R. Macintosh and J. S. Stewart. Edinburgh: T. and T. Clark, 1986.

———. *On Religion: Speeches to Its Cultured Despisers*. Translated by John Oman, with an introduction by Rudolf Otto. New York: Harper and Row, 1958 [1893].

Scholder, Klaus. *The Birth of Modern Criticism: Origins and Problems of Biblical Criticism in the Seventeenth Century*. London: SCM, 1990.

Selby-Bigge, L. A. "Introduction." In *British Moralists, Being Selections from Writers Principally of the Eighteenth Century*, edited by L. A. Selby-Bigge, 1:xi–lxx. New York: Dover, 1965.

Shaftesbury, Third Earl of [Cooper, Anthony Ashley]. *Characteristics of Men, Manners, Opinions, Times, Etc.* 2 vols. Edited by John M. Robertson. Gloucester, Mass.: Peter Smith, 1963.

———. *An Inquiry Concerning Virtue or Merit*. In *British Moralists, Being Selections from Writers Principally of the Eighteenth Century*, edited by L. A. Selby-Bigge, 1:3–66. New York: Dover, 1965.

Shea, Daniel B., Jr. "The Art and Instruction of Jonathan Edwards's *Personal Narrative*." In *Puritan New England: Essays on Religion, Society, and Culture*, edited by Alden T. Vaughan and Francis J. Bremer, 299–311. New York: St. Martin's Press, 1977.

———. "Deconstruction Comes to Early 'America': The Case of Edwards," *Early American Literature* 21 (1986–7) 268–74.

———. "Jonathan Edwards: The First Two Hundred Years." *Journal of American Studies* 14 (1980): 181–197.

———. "Jonathan Edwards: Historian of Consciousness." In *Major Writers of Early American Literature*, edited by Everett Emerson. Madison: University of Wisconsin Press, 1972.

Sidgwick, Henry. *Outlines of the History of Ethics*. London: Macmillan, 1931.

Simonson, Harold. "Typology, Imagination, and Jonathan Edwards." In *Radical Discontinuities: American Romanticism and Christian Consciousness*, 19–43. Rutherford, N.J.: Fairleigh Dickinson University Press, 1983.

Smith, Claude A. "Jonathan Edwards and 'The Way of Ideas'." *Harvard Theological Review* 59 (1966): 153–73.

Smith, John E. "Editor's Introduction." In Jonathan Edwards, *Religious Affections*. Vol. 2 of *The Works of Jonathan Edwards*, 1–83. New Haven: Yale University Press, 1959.

———. "Jonathan Edwards as Philosophical Theologian." *Review of Metaphysics* 30 (1976): 306–24.

Smith, Norman Kemp. *John Locke*. Manchester, England: Manchester University Press, 1933.

Smith, Robert Doyle. "John Wesley and Jonathan Edwards on Religious Experience: A Comparative Analysis." *Wesleyan Theological Journal* 25 (1990): 130–46.

Smyth, Egbert. "The Theology of Edwards." In *Exercises Commemorating the Two-Hundredth Anniversary of the Birth of Jonathan Edwards*, edited by John Winthrop Platner, 73–93. Andover, Mass.: Andover Press, 1904.

Spengler, Oswald. *The Decline of the West*. Translated by Charles Francis Atkinson. New York: Alfred A. Knopf, 1926–28. From the German edition *Der Untergang des Abendlandes: Umrisse einer Morphologie der Welgeschichte*. Munich: Beck, 1919–22.

Spiegler, Gerhard. *The Eternal Covenant: Schleiermacher's Experiment in Cultural Theology*. New York: Harper and Row, 1967.

Spinoza, Benedict. *The Chief Works of Benedict de Spinoza*. Translated by R. H. M. Elwes. 2 vols. New York: Dover, 1951.

Spohn, William C. "Sovereign Beauty: Jonathan Edwards and *The Nature of True Virtue*," *Theological Studies* 42 (1981): 394–421.

Stephen, Leslie. *History of English Thought in the Eighteenth Century*. 2 vols. New York: G. P. Putnam, 1876.

———. "Jonathan Edwards." In *Hours in a Library*, 2:42–102. 4 vols. London: Smith, Elder, 1907.

Stein, Stephen J. "Editor's Introduction." In *Apocalyptic Writings*. Vol. 5 of *The Works of Jonathan Edwards*, 1–93. New Haven: Yale University Press, 1977.

———. "A Notebook on the Apocalypse by Jonathan Edwards." In *Critical Essays on Jonathan Edwards*, edited by William J. Scheick, 166–76. Boston: G. K. Hall, 1980. Reprinted from *William and Mary Quarterly* 29 (1972): 623–34.

———, ed. *Jonathan Edwards's Writings: Text, Context, Interpretation*. Bloomington: Indiana University Press, 1996.

Stout, Harry S. *The New England Soul: Preaching and Religious Culture in Colonial New England*. New York: Oxford University Press, 1986.

Stromberg, Roland N. *Religious Liberalism in Eighteenth-Century England*. Oxford: Oxford University Press, 1954.

Sullivan, Robert E. *John Toland and the Deist Controversy: A Study in Adaptations*. Harvard Historical Studies 101. Cambridge: Harvard University Press, 1982.

Suter, Rufus. "A Note on Platonism in the Philosophy of Jonathan Edwards," *Harvard Theological Review* 52 (1959): 283–4.

Thomas à Kempis. *The Imitation of Christ*. Translated by Leo Shirley-Price. London: Penguin Books, 1952.

Thomas Aquinas. *The Summa Theologica of St. Thomas Aquinas*. Translated by Fathers of the English Dominican province. 5 vols. Westminster, Md.: Christian Classics, 1981 [1911].

Tillich, Paul. *Systematic Theology*. 3 vols. Chicago: University of Chicago Press, 1951–63.

Tomas, Vincent. "The Modernity of Jonathan Edwards," *New England Quarterly* 25 (1952): 60–84.

Track, Joachim. "Analogie." In *Theologische Realenzyklopädie*, edited by Gerhard Krause and Gerhard Muller. 27 vols. to date, 2:625–6. Berlin and New York: Walter de Gruyter, 1976–.

Tracy, Patricia J. *Jonathan Edwards, Pastor: Religion and Society in Eighteenth-Century Northampton*. New York: Hill and Wang, 1980.

Tuveson, Ernest Lee. *Redeemer Nation: The Idea of America's Millenial Role.* Chicago: University of Chicago Press, 1980 [1968].

Van Beek, M. *An Enquiry into Puritan Vocabulary.* Groningen: Wolters-Noordhof, 1969.

Vetö, Miklos. *Le pensee de Jonathan Edwards.* Paris: Les Editions du Cerf, 1987.

———. "Spiritual Knowledge According to Jonathan Edwards." Translated by Michael J. McClymond. *Calvin Theological Journal* 31 (1996): 161–81. From "La connaissance spirituelle selon Jonathan Edwards." *Revue de theologie et de philosophie* 111 (1979): 233–45.

Wainwright, William J. "Jonathan Edwards and the Sense of the Heart." *Faith and Philosophy* 7 (1990): 43–92.

———. *Reason and the Heart: A Prolegomenon to a Critique of Passional Reason.* Cornell Studies in the Philosophy of Religion, ed. William P. Alston. Ithaca, N.Y.: Cornell University Press, 1995.

Wakefield, Gordon. *Puritan Devotion: Its Place in the Development of Christian Piety.* London: Epworth, 1957.

———, ed. *The Westminster Dictionary of Christian Spirituality.* Philadelphia: Westminster Press, 1983.

Walker, D. P. *The Decline of Hell: Seventeenth-Century Discussions of Eternal Torment.* London: Routledge and Kegan Paul, 1964.

Walton, Craig. "Malebranche's Ontology," *Journal of the History of Philosophy* 7 (1969): 143–61.

Ward, J. Neville. "Contemplation." In *The Westminster Dictionary of Christian Spirituality,* edited by Gordon S. Wakefield, 95–6. Philadelphia: Westminster Press, 1983.

Weber, Donald Louis. "The Image of Jonathan Edwards in American Culture," Ph.D. diss., Columbia University, 1978.

Weddle, David L. "Jonathan Edwards on Men and Trees," *Harvard Theological Review* 67 (1974): 155–75.

———. "The Melancholy Saint: Jonathan Edwards's Interpretation of David Brainerd as a Model of Evangelical Spirituality." *Harvard Theological Review* 81 (1988): 297–318.

Wesley, John. "A Plain Account of Genuine Christianity." In *John Wesley,* edited by Albert C. Outler. New York: Oxford University Press, 1964.

Willey, Basil. *The Eighteenth-Century Background: Studies on the Idea of Nature in the Thought of the Period.* New York: Columbia University Press, 1950.

Wilson, John F. "Editor's Introduction." In Jonathan Edwards, *A History of the Work of Redemption.* Vol. 9 of *The Works of Jonathan Edwards,* 1–109. New Haven: Yale University Press, 1989.

Wilson-Kastner, Patricia. "God's Infinity and His Relationship to Creation in the Theologies of Gregory of Nyssa and Jonathan Edwards." *Foundations* 21 (1978) 305–21.

Winslow, Ola. *Jonathan Edwards, 1703–1758: A Biography.* New York: Farrar, Straus and Giroux, 1940.

Wisner, William C. "The End of God in Creation." *American Biblical Repository,* 3rd series, 6 (1850): 430–56.

Wolterstorff, Nicholas. *John Locke and the Ethics of Belief.* Cambridge Studies in Religion and Culture 2. New York: Cambridge University Press, 1996.

———. "Locke's Philosophy of Religion." In *The Cambridge Companion to Locke,* edited by Vere Chappell, 172–198. New York: Cambridge University Press, 1994.

Woodbridge, Frederick J. E. "The Philosophy of Edwards." In *Exercises Commemorating the Two-Hundredth Anniversary of the Birth of Jonathan Edwards*, edited by John Winthrop Platner, 47–72. Andover, Mass.: Andover Press, 1904.

Yarbrough, Steven R., and John C. Adams. *Delightful Conviction: Jonathan Edwards and the Rhetoric of Conversion*. Great American Orators 20. Westport, Conn.: Greenwood Press, 1993.

Index

God *(Continued)*
    cause of creatures' knowledge, 33, 128–9
      n.53
    church's importance to, 63
    created for his own glory, 52, 54–5, 103,
      137 nn.24–5,27
    cosmic role of, 148 n.9
    deistic view of, 83–4, 93
    deliverances by, 71–2, 98
    diversity of views on, 94
    does everything, 93, 110, 155 n.88
    Edwards's preoccupation with, 29
    Edwards's view of criticized, 114 n.7
    election by, 20, 64
    enemies of, 78, 104
    as Epicure, 62
    esteems the esteem of others, 60–1
    ethicized by Edwards, 52, 58–61, 59, 64,
      103
    ethics based on, 50, 52
    exalted but not remote, 30
    as First Mover, 82
    freedom to create in, 53, 61–2, 139–40
      n.57
    goal-directedness of, 55
    glory of, 20, 52, 78, 103, 124 n.91, 137
      nn.24–5, 138 n.31
    as goal of history, 76, 79
    as "God of the gaps," 88, 92, 111, 150
      n.36
    goodness of, 139–40 n.57
    heavenly illumination by, 48
    historical design of, 67, 72, 75–9
    humanity's distinctness from, 13
    immanence or presence of, 10, 24, 28,
      39, 92, 102
    as the Infinite, 91
    innate ideas of, 81–2
    inscrutability of, 58, 64, 89
    knowledge of the end of creation, 33–4,
      55–6, 77, 96, 155 n.94
    knowledge or wisdom of, 20, 33, 99
      –100
    known by revelation, 58, 94–5, 99, 121
      n.59, 138 n.43
    love toward, 39, 105, 134 n.59
    marginalizing of, 51, 80–4, 90, 107–8
    as the measure of all things, 29
    moral government of, 89–90, 94, 96, 99,
      104

    objective basis for religious experience
      in, 16, 120 n.42
    pagan view of, 94, 99
    power of, 33, 145 n.58
    proofs for, 95–6, 105, 149–50 n.21, 154
      n.70, 155 nn.88–9
    punishments of, 89, 96, 100, 140
      nn.62,65
    redemption by, 69
    Schleiermacher's view of, 23, 92–3, 123
      n.78, 152–3 n.62, 153 n.68
    secularizing interpretations of, 8, 92–3,
      153 n.68
    self-knowledge of, 95
    self-regard of, 56, 60
    self-sufficiency of, 55–7, 62, 137 n.27
    "substance" of, 33, 126 n.29, 128
      nn.48,50
    symbolized in nature and history, 68–9
    as Trinity, 32, 157 n.132
    triumph of, 78, 104
    unity of world in, 85
    unknowability of, 23
    vantage point of, 20, 75–9, 96
    virtuousness of, 59–61, 64
    vision of, 38, 48–9, 104, 111, 124 n.89, 135
      n.63
    will of, 33, 39
    see also Beauty, Calvinism, Christ,
      Creation, "Excellence," Spirit
God Glorified in Man's Dependence, 29
Goen, C. C., 67, 69, 78, 132 n.33, 141 n.4,
    142 n.14, 145–6 n.63
Grace
    external means (or sacraments) of, 20,
      40, 121–2 n.65
    inconsistent with proportionate regard,
      62
    known through signs, 39
    needed for religious experience, 10, 22,
      24
    operates through mental notions, 120
      n.52
    pagan view on, 99
    perfects nature, 22, 154 n.73
    preceded by humiliation, 40
    preciousness of, 20
    salvation based on, 13
    selectiveness of, 53, 63–4, 121–2 n.65, 140
      n.66